THE CARE
REVOLUTION

A Proven New Paradigm for Pastoral Care

by
DR. JOHN W. BOSMAN

Foreword by Reinhard Bonnke

EQUIP PRESS
Colorado Springs, Colorado

THE CARE REVOLUTION

A Proven New Paradigm for Pastoral Care

First Edition: Year 2019
The Care Revolution / Dr. John W. Bosman
Paperback ISBN: 978-1-946453-34-1
eBook ISBN: 978-1-946453-35-8

THE CARE REVOLUTION
A Proven New Paradigm for Pastoral Care
Dr. John W. Bosman

Having been a pastor for many years, I believe the effectiveness of any healthy church is determined by church members and their pastor partnering together in ministry. The responsibility and demands are far too great for only one person, or even a select few, to accomplish. This rings especially true when it comes to pastoral care. Our churches will once again be reignited with new passion when we decide to get congregational care right. The contagious churches of the next century will be different from traditional churches today. One revolutionary difference will revolve around pastoral care. The exciting prospect is that everyone in the congregation will receive regular pastoral care from a gifted and trained layperson.

—Dr. Jim Garlow
Lead Pastor
Skyline Church, La Mesa, California

It is with great joy and elation that I write this recommendation for John Bosman who I regard as the consummate pastor. We have known each other for many years and had the privilege of ministering together at different events. I had the pleasure of preaching at his church on more than one occasion, which availed me the opportunity of seeing their church in action. I was not surprised to realize why it had become such a significant congregation with so many people involved in ministry. As my friend, he has also ministered at Church of His Presence and has furthermore faithfully served on our church's Board of Directors for many years. The Scripture declares, *there are not many fathers.* I regard John as an apostolic father in the church today and is the reason I value his insight so much.

—Pastor John Kilpatrick
Lead Pastor
Church of His Presence, Daphne, Alabama

If anyone is ever qualified to write a book on pastoral care, Dr. John Bosman is that person. He has built a pace-setting church under challenging circumstances and ascribes its success to the scores of committed believers in the congregation. If every church would get a hold of the simple truths John conveys in *The Care Revolution*, I am convinced pastoral care in the church in America would be revolutionized. For a church to increase its relevance and become effective in any community, we must once again enable all of God's people to take back the work of the ministry and allow their pastors to lead the congregation, cast the vision, and become their ministry-coach.

—Pastor Denny Duron
Lead Pastor
Shreveport Community Church, Shreveport, Louisiana

You hold in your hands a book that comes out of the heart of a man with compassion, a demonstrated pastor, and a superlative communicator. I know John Bosman up close and personally from sharing the speaker's platform with him on numerous occasions. He speaks and writes with clarity, precision, and insight. John built a dynamic congregation in Lake Charles, Louisiana by utilizing the gifts and abilities of the members. He thoroughly believes that *the church should not run on the feet of the clergy, but on the feet of the laity*— (one of his own quotes). *The Care Revolution* will undoubtedly become a prized directive for pastors and churches. In it, he shares proven principles for congregational care and clarifies the valid reasons we need *A Proven New Paradigm for Pastoral Care,* and especially how we can bring it into reality. He has done it; he knows how.

—Pastor J. Don George
Lead Pastor
Calvary Church, Irving, Texas

DEDICATION

I dedicate this book first and foremost, to my wife, Anne, who is not only my spouse and ministry partner but also my best friend and confidant. We have spent many wonderful years together, and I realize today, more than ever before, that without her I would never have made it through life. Her encouragement and dedicated prayers have been the catalyst that kept me reading, writing, and researching.

Thank you, Sweetheart, for being willing to spend so much time alone, and keeping yourself occupied so I could devote my time to study, reflect, and compose chapter after chapter. Thanks for the many Scriptures and insights you brought to me and also for listening to my bursts of inspiration and joining with me in joy when I was so elated about something new I discovered. In that same vein, I also want to thank you for bearing with my frustrations and annoyances that seemingly are part of the territory in a project such as this.

You listened to me teaching the material over and over in so many training conferences across America and never complained. You need a medal for that! But most of all I appreciate your love and devotion, and your never-failing commitment to the Kingdom of God and me. You are indeed a Proverbs 31 woman, and I love you dearly. The best is yet to come!

I gladly also dedicate this book to my children and grandchildren. They are the joy of my life and the stimulus for my living with purpose. Thanks, John, Jayce, and Debbie for faithfully reading excerpts of what I had written and made me believe it was terrific. Thanks for your ideas and insights and also for listening to me when I would share my heart with you. My grandsons, John, Andrew, Jaren, Colin, and Nicholas, are the best in the whole wide world. I have always said, *If I had known they were going to be that grand, I would have been kinder to their parents!* Love all of you!

ACKNOWLEDGEMENTS

Having been in the ministry for many years, I realize how many people have influenced me, formed my life, and shaped my thinking. How do you ever find a way to thank them? I guess there is no real and practical way to be able to appreciate them appropriately.

The input my parents have had in my life need to be acknowledged. My Dad was a pastor before I was even born. He was one of the most outstanding preachers and prolific leaders you could find anywhere. God had blessed him with more talents and abilities than I can mention in a brief reference such as this. My Mom was one of the kindest and sweetest ladies you could ever meet. People often referred to her as, *The Lady*. She was tender, but she was strong. I learned many life lessons from her. I cannot omit also mentioning the significant influence Anne's parents had in my life. *The Captain* had more wisdom in his little finger than most people have in their entirety. *Mom* was the joy of the family and the best cook one could wish to have. They loved me as their son, and I eagerly loved them back.

Since the genre of this book is about pastoral care, I gratefully acknowledge Dr. Mel Steinbron. First, in person, and secondly for his many writings that have undoubtedly been the inspiration for me to pursue care ministry. We met about twenty-five years ago while I was the Lead Pastor of Glad Tidings Church in Lake Charles, Louisiana. Dr. Steinbron presented our first *Equipping Seminar* and also did some follow-up seminars during that time. I have taken several quotations in my book from Dr. Steinbron's works for which he gave me personal and written permission. I want to provide all necessary recognition to him for his valuable friendship and mentorship, and sincerely thank him for enriching the Body of Christ with his godly influence. For several years, until his passing in July 2017, at the age of ninety-five, I visited Mel at his home almost every year.

My acknowledgments will be incomplete if I do not mention Mary Humphries for her hours and hours spent in proofreading my material over-and-over and making the necessary corrections and suggestions. Her excitement for the contents became an inspiration to me to continue rolling out another chapter. She and her husband, Ric, were part of my pastoral staff at Glad Tidings and consequently knew the functions of the care ministry. Their insights were most helpful in shaping my thoughts and influencing my approach to the subject.

Having been a pastor for many years, and having focused on congregational care, it is evident that I have had to read many books, magazines, and other periodicals on the subject and have incorporated much of it into my preaching and teaching. It has been my joy to also attend several seminars, conferences, and discussions on the subject, and as a result, many of the principles and thoughts have become *my own*. I feel sure that I may have included some of these learned values without realizing from where they originated. I want to thank all who have contributed to developing the subject of congregational care in my spirit. If I inadvertently did not give anyone deserved recognition, I sincerely apologize. I commit to rectifying it in future publications if notified.

—Dr. John W. Bosman

IN LOVING MEMORY

It is my great joy and delight to recognize and honor my friend, James Fontenot, of Lake Charles, Louisiana. He will forever live on in my memory as a kind, gentle, and gracious gentleman. James loved the Lord, His Church, and His people. He was a devoted follower of Christ, a loving husband, a caring father, and a compassionate grandfather. James was my friend.

James loved people. More than simply loving people from afar, he cared much about their well-being. We often talked about the necessity of the church to reach out to its members — and to meet their needs. He was quickly disturbed when he noticed neglect or a lack of attention. That was true not only of his church family but also his own family. For as long as he lived, he retained a concern for them. James' life epitomized, *loving God, loving people.*

James' parents were pastors for many years. They built a great church — both spiritually and physically. As a direct result and to a great extent, he knew what ministry was about and understood the manifold challenges pastors face. He loved his parents dearly, as did his siblings.

Life dealt James some heavy blows. His older son died of a massive heart attack at a young age. This tragedy devastated him and became a tremendous battle to fight. Soon after that, James' brother died, and in 2017 his mother and sister also died within eight days of each other. James somehow began to love the Lord in a more personal way. Heaven became his heart's desire. His last years were not sad and discouraging—he kept the faith and lived life to its fullest.

He and his wife continued their special love for each other while their younger son continued to lead the family business quite successfully. Grandchildren, special family members, and close friends extended his quality of life. They all helped each other until his death on November 10, 2017.

In loving memory of James, the Fontenot Family underwrote the publishing of this book with the prayer and deep desire that it would help many pastors, churches, and members to care for the household of faith. With great gratitude, I express my most profound appreciation to them. I miss my many conversations with James — especially his laugh! Rest in peace, my friend, rest in peace, until we meet again.

FOREWORD

Ever since I was young — both in years and in ministry — I have been an evangelist. During my lifetime, I have been blessed to see literally millions of people receive Christ. In this season of my life, looking back, I realize that I likely never would have been an effective local-church pastor. Evangelism has always been the grace-zone of my calling and I thank God for that wonderful privilege. For that reason, I find myself somewhat *inadequate* to write the foreword to a book on pastoral care.

Having said that, I realize fully the importance of all the five-fold ministry gifts working together in the body of Christ. The role of the evangelist is to win souls, and it is then the role of the pastor to nurture and disciple them. It is within the local church where people experience the ongoing love of God from and through people who care. It is here where they have the privilege to participate in the ordinances of the Church, learn to cultivate the Fruit of the Spirit, receive help to discover their spiritual gifts, and accept guidance to eventually also become faithful ministers in the body of Christ. When a church operates like this, evangelism becomes more effective and the role of the evangelist becomes imperative.

In his book, *The Care Revolution*, John Bosman captures the value of pastors and members collaborating to nurture new believers and care for the sheep God has entrusted to them. Taken from the *Great Commandment*, he extrapolates two streams he refers to as *Loving God* and *Loving People*. In the first, he emphasizes the *Great Commission*, and in the second, the *Great Commitment*, which is built on Peter's acceptance of Christ's charge to take care of the sheep (John 21:15–17).

Throughout the book, Dr. Bosman advocates that it is only a nurtured and cared-for church that will have the requisite ability to evangelize the lost effectively. He holds that a hurting and/or dysfunctional church simply cannot do it. This premise makes us realize that evangelism and pastoral care are not contrary to each other — the one depends upon the other! As Dr. Mel Steinbron says, "Caring and nurturing follow evangelism in the spiritual order in the same way that nurturing follows the birth of a child in the natural order." We can never leave a newborn believer to survive on his or her own, just as we cannot leave a newborn baby to survive on a sidewalk.

Evangelism is the lifeblood of the Church and no local congregation will ever grow without reaching the lost intentionally. Likewise, the successful outcome of any evangelism effort depends on the ongoing endeavors of the local church to follow up on the new converts, discipling and nurturing them with loving care.

—Evangelist Reinhard Bonnke
President/Founder
Christ for All Nations
Orlando, FL 32859-0588
USA

INTRODUCTION

I had been a pastor for several years before I received the revelation of effective congregational care as I have articulated it in this book. It hit me like a ton of bricks and soon became a revolution that changed my life and ministry forever. I often said, *I wish I had known these principles when I started off in the ministry.* This eye-opening endeavor came to me shortly after I had become the Lead Pastor of a church that was facing incredible challenges. They had gone through a sudden valley of grief and pain, heading for a split, with unbelievable tension and strife. The Sunday morning attendance had dwindled from almost a thousand to less than four hundred, and people were still leaving.

They were facing an overwhelming dilemma, which I summarized as the tail wagging the dog. It seemed as though the people were finding themselves in gridlock and nobody was willing to surrender, which consequently caused unreal stress and strain. I say more about that in the book. Not only did God graciously help me bring restoration to the church but also gave me divine wisdom to deliver a solution to the apparent problem. What once was defeat became one of the most significant victories you could ever imagine.

Against all the odds, the church grew exponentially within the first year to the point where we had to provide four hundred additional seats in the sanctuary immediately. Many people who had left the church, returned almost overnight, and as a result of this significant momentum, caused scores of new people to be drawn at the same time. That was incredible. The revolving door had swung in the other direction. But as exhilarating as this was, it created a daunting challenge for me to connect all the many individuals with each other in this volatile environment. Many things naturally demanded my attention as a new pastor, while at the same time, I was working on constructing an inspiring vision for the church. After having gone through such a tough time, the influx of so many people caused the enthusiasm among the congregants to soar. Deep down in my heart, I knew, however, that real ministry is about people, and if we miss connecting with them, we could lose the God-given momentum. It was at this crucial moment that we discovered the powerful concept of *people caring for people.*

With the excellent help of my leadership team, we put a system in place whereby our members were trained and developed to connect and care for one another. The more we researched this concept, the more we came to the understanding that it not only meets a crucial need, but that it's entirely biblical, and should be part of the ongoing ministry of every congregation. 1 Corinthians 12:25-26 says, *But that the members should have the same care for one another. And if one member suffers, all the members suffer with it; or if one member is honored, all the members rejoice with it.*

Somewhere along the line, we have missed this reality in the body of Christ and erroneously made pastoral care the sole responsibility of the pastor. This mindset held on over centuries and became the traditionally accepted norm for congregational care to most people. In spite of the restoration of the priesthood of the believer during the

First Reformation, the conviction remained that the clergy are the ones that *do* ministry, while the laity *watch* ministry being done. For church members to be involved in pastoral care was almost viewed as heresy. Unfortunately, this mentality remains stuck in many people's mind even to this day.

As pastors, we deprive ourselves of a wealth of resources by not utilizing the gifts of grace and mercy our people have received from the Holy Spirit. Simultaneously we rob them of the excellent opportunity of being involved in a ministry that will provide them with decisive fulfillment. Once we mined the treasure of capabilities our church members already had, we tapped into a vein that became the catalyst for growing a large church in a relatively small city. We finally had to build a worship center that could seat more than three thousand people. Looking back, I know today that the care system we designed became one of the two main tracks that helped us reach a community for Christ.

One of the challenges we still face today is the conviction of most pastors and churches who believe that they actually do provide adequate pastoral care to their congregation. Looking at it a little closer, we will discover that they are not, in reality, providing *pastoral care* but instead only *crisis care.* This perspective means that people usually have to face a crisis before they receive attention, but once the crisis is over, so is the care. That's not the way to connect people and is most probably not the way to care for the flock God has entrusted to us. Is it any wonder that so many people in our churches, these days, feel unattached, insecure, and neglected? The challenge increases when we realize how many people fall through the cracks or slip through the proverbial back door, and for the most part, realize too late they had left. There is a missing link in our ministry efforts.

Dr. Mel Steinbron asks the question in his book by the same title: *Can the Pastor Do It Alone?* And we know the answer to that statement-question is an unequivocal, no! But when it comes to pastoral care, it seems we, as pastors, just press on, having made peace with the traditional mindset that we have no option other than to do it on our own. Now, we know, there is an option! The sad part is that in the modern-day church, with all the busyness we face, pastoral care has become a neglected necessity even for pastors. We only have time to handle crisis situations, and even at that, often miss the opportunity. We often see the results in the many burnt-out pastors and frustrated church members around us.

Pastors have been called to shepherd the flock that God has put under their care (1 Peter 5:2) which is no light responsibility. According to Hebrews 13:17 they will one day have to give an account to God for the way they have watched over the sheep. I discovered a long time ago that it's not possible for pastors to do all the work of the ministry by themselves. It's just not possible, and it's undoubtedly not Scriptural. The same applies to pastoral care. Paul says in Ephesians 4:11 that Christ gave some to the Church *to be pastors*—to shepherd the flock, and then to *equip the saints* to partner with them in the ministry of caring for the congregation.

Pastors often impede the health and growth of their churches by having the notion that they should be available to all the people all the time. Wrong mentality. An exceptionally gifted pastor can do most of the pastoral care up to 200 people, but when it goes beyond that number, he or she burns out, or the church collapses. There should be a meaningful system of pastoral care in every congregation, regardless of its size. Sincere care is at the heart of the life of a congregation; if your pastoral care fails, so will your mission. The solution is to enlarge the footprint of your ministry by involving church members to provide ongoing congregational care to each other.

It is often difficult to get from where we are to where we ought to be if we continually allow the overwhelming demands of a congregation to strangle us. Unless we deliberately take steps to change from the *lone-ranger* style of pastoring to a *shared-pastoring* style, we will remain frustrated in our goals and stagnate in our development. When I saw this revelation, it soon became a revolution that positively changed the culture of our church and set us on the highway for becoming pace-setting in our entire region.

Being aware of a need such as this in itself is not good enough. We have to set our minds to developing and training our people according to a proven system. After having found the solution, our team designed teaching manuals and conducted regular training conferences. We developed leaders who developed leaders and methodically covered the whole congregation. The principle was to provide care for each member continually and to make sure people experienced a sense of belonging and acceptance. We established an efficient and workable system that connected members to each other and found practical solutions to assimilate new members. What was furthermore uplifting was to see the large numbers of people who enthusiastically participated in this life-giving ministry—greater than any other ministry activity we ever launched. There is nothing that can catapult the enthusiasm of a congregation quicker than getting people involved in the life of the church.

There are scores of people in all of our churches who have the giftedness, heart, and willingness to provide care to their fellow church members if given the opportunity. They are chomping at the bit to be involved and feel slighted when their particular gifts are not recognized.

It is this oversight that causes so much apathy in our churches. Our members are involved in evangelism, missions, intercession, outreaches, etc., why not congregational care? I am convinced that we will be much more effective and reach many more people if we change the way we do pastoral care.

Our focus on developing an active care ministry is not so much about growing our churches larger than it is developing them healthier. Any biological family that does not show love, care, and concern for each other have become known as dysfunctional families. We can say the same of a church family. If they are not showing the love and care to each other as they should, they have likewise become dysfunctional. The question then arises: how wise is it to add more people from the world to an already dysfunctional church family? Should we not first concentrate on making the church family healthy? Jesus said it is only when people see the love we have for each other that they will know we are followers of Christ.

If we desire to build healthy churches with excited people worshipping God, loving each other, and reaching out to the lost, we should embrace the truth that *the love of God has to flow down the aisles of our churches before it will flow down the streets of our cities.*

With that thought in mind, I find myself amazed at many pastors who are of the opinion that we should not spend time, resources, and energy on ministering to church people. They center all their efforts on reaching the lost—which, of course, is the mission of the Church. But a sick church cannot efficiently do evangelism, missions, outreaches, etc., as they should. I have carefully observed many churches who have taken on the approach of implementing evangelism only, and with dismay noticed at the end of any given year, they added few to none people to the flock. In the meanwhile, their established members feel hurt, abused, and neglected. Pastors and churches who have this *forever-knocking-on-every-door-mindset* seem to be more driven by guilt than reality and often reap the harvest but seldom keep the fruit. There is no connectivity. They have no way for people to bond with the congregation and no way to care for them in the event they do connect.

On the other hand, there are again pastors and leaders who assume they do not need a system of care and reason that their church consists of loving people who are already concerned about each other. The truth is that most churches are friendly and warm, but the question is whether there is any intentionality in their caring for each other. Let's be honest: people are not looking for a friendly church; it's friends they are after!

Observing church folk a little closer, you will almost always find that they spend blissful moments together on a Sunday, love one another, pray for each other, shake hands during fellowship time, but when the final amen is said, they each go their way, and nobody cares about someone else. The strength of a care ministry is evaluated not by what happens in church on Sunday, but by what happens between Sundays. Unless we are deliberate in the way we provide care, caring will not occur. That's why we need a proven system and develop people accordingly. Question: if we do not take care of the people God has already given us, why should He send us anymore?

The more we developed our care ministry, the more we came to realize that care should never be seen as an event, but rather as a way of living. By that, I mean that however much it may be a one-time blessing, we won't apply adequate care to our congregations by just calling a group of believers together for a weekend or two to visit members at their homes. Meaningful relationships can never be developed by means of a singular event. We have to have a systematic approach by which we provide care for our people when they walk through the valleys of life, but also even when things are going well with them. The key to the success of effective congregational care is consistency.

After we had operated the care ministry system in our church for some time, we then began also to equip pastors and members from other churches who likewise testified of the enormous benefits they gleaned from involving their members in caring for one another. It is practical, and it works. A few years ago, I re-designed the system to fit modern-day expectation, wrote new manuals, and created an adaptable system for churches in the twenty-first century. That was also the time when I coined the phrase, *The Care Revolution,* and changed the name of the local church application to *The Care Ministry Network.* I then asked several churches to run pilot programs on our behalf. The results were phenomenal. With this in place, I began teaching the principles of the concept to churches across the United States and simultaneously released the idea in South Africa through my younger brother, Pastor Stephan Bosman. It became overwhelming!

Through this book, and other publications soon to follow, we are now entering a brand-new season of the *Care Revolution.* We are going to release all the information of the concept to pastors and churches in an easily understandable and reproducible format which will make it possible for them to develop and equip their people to find their fulfillment in providing congregational care. We have done all the work for you—all you must do is cast the vision (and we'll help you with this too), prepare your people, and then launch your own *Care Ministry Network.* You also will say, "Why did I not know about this concept years ago?"

As you read through the pages of this book, you will see how I expand on the things I have touched on in this *Introduction*. I have included unbelievable amounts of information for pastors and leaders because I am convinced that the more material we have, the easier it is to cast the vision to our congregations. As one pastor said, "This book has more preaching material in it than I have time to preach." One chapter deals with the basic needs all people have and touch on a nerve that has been sorely neglected by the church. I have also included practical applications to prepare people for the work of the ministry and made sure we underscore the fact that our care concept is founded on the Word of God and not just based on a good idea. I have added many Scriptures to validate the authenticity of the care ministry and continue to find much more as I continue to study this subject.

Taken from the Great Commandment in Matthew 22:35-40 we develop the thought of two streams flowing from it, identified as *Loving God* and *Loving people*. The first flows into the well-known Great Commission and the second into our newly derived concept, the Great Commitment. It was from this commitment to Jesus, to care for the sheep, that Peter gave the charge to the elders, and the church-at-large, to watch over the flock (1 Peter 5:2). He ends the charge by reminding those involved that their faithfulness in shepherding the flock (the congregation) will receive a reward from the Master, reserved exclusively for them. I had read this portion of Scripture so many times, but it never struck me so profoundly that it had to do with caring for the congregation of which God had made us responsible. I assumed heaven was reserving the reward for being a good pastor and never considered the responsibility of church members who likewise had giftedness towards that end.

In closing, I would like to mention a few things regarding our Care Ministry Network briefly. First off, I want to state that the *Care Ministry Network is an authentic and proven system of congregational care that enables believers to care for one another.* The new paradigm I propose is developing a healthy partnership between the pastor and the church members who together provide the necessary care to the flock (congregation). It is a collaborative effort between them. The members don't *help the pastor* to care for the people; they come alongside him or her and perform actual works of ministry. The pastor is the one that *helps the people* to develop their gifts and skills to provide systematic and meaningful care. This can only effectively be accomplished when there is a demonstrated training course through which members are equipped and trained. There must be levels of expectations, which include personal commitment, and once these anticipations are made, they become the standards by which members perform their ministries. It is important to state that church members, providing congregational care, do not *replace* their pastor, they *represent* their pastor.

I have tried to cover all the bases. Previously, similar care models have seen the light but did not succeed, and one of the main reasons it failed was that they never afforded a way whereby those who provided care could likewise receive care. I have taken this into consideration and have made provision for every member to get the attention they deserve—from the leaders to each family member; from the directors to every worker.

Throughout the book, I use selected vocabulary to describe the workings of the care ministry as well as *titles* for those involved. These descriptions are not cast in concrete—only means of identification. Should pastors or churches prefer to reference their care ministry by any other name, or ascribe different *titles* to their workers, they should feel free to do so—for as long as it makes sense. Names and titles are not what's important; the concept is.

My prayer is that this book, and especially what it stands for, will be a blessing to many pastors, leaders, churches, and faithful believers who have taken up the charge to care for the flock. There is a huge reward waiting at the end of the journey!

CONTENTS

Dedication		7
Acknowledgements		9
In Loving Memory		13
Foreword		15
Introduction		17

1. A Needed New Paradigm 31
2. My Discovery of the Care Revolution 67
3. The Great Commitment 89
4. A New Paradigm 109
5. Why Have a Care Ministry? 129
6. If It Ain't Broke, Break It 153
7. The Care Revolution Revelation 175
8. It's Not Only a Concept—It Works 201
9. Why People Act the Way They Do 223
10. The Role of the Pastor 261
11. There is a Shift Going On 283
12. Let the Bible Speak 311
13. The Restoration of the Ministry of the Pastor 339
14. The Church in Action 359

So far as the Christian faith is concerned, the solid handle in our time is laity religion. If in the average we would suddenly take seriously the notion that every lay member, man, or woman, is a minister of Christ, we would have something like a revolution in a short time; it would constitute both the big dose and the required novelty. Suddenly the number of ministers in the average church would jump from one to five hundred. It is the way to employ valuable but mostly wasted human resources. Elton Trueblood.

(Your Other Vocation, Harper & Row, Publishers, San Francisco, 1952)

1

A NEEDED
NEW PARADIGM

We are living in a different world. In the late 1960s, Louis Armstrong mused, "What a wonderful world." Fast forward two decades and, in the late 1980s, you'd have heard Aretha Franklin offer, "I know my parents love me, stand behind me come what may . . . It's a different world."[1] Fast forward another two-and-a-half decades or so and hear NFL general manager Sonny Weaver (actor Kevin Costner's fictional character in *Draft Day*) quip, "We live in a different world than we did 60 seconds ago".[2]

We are living in a different world, indeed. Everything seems to be changing faster than we have ever anticipated and it's undeniably affecting our church-world also. Even our culture and is changing rapidly and necessitates that we reevaluate our approach to the way

---

1   https://www.lyricsondemand.com/tvthemes/adifferentworldlyrics.html

2   http://shepherdproject.com/draft-day

we do ministry. The demands on local churches are not the same today as they were only a few years ago. When it comes to their worship preferences, people are no longer focusing their attention on religion, but rather on relationships. They are searching for a church environment that offers acceptance, meaning, and purpose—regardless of their religious background.

Although it is the sense of belonging that provides the stimulus for generating stability and constancy to any local congregation; we do not find it readily everywhere. We don't have to go too far to realize that the crying need of scores of people is a heartfelt desire to build deep friendships and foster genuine relationships. To be sure, actually developing and promoting those have become more challenging than most people care to admit. But that should not have been the way we operate. People are longing for meaning and community and the church is where people should be able to find the answer. Unfortunately, we don't always seem prepared to respond to the need.

There is a good chance that a church member left your church on Sunday thinking, "I wonder if my pastor even knows I was here today?" While walking across the parking lot, feeling rather lonely, the thoughts continue to roll: "I wonder if **anyone** knows I was here today? If I had to leave this church, I wonder how long it would take for them to notice I am no longer attending—that is, if anyone would ever realize I had left." A guest may have come with hurt and pain; hoping to find encouragement, love, and support; yet left without anyone even paying attention to him or her. It happens all the time.

Despite modern technology and new methods of communication, we find that people today are lonesome and desperately in search of meaningful interaction. We are more connected than we have ever been and yet have never felt more alone. The question is, how do we solve this? The frustration of many pastors lies within the uneasy feeling of not knowing how to resolve the problem of crossing the chasm between them and attendees, finding ways to stay in touch with them. It keeps pastors out of their much-needed sleep and often dampens their enthusiasm. But what if I told you there is a solution—an authentic and proven new paradigm that will remedy most of these challenges and likewise provide you with answers to many other similar problems—would you be interested? If so, I invite you to embark on an exciting journey with me.

People Are People

Seeing people as individuals and meeting them at their point of need should remain the clarion call of our mission. We have become comfortable *inviting* people, but we are no longer willing to be *involved* with people. We need a mind-transformation and a heart-regeneration to begin to understand where people find themselves honestly. This transformation and regeneration may well call for a renewed strategy of connectivity in most churches. God created humankind to live in community, and where there is an absence of essential cohesiveness, people get lost in the shuffle.

Observing reality all around us validates the urgency for a new paradigm in most of our churches. We are almost two decades into the twenty-first century, and it has become abundantly clear that the church is facing some severe challenges most of us never anticipated. We were all expecting the falling away the Bible refers to but have not prepared for the radical nature of today's challenges. Many are saying that the church has become irrelevant as prior approaches have lost their effectiveness and attraction.

What once was the ideal for the church is no longer realistic to most people. In today's lonely world people are desperately reaching out to anyone who genuinely cares, and when you ask them, they will tell you that they are in reality not looking for a friendly church; it's friends they are after. This search has become one of the loudest outcries of scores of people and many churches seem to have no practical solution. The truth is that there are many friendly churches available everywhere, but that does not mean they necessarily always provide the required environment wherein people can cultivate sincere friendships and develop meaningful relationships.

> People are not looking
> for a friendly church,
> it's friends they are after!

To be more capable in reaching people, as well as keeping them, we need to move beyond the models or techniques of the past and come up with a renewed way of solidifying those who come to our churches. People are starving for genuine relationships and are desperate for community. They have become cognizant of needs they had not been aware of before and are keenly searching for churches that meet these requirements. People want to connect in meaningful ways with others and in so-doing develop interactions that will mutually benefit each other to reach their potential.

Astonishing as it may seem, in this search, people are no longer steered by denominational labels in their choice of a church for themselves or their family. That sentiment has mostly dissipated. The way a church provides opportunities for interaction and has developed means of connection among people has become the more vital criteria in their choice of a congregation. The dictates of life have forced people to adjust their need-cries which have caused them to focus on those things in a church that will provide the essential interaction for them and their families as a whole. Churches willing to adjust their approach to ministry in a way by which they can accommodate these seeking individuals will be the ones that become the life-giving churches of the future. That does not mean lowering our standards or forsaking our core values. As the adage goes, "The message never changes, but methods do!"

Alarming Tendencies

According to a May 2015 report from Pew Research Center, the number of Christians in America has been dropping at alarming rates over the last eight or more years. The report further states that during that same time frame, people who didn't affiliate with any religion continued to grow noticeably in numbers. This research introduces us to a group of individuals sociologists refer to as *Nones*—people who answer *none* when asked about their religious affiliation. And the shocking reality is that we are not talking only about a few. The numbers are becoming staggering. In many ways, this sounds amazing and almost unbelievable to be right in the United States of America. Because of the rise of these religiously unaffiliated people, social platforms like Facebook believe there is a gap in religious participation and that their social network can fill that vacuum.

This alarming tendency doesn't stop there, however! There is another extraordinary group of people who we identify as *Dones*—people who say they are *done* with the local church. The Dones are not only former church members but also pastors and church leaders, people who at one point were the pacesetters and visionaries of their congregations in their own right. In many cases, they were the ones who pioneered new churches and funded the dream. "Dones" are no longer meeting in churches but in coffee shops, in workplaces, and their homes. They are studying Scriptures together, praying for each other, serving one another, and enjoying genuine fellowship they once knew. These people have not abandoned Christ or His message. They have not stopped praying or reading their Bibles; they are just *done* with being part of a local church. The reason many people are leaving the church is that it no longer holds that sense of community it once did.

Together, these trends give us much reason to be concerned. Let's look a little further: Why did approximately 80 percent of people in America say in 1992 they regularly attended church but now only 59 percent? Why are so many saying that the church no longer makes any difference in their lives? Why are people saying churches have become irrelevant? Why are 70 percent of our churches in decline or stagnated? Why are only 30 percent of our churches showing signs of growth in spite of population growth? Why do families no longer arrange their activities to revolve around the church as was previously the case? Why are Millennials avoiding church participation?

These questions are real, and we cannot ignore them, and if we're not careful, we can ignore what is occurring, stick our heads in the ground, and hope things will get better. But they won't, and we already know that. Or, we could foolishly continue to do the same things we've always done and hope the results will be different. If we want to move to the cutting-edge of church life and restore our relevance, we have no option other than to face reality and change what we need to change, remove what we need to remove and replace what is needed. We cannot just disregard what's going on, because ignoring a problem won't make it go away and, indeed, won't produce any positive results.

The Church Is Not Dying

In the face of all these challenges, let us be real and firmly agree: The Church (the universal body of Christ) is not dying, and has not lost its mission. God has not given up on the Church, and neither should we. Many positive things are happening in many churches despite the troubling landscape around us. For the Church to die is off-course theologically impossible. Jesus said, "I will build My Church, and the gates of hell shall not prevail against it . . ." (Matthew 16:18 KJV). If Jesus said He would *build* His Church, then obviously it's never posed to die. The Church has stood the test of times over the ages and will remain triumphant until Jesus returns. They have tried to ridicule Its message and silence Its voice. They have sought to blaspheme Its leader and kill Him on a cross. But still, the Church is triumphant, alive, and doing well and remains an unstoppable force in the world. Our God remains a God of hope, faith, and restoration. Our present responsibility is to continue with Christ's powerful message by hearing what the Holy Spirit is saying, getting in step with what He is doing, and follow where He is directing.

Considering all the demands and pressures on churches added to changing cultures and social strains, we can all readily agree that something fresh will have to break forth on the horizon. We will have to make some significant changes. Vibrant and growing churches are just not the norm any longer, and we had better not settle for that status quo. I remain convinced that the American Church still has a compelling future, but it will much depend on our ability to create a renewed means of close, spiritual community that cannot be replaced by any form of electronic media.

Another reason we see the forming of groups, primarily such as the Dones, may be the result of many churchgoers having slipped into the propensity of merely attending church on Sunday, but no longer being involved in ministry in one way or another. There may be many reasons for this, and we'll say more about it later, but this trend could most likely have developed from the unfortunate truth that churches have not engaged their members strongly enough in practical ministry—more than casual volunteering. This disengagement caused them to lose their sense of belonging and their need to be needed, and the result was that they moved on. We will have to engage people more deliberately in meaningful ministry and develop them efficiently in servant-leadership. Life-giving churches have proven that those people who are purposefully involved in ministry have the sense of being on mission with their pastor and are liable to be much more committed to constant attendance, financial support, and unfailing loyalty. They have developed a sense of "buy-in." The strength of a church lies within its people. That is why I have always said: The church should not run on the feet of the clergy, but on the feet of the laity.

> The church should not
> run on the feet of the clergy,
> but on the feet of the laity

You Are Here

If you visit a large shopping mall, you will usually find a display board, called a directory. On it, you will locate a red dot with the words; "You Are Here." Once you have seen where you are, it's much easier to know how to get to where you want to go. As church leaders, it may be helpful first to determine where we are, so we can resolve how to reach our destination.

Traveling extensively across America and using the opportunity to ask some pertinent questions to pastors and leaders underscored to me a greater present-day confront concerning local church ministry. One of my first and honest questions to these pastors dealt with the process they were following in their churches to make it balanced and healthy. I was blown away by most responses. In short, if a church had a working process, the pastor could easily articulate it and excitedly explain the functions when asked. If they did not have a designed process, they usually never understood the question, or began to fumble, trying to make it up along the way until finally, they would say something like, "I guess we don't have a process!" When a pastor or leader responded by asking, "What do you mean a process?" I readily knew the answer: they did not have one.

I was sitting at a table with a pastor at a nice restaurant one day. It seems most of these conversations occurred around a dining room table! He requested this meeting to discuss with me the practical ways of developing a healthy church. "We need a move of God, and we need it now" was the way he approached the subject. His statement made me uncomfortable because I knew where this would typically take us. After talking about the weather and the hopeless football team we both thought would do great, I asked the pastor, "What is your congregation's vision?" Without flinching, he said, "Our vision is revival; we are desperately seeking revival!"

It felt as though the blood drained out of my head. Of course, I understand we all desire a move of God, but if all we want to do is sit back and wait for something supernatural to happen, it may never come. After all, Jesus never told us we should wait for people to come, He said we should *Go, and make disciples*. To do that, we should begin by training our members in evangelism, organize substantial prayer, and start getting a process in place for when the people come. Revival does not just happen, but when it does, we should be ready to accommodate the harvest and provide the essential care for them to develop personally and grow spiritually.

When we experienced a divine visitation of God's Presence at Glad Tidings we saw more than 4,000 people make a commitment to Christ over only nine weeks. This was the result of an extensive prayer process among the church members and not the mere desire of the leadership. Among several other things, our prayer initiative included a 24-hour prayer room—168 hours of prayer, non-stop every week, led by my wife, Anne. I realize God can do whatever is needed, whenever He wants, but prayerful preparation has always been a prerequisite for any move of God.

I'm afraid that too many pastors and churches are operating without a proven system of discipling people and likewise caring for people. You cannot build a healthy church without having workable systems in place. John Maxwell quotes Urban Meyer of The Ohio State Buckeyes as saying, "Average leaders have a quote. Good leaders have a plan. Exceptional leaders have a system." [3]

A few years ago, I made it a point to involve pastors in engaging conversations regarding the state of the church in the twenty-first century. The knowledge I gained from these many discussions, caused me think intensely and made me dig deeper into what churches are

---

3   *Above the Line: Lessons in Leadership and Life from a Championship Season.*

A NEEDED NEW PARADIGM | 41

facing. Often, these discussions became distressing. I was quite frankly shocked to discover so many well-meaning pastors and churches who were merely going through the motions and being seemingly content with where they were regarding managing their churches. In many cases, they could not remember when they last saw someone saved. Those who were still winning the lost could rarely give any account of those who accepted Christ. Questions concerning discipleship were responded to, in many cases, as though it belonged to a by-gone era. And let me be clear: this was not the case in all churches, and neither was it the case in only small churches.

The Absence of a Common Thread

Apart from the obvious things we find in a local church, I discovered through this experience, the absence of a common thread that I have coined *the missing link*. I call it "missing," because it's not a new discovery, it's a lost reality. This lost necessity has been in existence from the days of the early church and is a stated expectation in the Bible but has now become nonexistent in so many of our churches. I have no idea how we have missed it. But when you rediscover this truth and implement its reality, every church becomes balanced and healthy, and will not be able to do anything other than grow. The fact is that no congregation can afford to function in the absence of this *missing link* and that's why I am going to introduce you to this new paradigm.

A New Reformation

It's amazing how history tends to repeat itself, even for the Church. The first Reformation is now five hundred years behind us. One of the essential themes Martin Luther addressed during the first Reformation was *the priesthood of all believers*. He based the essence of this principle on the truth that believers did not need an earthly priest as a prerequisite for them to enter into the presence of God but, being made priests themselves through the redemptive work of Christ had free access to the Father. The priesthood of believers—direct access to God through Jesus Christ—was thankfully acknowledged and put into practice, albeit limited in scope. This truth, however, never expanded beyond the expression of personal faith.

Unfortunately, the further expansion of this truth never entirely took root. This truth distinctly referred to the involvement of believers in the work of the ministry and clarified that there was no class difference between the clergy and the laity. In the days of the Reformation, paid professionals were expected to do the work of parish ministry, while the laity had to sit back passively and be satisfied to be mere spectators—which became the accepted norm. Missing was an understanding that every believer is a minister, the fact that the priesthood of each believer affects both worship and work. Much of this misperception still lingers in our churches today. The ordinary believers were furthermore deemed unqualified to understand the Word of God and consequently had no Bibles of their own.

Just like during the first reformation there is once again a swelling tide of restlessness in the church-world. I believe God is preparing us for another transformation, another grave, but a necessary makeover. Something new is about to be birthed. And just as a newborn child entails significant adjustments in a household, so this re-applied truth requires some of our traditional thinking to change. Among the qualities we will most certainly have to restore at-large, is the fact that ministry is meant to be a shared effort between vocational ministers and church members alike. And this means more than people just volunteering in some minor role. It refers to actual functions of ministry, which in the past, for the more significant part, were exclusively held by credentialed ministers. Through involving people in ministry-partnership, incredible enthusiasm is going to be released, which will become the catalyst for significant numbers of individuals participating in building the Church.

The general idea of partnership in ministry does not come easy for everyone—especially regarding the new paradigm, I will be introducing. We are facing high traditions and deep convictions that will most likely have to change, but the results will undoubtedly be worth the effort. If churches are going to survive in the next century, pastors and leaders will have to obey the Holy Spirit, follow the instructions of the Word of God, and release the people of God to do the work of God. There are scores of capable and willing people in our churches who would gladly make themselves available for tasks of service. They are accomplished and instrumental and are purely waiting for an opportunity. Not involving church members in ministry will most certainly result in declining membership, which could potentially lead to dying congregations.

A Breath of Fresh Air

The good news is that there is a breath of fresh air blowing through the body of Christ, an awakening, a thrilling awareness in the hearts of many people across the country bringing new hope for the future. A spiritual revolution has begun, and it holds in its wings the promise of a bright new tomorrow! Both leaders and church members alike are sensing this. Through this revolution, they are discovering the solution to the missing link. The Bible has laid out the resolve and given us the answer—a straightforward, but useful, answer.

The sleeping giant called the body of Christ is rising to take its rightful position. This breath of fresh air we are talking about is God's intentional means of having the saints arise and letting the Church be the Church! We can already see positive results through churches building community through developing meaningful relationships and strategically bonding people with each other. Developing relationships is becoming the catalyst for restoring strong interconnection among church members that will result in new life. You can already hear references of restoration to a missing link expressed in the words of influential Christian leaders who are beginning to refer to this theme with great enthusiasm. You can read about their actual attempts on the pages of magazine articles and blogs. It's starting to surface more and more as the experts of church strategy are referring to a vacuum in churches and enthusiastically recommending how we could get back to basics and pay attention to the principles Jesus taught.

Not everyone is necessarily using quite the same terminology, but the revolution has begun. It's directly attached to what I call the Great Commitment—a term I will fully explain as we proceed! You can already detect the revolution in words such as community, connection, caring, etc. They are all pointing in the same direction. I believe the Holy Spirit is saying the same thing to many different people across the land; something is stirring, and we have the glorious opportunity to respond.

Something is
stirring and we
have the glorious
opportunity to
respond

The Revolution

Before I introduce you to the missing link itself, allow me, for clarity's sake, to mention first that I refer to the entire process of what we are dealing with as a *revolution*, since it has every potential of bringing wholesome transformation to churches. I refer to this revolution as the *Care Revolution*! As the designation indicates, it means in its purest form: a revolution of care—but care on a significantly different level than we have become familiar with in the past.

- The *Care Revolution* is the spark that ignites the solution to the missing link and provides a process through which we can remedy this nagging lack. It unfolds a means of bringing a church to a place of health and vitality, with practical ministry accomplishment as the beneficial outcome. It simultaneously releases compelling cohesiveness through developing sustaining relationships within any given congregation. The *Care Revolution* is more than a mere one-line statement and takes more than a single paragraph to describe.
- The *Care Revolution* promotes a strategically designed concept that empowers the local church to create a culture of care and genuine community. This robust system of congregational care has its roots deep in the Great Commitment. It is a well-designed network system that connects people to each other quickly and methodically, bringing both unity and trust in the church, regardless of its size.
- The *Care Revolution* concept releases incredible energy among church members and consequently attracts many

to be part of the momentum. It creates an environment for health and growth for all church members while at the same time opens the door for many new people to come in. Although what I am talking about is not necessarily a new *revelation,* it has indeed begun a new *revolution.*

- The *Care Revolution* is touching a nerve that's magnifying so much of the void that's present in so many churches. The model is not complicated. It is so simple that if we're not careful, we may just overlook it, brush it off, and continue to miss it. If that happens, we will still be asking, "What is missing in our churches? Why are people coming, but they're not staying?"

The Missing Link

The *missing link* I am referring to is primarily the absence of a systematic unfolding of the Lord's Command, *love your neighbor as yourself* which eventually became the catalyst for the appeal of Peter who said, *Take care of the flock . . .* That is why I said it's not a new discovery, but rather a lost reality. But hang in there with me, and I will show you the depth of what this all means.

Somewhere along the line, we have lost our focus on adequately caring for the people God has entrusted to us, as we should. It seems we have become more interested in programs than people. We tend to be focused on adding more and more people to our churches, but in the process, disregarded those sheep who are bleating for attention. We forever want to go beyond, build more prominent churches, and gain more people, but we never seem to get there, because more people are falling off the back of the wagon than we are trying to load on the front end. That is frustrating, but why is that happening?

What adds to this already crippled function of ministry is the belief of many church members that providing care to one another systematically is not their responsibility, but exclusively that of the pastor. And it's not that they don't love other people, because that is not the case. It's more a matter of them not understanding that they too have a role to play in providing congregational care.

Bottom line up front: Consequent to speaking in a different church nearly every weekend—across the United States and abroad—my research (or, at least, my intentional and deliberate *fact-finding* journey) has identified five critical attributes that are absent in most local churches.

The lacking vital traits are:

1. The *core value* of providing *ongoing* care to each congregant in bad times as well as in good times;

2. A stated and practiced *philosophy* that church members are the ones to supply congregational care and not only the pastor;

3. A culture of *intentionality* in caring for one another;

4. Deliberately *maintaining contact* with every member between Sundays, and, most of all,

5. A *proven system* to train and develop church members to provide authentic care to each other.

Practicing these above-mentioned attributes fulfills Paul's directive when he says, "The members should have the same care for one another" (1 Corinthians 12:25(b)) to which he then adds, "And if one member suffers, all the members suffer with it; or if one member is honored, all the members rejoice with it" (1 Corinthians 12:26b). These statements express the standard of community the early church held, but for the most part, no longer exists in the modern-day church. Many leaders who know, will agree with me that our churches will again become healthy and grow when we change the way we do pastoral care.

While, at first, this premise (as it relates congregational care) may sound overly simplistic to some and, to a degree, it might be, when we consider its full implication, however, we will discover its intrinsic value and regard it anew in an entirely different light. Seemingly, one reason we have missed it is that it is so simple. (Let me offer two thoughts on *simple* things: Remember, (1) simple does not mean easy and (2) it certainly does not mean shallow.) We are going to take this simple concept—and, yes, it really is—and build it out to its fullest expression, without making more of it than it should be. You will be amazed to see the unfolding of this vital and missing Scriptural link.

First things first: You need to settle in your mind that we are not talking about creating some artificial *lovey-dovey*, *cushy-cushy* atmosphere in our churches. (The end game is not for everyone to stand around, hold hands, and sing *kum ba yah!*) We are talking about an intentional and workable biblical system of taking care of the people the Lord has entrusted to us. We intend to make sure we are nurturing church members on a regular and meaningful basis—during the good times as well as the tough times. It's the kind of caring that goes hand-in-hand with discipleship and holds firm to the expectation of Christ.

Most people in most churches nowadays do not receive ongoing care. They just don't. This fact is even sadly true when it comes to our outreach efforts: Collectively, we tend to reap the harvest, but, for the most part, do not keep the harvest. The reason we don't keep them is that we don't nurture them. It is true not only of new converts but also of longtime members—especially longtime members!

The statement-questions we made at the opening of this chapter are typical and occur more often than we would like to know or admit. A disconnect has somehow developed. In a world of competition and comparison, church members feel more and more like numbers on a roll instead of living human beings with feelings and emotions. Is it any wonder why we now have the *Dones* and the *Nones* as I referenced?

We realize that most of these troubling situations are the result of our enduring busyness, packed lives, and overfilled calendars. In its wake, this trend has left many people feeling isolated, which created a vacuum in our closeness, that is so crucial in building unity. This desertion has caused many people to feel lonely and rejected despite being surrounded by many other people. We can often see it in the prevailing atmosphere of member-self-centeredness, which, thus, stifles the building of authentic, genuine fellowship that is supposed to last beyond Sunday morning.

The missing link does not lie so much only within the lack of *providing* care, but even more so in the absence of a well-designed *congregational care system.* We have systems for everything else in the church, but not for taking care of people in meaningful and significant ways. We usually are clear on our mission and vision, our churches are mostly friendly and kind, but if there is no *intentionality* in reaching out to others in love, and paying attention to their hurts and needs, we will never experience the cohesiveness we need for developing a healthy church body. To accomplish meaningful community, we need a strategy—a well-defined system. It just will not happen by itself. In some cases, it may require leaders to revisit their mission and vision statements and make sure *taking care of the flock (the household of faith)*, is even anchored in a reliable system. Pastors and members alike should know how they will provide effective care to all who relate to their congregation.

It's a well-defined
system that's
lacking

Member Involvement

During my journey of interviewing pastors, I have found that one of the most crucial care-disconnects among church members is the traditional mindset most of them have of believing pastoral care should entirely be provided by credentialed ministers. We are saying it here and will say it often: ongoing care, to all the members of a congregation, cannot be provided by the pastor alone. That is just not possible. Trying to invite additional staff, in most cases, is not an option either, because most churches cannot afford to employ enough staff to adequately get the job done. The solution lies in creating a platform for church members to partner with their pastor to provide the required care to all who relate to the congregation. I will introduce you to a strategy that effectively develops God's people to care for one another and in the process, builds loyalty and unity.

If we are serious about following the direction of the Holy Spirit and devoted to the conviction of disbanding the two-tier caste system, we must be willing to abandon our persuasion concerning ministry exclusivity. It is the prohibition of church members in ministry that has made many people apathetic, unconcerned, and uninvolved. The *Care*

Revolution calls for pastors, leaders, and church members to challenge the traditional thinking of pastoral care and create a new paradigm for taking care of the congregation. And I'm not suggesting that members help their pastor in caring for the flock, but instead coming alongside and partnering with their pastor to provide essential care.

It's Not What You May Think

In my presentation of this subject, I don't want you to get the impression that I am only underscoring the relevance of pastoral care, but rather that I am beckoning the church to break with the antiquated model and to instead equip members to provide the necessary care systematically. It's not so much a matter of *what* should be done as it is about *how* it should be done. My approach is to utilize church members, who have the proper gift-sets, to take on this responsibility and provide care to their fellow congregants in organized group settings. All the way from Moses (in the old Testament), as we will see later, this is the biblical and workable model. I challenge you to be open-minded and begin to think differently about the subject of pastoral care. If you want your church to be healthy and grow, you must change the culture of people expecting their pastor to be available for every birthday party, every hospital visit, and every family celebration. This will not be easy for all people to accept, but if the church wants to break through any growth barrier, it must happen. That is why we refer to it as *a new paradigm for doing pastoral care*. The bottom-line is that everybody needs somebody to care for them, but it does not always have to be the pastor.

Pastoral Care or Crisis Care

Many well-meaning pastors and churches today believe they are indeed providing the required care. What is true is that we have created a *tradition* of pastoral care and have accepted it to be the sum total of what is required. The veracity of the matter is that the traditional way of doing pastoral care generates a means of co-dependency among church members, relying on their pastor for all their need-fulfillments, while the pastor, on the other hand, depends upon the congregation to provide their personal sense of worth. It has created an unhealthy scenario.

Following the traditional model, some churches have appointed people in vocational positions calling them *Minister of Pastoral Care* or the likes, and most of them are doing a great job. The truth, however, is that even this approach still does not fill the ticket or provide the care needed by all and does not answer the question we are addressing. When in fact, you look at it a little closer you will find that in most cases, if not all cases, churches are not providing *pastoral care*—they are only providing *crisis care*. I fully realize that this statement may well raise some eyebrows and evoke some questions, so allow me to demonstrate the point for you in a real-life situation.

Let Me Illustrate

I received a call from a lead pastor of a large church one-day, requesting that I would come and explain to him what I was doing in coaching other pastors that is causing so much excitement. I naturally accepted the invitation and made my way to their church on a given day. The pastor received me kindly and welcomed me into his large and comfortable office. We sat down each with a cup of hot coffee in our hands. After we had talked about everyday things that happen in all our lives, he asked the question:

> "So, John, what is it that so many pastors are saying that you
> are helping them to build their congregations? Everywhere I

go someone is saying something about some new paradigm. What is this they're saying?"

I appreciated the opportunity and enthusiastically introduced our designed system of care. I made sure I articulated the definition clearly and explained the concept systematically. I noticed the pastor leaning further and further back into his chair as I was talking. His body language was evident that I am not ringing the bell.

When I got through, he said, "Is that all that you have? Is it all just about pastoral care?" He was obviously disappointed.

"Yes," I replied, "our care ministry system has to do with providing authentic pastoral care to every member of the congregation in an ongoing way, and churches are bursting with excitement!"

"Oh well, John," he said, as he fell back in his chair, "I think we have pastoral care covered in our church. We won't need any care system at our church."

"That's great," I said. "If you indeed have it covered, you are one out of thousands. Since I want to be sure I have included all essential aspects; please tell me what you are doing. I am more than willing to listen and learn. I may have missed something."

He slid forward in his chair, and with his elbows on his desk said, "We have a large church, as you know, and therefore have a large team of pastors. I have a pastor on call 24 hours of every day (and he explained how each of them operated) and therefore people who face any crisis can call them at any time."

He glided back into his chair again as he continued, "We have a single phone number that is transferred to each pastor on call, so church members have only one phone number to remember. And then we have a full-time minister of Pastoral Care who does regular hospital calls, visits people who are going through some crisis, and does some counseling if people are struggling. He marries some and buries others."

I now knew where he was going but continued to listen as he added attentively, "And then, of course, I am still there. I also even do pastoral care, especially if there is a crisis. Besides these, we also have a professional counselor on staff that takes care of all the emergencies people face in their lives. If someone faces a financial crisis, a marriage crisis, or some trauma in their family, or whatever crisis may be going on, they can see our counselor."

He meticulously expounded on the way they function in their pastoral care ministry, sighed, and said, "So, John, as you can tell, we have pastoral care pretty much covered. I think we're okay."

And he was correct. They indeed did have much more in place for pastoral care than most churches. I smiled, and being just a little facetious, asked, "Is that all you have?"

"What do you mean? I think we're doing a good job!" He was noticeably confused by my question.

"Yes, you are. It's way more than most churches are doing. But do you realize, that in fact, you're not providing pastoral care? You are only giving crisis care."

Now he was even more puzzled. "I don't get it. What do you mean?" He asked, somewhat appalled.

I secretly hoped that would be his response. It opened the door wide for me to state my premise. I said, "Do you realize that as you explained how you and your staff members provide pastoral care, you said every time 'when people face a crisis' they can call; or they can see one of your team, 'when people face a crisis they get attention.' But what about the 95 percent of your members who are not experiencing a crisis? Should they not also be cared for, do they not even matter?"

I continued to address what could have become a tender moment carefully and added, "The problem with merely providing crisis care means that once the crisis is over, so is the care! And furthermore, many times, as good as our intentions may be, when people receive 'crisis care,' it spoils them and makes them wonder why they do not always get this kind of attention. It creates a vicious cycle. That is why we are tediously training pastors and church members to develop a system that provides sustainable care to all of our people all of the time."

"I honestly have never seen it that way before, but every member? Is that even possible?" His mind was spinning like a dry sock in an enthusiastic clothes dryer.

"I am glad you asked. The answer is an emphatic 'Yes,' if you create a platform, have a proven system, and if you train your people on the biblical principles, you can!"

The penny seemingly dropped, and he slid back into his chair, and said, "Wow, I think I get it. I've never heard of anything like that before. Perhaps you need to tell me more." And, of course, I did.

And this real story, my friend, is the perception of most pastors and churches. It's an engraved mindset, and we must change the paradigm of providing pastoral care to our people. The tragic fact is that churches often do not even know how many members are falling through the cracks because they have no notion of a system of intentional congregational care. They only notice the shrinking attendance and the disappointing stats of church growth. By the time they become aware of the absence of actual bodies, it's too late.

But let's not be too harsh on churches. Conventional pastoral care, as such, is a well-known subject, but a proven system of care, provided by church members, to the entire congregation, on a regular basis, is not. Attracting people is not difficult but retaining them could be. If we succeed in drawing people to our churches continually but fail to assimilate them efficiently, we may understand what Rick Warren means when he says: "It's like pastoring a parade!" We will say more about this later.

The Greater Missing Link

Although I have cited some practical reasons for the cause of the missing link, which are real and require our attention, my persuasion is more fixated on an overlooked, biblical aspect that, in my opinion, is the *more significant* missing link in churches. I have coined the more significant missing link the *Great Commitment*[4] and have briefly

---

4   The author recognizes that Rick Warren in his book *The Purpose Driven Church*, also uses this expression, but in another context. My application takes on a unique perspective and addresses the subject in an entirely different scenario.

mentioned it before. The truth about the *Great Commitment* is, however, so vital and significant that I dare not attempt discussing it in capsulated form. For that reason, I am going to devote an entire chapter to this revelation. It is a real exposé of how we should function as churches, and, once you grasp this interpretation, the reason I call the concept *the missing link,* will become apparent.

The Great Commitment concept is not about the latest new thing or the hottest flavor-of-the-month. It's not another program to add to your already overloaded schedule. The Great Commitment is a scriptural expectation we should have been fulfilling all along but have somehow missed. It is a charge directly given by Christ and stands firmly in relationship to the Great Commission. At first glance, we may assume that we have understood this command and have implemented it, but at closer examination will find that we have most likely never had a complete revelation of what it meant. Although in its purest form, we can describe it as congregational care, its implications go way beyond the traditional understanding of that expression.

Churches Do Not Become Ingrown or Self-Centered

When we emphasize the critical aspects of a congregational care system as we present it could quickly create the impression that it will result in a church becoming ingrown, disparaging evangelism, dismissing discipleship, or disregarding missions, but that is not the case. It is quite the opposite. Our genre is emphatically caring for each other, but as we continue, you will discover that the intent of this concept is meant to actually develop a balanced and healthy church, which creates the desired environment for us to execute our mission of influencing the world around us. Our focus should therefore not only be on having good fellowship and being kind to people but even more so on developing meaningful interconnection within a congregation where the love of Christ prevails and permeates all we do in ministry. This atmosphere becomes the catalyst for people to feel emboldened to reach the unsaved while it simultaneously creates an environment where strangers feel welcome.

An unhealthy, unfriendly, and sometimes hostile setting is probably not conducive to attracting people to a church. A good analogy would be a biological family. When the members of a family are disconnected, do not love each other, don't care about the well-being of the other family members, and neglect their children, we refer to them as a dysfunctional family. They will never qualify to adopt any children. *Dysfunctional* may, in many cases, be an exaggerated way of describing some of our churches, but again may be fitting for others. Some bicker and fight, others split because they cannot agree on the color of the carpet, business meetings are unruly, elections are politicized, leadership is criticized—and they still expect the church to grow! How can we possibly think of inviting more people to attend an already dysfunctional church? It seems the best place to express the true, felt love of God would be to begin with the household of faith. Did Jesus not say our love for one another will prove to the world that we are His disciples? (John 13:35).

The Atmosphere We Create, Determines What Grows

The key to the effectiveness of our God-called mission lies within the healthy relationships and attitudes we display among each other as believers. That then makes good sense to start first by cultivating an atmosphere of love and acceptance among the people of God before we attempt to reach out to people in the world. It is when we create an atmosphere of genuine God-kind-of-love, that a healthy, spiritual environment begins to develop. A church that finds itself here is on the way to breaking through every barrier and overcoming every obstacle. Paul urges the church in Galatia by saying, "Let us do good to all people, especially to those who belong to the family of believers" (Galatians 6:10 NIV). This Scripture places emphasis on the importance of the family of believers. In today's world, people are responding overwhelmingly to love, family, and genuine acceptance. People crave this, both inside and outside the church.

We base the value of our strategy for growing healthy churches on our ability to bring a balance between caring for the household of faith and reaching the lost. The one is dependent upon the other. Through the enablement of the Holy Spirit, built on Scriptural values, we foster a loving family emboldened to win people to Christ, to whom they then display love through care and discipleship. Once they are embraced by the family of God, these disciples are developed to likewise love each other, and then go out into the world to share the love of God. The important point to note here is that the incentive should always start within the church. We may have had it turned around all along. We have concentrated primarily on winning the lost but have not necessarily brought the church to the level of love and concern for each other first. That may be one reason so many of our outreaches have failed. That may also be why people come, get saved, and then move on to another church. Referring to Rick Warren again, I remember him saying something like, "If God gets ready to bring many new souls into the Kingdom, He first looks for a church that has a warm incubator of care to nurture the new babes in Christ." We must begin getting it right: the love of God must flow down the aisles of our churches before it will flow down the streets of our cities.

The love of Christ must flow down
the aisles of our churches before
it will flow down the streets of our cities!

The Bottom Line

Here is the reason for our frustration: We have for too long concentrated primarily on increasing our church attendance by continually searching for new people without ever paying attention to those we already have. To add to this frustration is the propensity of so many church leaders to erroneously believe they should not spend any time, energy, or resources on ministering to the needs of the existing church members. They do not see this as their priority. They assume that all their efforts should be aimed only at winning the lost and growing the church. They feel guilty when they spend time and resources on the membership. They are instead driven continuously to get outside the church building and knock on every door in the community. And this is understandable because every pastor and church want to create the best opportunities to reach people with the good news of Jesus Christ. They should, however, couple this essential purpose of the church with genuine care for the people who are already part of our congregation at the same time. It is through them that we prepare a warm incubator for the converts on the way.

The Need to be Needed

Keeping a sharp focus in ministry is an essential principle. We should never lose out of sight the importance of what ministry is all about. It's not about statistics, numbers, or things; it's about people. Always. If we are not careful, in our pursuit of success, we may find ourselves concentrating more on preaching than on the people we intend to reach. As pastors, we know the best way to help people is to know people. Medical doctors, psychologists, and sociologists all concur. Many churches, however, don't realize what makes people tick in a real world. We expect people to sit down each Sunday and listen to us and do what we hope they would do, yet we don't really know what is shaping their emotional world, and neither do we include them in our ministry efforts.

People want to feel they are part of the team and want to serve in one way or another. All people need to be needed, and the way they serve, produce their significance. It's in their sense of belonging that people feel secure and start thinking more about their fellow church members than their circumstances and willingly give their life away.

Reality Check

It may serve us well to pay close attention to these matters because the truth is that most churches have stagnated and are not growing. That should make us wonder if we haven't missed something. Our message is solid. Our teachings are great. Our people are committed, but where is the fruit? If preaching and programs could have gotten the job done, we should already have experienced the breakthrough we all so desperately desire. But we know these alone cannot be the answer.

Reality check: If all the people that have come to your church over the past *ten* years had stayed, how many people would there have been today? Perhaps that sounds a little far-fetched, so, let us draw the circle a little closer and ask, if all the people that have come to your church over the past five years had stayed, how many people would there have been today?

And I'm not talking about those who have casually come to attend a musical presentation, or an Easter or Christmas performance. I am referring to those who had seriously come intending to make your church their spiritual home. What if most stayed? How come they did not stay? If we are not taking care of the people the Lord has already given us, why should He send us anymore?

> If we are not taking care of the people
> the Lord has already given us,
> why should He send us anymore?

Consider this: if you have four people per week who would visit your church and two of them stayed, you'd have an attendance increase of more than 100 in a year. How difficult is that? If you have a larger church, off-course, the numbers should be exponentially higher. The truth is, however, that most churches don't retain visitors. They fail to connect with their guests and either drive them away unintentionally or worse still, don't have a system or efficient process in place to retain them. The one huge factor that feeds into this dilemma is the fact that most of this work is done by the pastor and probably a handful of people who are frantically trying to make ends meet. We have all tried this routine and by now should know it's not working. We have indeed also learned over many years that retaining people is by no means easy and assuredly never happens by itself. People come, and people go. All churches should have some assimilation process, and if they do not, people may still come, but they will not stay. Unless we create a system of connecting with people and find ways of closing the *backdoor*, the church will still not grow. That's probably why so many churches in America are stuck with less than 80 members and have been there for the longest time.

As pastors, we have tried for too long to do ministry to the exclusion of our church members. The only way we can solve this problem is by effecting a new paradigm and drastically enlarge the size of our ministry-base. To provide continued care to all our people will take more than merely encouraging church members to be friendly towards guests on a Sunday or by purely shaking hands with each other during fellowship time. It will require us to invite and encourage our church members to rise to the equation, be trained, and be willing to take up their responsibility, causing this new paradigm of pastoral care to take effect.

It's Transferable

We sometimes tend to make things so complicated in our churches, to the point where many people never get it. The concept we are presenting is not involved, and any church of any size can implement it. It has been verified, highly useful, and most definitely transferable to most, if not all, Christian denominations, or organizations, and cultures of different theological persuasions. Our care concept is biblical and proven practical. You will discover many Scriptural references and models in this book as we continue. At the root, it conveys the answer to the crucial need in the church of developing meaningful and sincere relationships. Not only will the pastor know the sheep of his or her pasture through this concept, but at the same time also be at peace, knowing the sheep are being cared for and not going astray.

The new revolution of care has begun, and the wave is hitting church after church, after church, is gaining encouraging momentum, and causing a real stir across America and other countries of the world. Believers enthusiastically realize that they too have gifts for ministry. Pastors, who now have a practical method of application and implementation, are eagerly seizing the moment to equip their people as never.

Join the Revolution

I am searching fervently for pastors, leaders, and church members who would like to join this life-changing revolution to see their churches become healthy, productive, and relevant again. Many already have. How about you?

> We are determined
> to not only raise up
> an audience,
> but to raise up
> an army!

- Pastor, you can be part of this revolution. It has the potential of positively transforming your congregation's dynamics. It is thoroughly scriptural and powerfully practical. Your church will experience such significant health that you would be able to replace attrition and discouragement with growth and excitement. The *Care Revolution* provides a safety net so compelling that no one should fall through the cracks. It can close your church's proverbial *backdoor* tightly and at the same time, get more people involved more rapidly than anything else.
- Church member, the exciting news is that the Holy Spirit is focusing His attention on you in this great revolution. Will you make yourself available to this movement that's causing more enthusiasm than anything else that has

happened for the longest time? This revolution is creating an opportunity for believers to become all God wants them to be. It may well be the season you have been waiting and praying for to come. It's entirely possible that the statement directed at Esther could be relevant in many church member's lives, *Yet, who knows whether you have come to the kingdom for such a time as this?* (Esther 4:14)

• In this fresh move of the Spirit, we are seeing new energy released as more and more self-sacrificing pastors and church members are committed to shaping their churches after the simple and efficient ways of Jesus who commanded us to love our neighbor as ourselves. The season we find ourselves in is indeed a blessed time to be alive and an excellent season to change our church paradigms to fit the call of the Holy Spirit *for such a time as this.*

For me, the revelation of establishing an authentic system of congregational care came as the result of unforeseen conditions. I know it may sound paradoxical, but it was at a moment in my life and ministry where I was experiencing tremendous anticipation and gratification, that I also faced challenging circumstances. Even though it was a good problem to have, it was still a problem—or perhaps more accurately, a challenge. But, as we have all discovered in life, those are the best times to break out of the mold and venture into exciting new and unfamiliar territory. That is the only way to break through restrictive barriers.

2

MY DISCOVERY
OF THE CARE REVOLUTION

My introduction to the *Care Revolution* mainly started after I had become the Lead Pastor of Glad Tidings Church in Lake Charles, Louisiana. Of course, we did not refer to the ministry as the *Care Revolution* at that point, but that is not the issue at this juncture. My journey brought me from the days of feeling overwhelmed by the ministry—trying to make ends meet in a distraught congregation— to the pleasure of seeing scores of people actively involved in joyful ministry. It has been one of the most thrilling experiences of my entire life and has, understandably, become indelible in my mind.

I will not belabor you with all the intricate details of our voyage because it's a long story, however, a fascinating one. The one remarkable thing I believe I need to mention in passing though is that we were not called to come to Glad Tidings, neither did we receive an invitation to consider the possibility. We were *sent* by God in an unbelievably divine way before we ever knew anything about the church or even the geographic location of Lake Charles. When God began to speak to us regarding going there, my wife and I had to buy a map to discover this *unknown world*. We had never been to Lake Charles before, which was probably a good thing! We were obediently following His marching orders at a time when we were not even looking for a church. At the time, we were functioning in the role of evangelists and were graciously being used by God in powerful ways. We found our schedule overloaded with appointments to the point where we had no wiggle room to add any further obligations. And when we least expected it, God sent us in a new and unexpected direction. Bear with me just for a moment, and you will understand why I am even telling you all of this.

It was, unquestionably, a miracle how our family ended up in Lake Charles, and I am convinced that in the natural, we would never have chosen to go there. But God knew He needed someone that was unfamiliar with the people, the community, and even the culture to bring healing and restoration at a crucial time.

Since my family and I are initially from South Africa, people often ask me why we chose to go to Lake Charles! My usual response has always been, "We did not decide to go to Lake Charles; God sent us!" And this assertion, my friend, played out to become the absolute truth. And as they always say, the rest is history! But in all honesty, we should also mention that even though it was a divine assignment, it was not necessarily a celestial journey. There were some daunting challenges that loomed up before us that could easily have made us doubt the leadership of the Holy Spirit. However, in this process, I did learn a compelling lesson, and that is that merely being in the will of God does not mean you will not face the storms of life. You can be right in the center of God's will and still face incredible trials, and your boat may still rock as it did for the disciples when they hit a storm at sea (Mark 4:35).

If you read this passage of Scripture, you will notice, amazingly so, that the disciples experienced this turbulence despite the fact that it was Jesus who told them to go to the other side. Following His orders, being where He wants you to go, doing what He wants you to do—even having Him in the boat with you—does not mean you are not going to face tough times. Now, if you're not careful, and listen to the religious folk, they will tell you, "If God is in on the matter, and if God asked you to do something, then nothing will go wrong, everything will be smooth sailing." Try to tell Paul that, or see what Peter or John would say about that philosophy. Let me repeat it: You can be in the center of God's will and still face the storms of life.

> You can be in the center
> of God's will, and
> still, face the storms of life.

Although I prefer not to be too descriptive concerning the details and circumstances of all that had transpired at Glad Tidings before we arrived, some brief comments may help you understand why our journey was so God-inspired. I had no idea what God was sending us to, but His grace has always been sufficient, and all the marvelous things that followed were all because of Him.

While I was fully aware of the fact that my predecessor had unexpectedly died of a heart attack, I did not fully realize the circumstances surrounding this tragedy. He preached the one Sunday, and the next was his funeral. He was not sick and was seemingly fit, being in his early fifties. It was a tremendous shock to the church and a blow to the community. Many people loved him dearly, but the stress and strain of ministry got the better part of him. He was widely respected and known to be a gracious man of God. To this day, I have never heard anyone say anything derogatory about him, although there were some loud, opinionated voices.

The church had gone through a tough time. Some people had more interest in their agenda than God's, which caused severe tension, uncertainty, and strife. I was told the attendance on that Sunday we were installed was 438—being up because of a new pastor. At that number, it was undoubtedly a great church, but if you take into consideration that they almost broke 1,000 in attendance the previous year, you would realize that we had taken over a troubled ship. And it was!

In truth, the church was heading for a split. There was still unbelievable anxiety when we came, and much of it was related to the day school that had become the tail that was wagging the dog. The sudden death of their pastor certainly did not help the congregation. Those who were opposed to him were stricken with guilt, while many of the faithful members felt hurt and pain and did not always know whom to trust. If it were not for the Official Board members who were decidedly in agreement, it would have been a terrible situation. Their support proved to be the catalyst for the many positive futuristic things that unfolded.

> Against all the odds,
> the church
> began to grow.

Against all the odds, and to my greatest amazement, within the first year, the church began to grow in unimaginable proportions.

Inspired by an enthusiastic board, we went ahead and increased the seating capacity from 1100 to close to 1500 during the first summer, and soon saw it filled. There was a significant influx of people, and God blessed us in unusual ways. Eventually, we had to go to two services in the morning.

Although scores of new people came in, some others felt it was time to move on. For people to leave always seems to be the case when there is a pastoral-change. That's just part of the territory. The good thing was that apparently many, many more people were coming than were leaving. This exponential increase, coupled with an innovative approach to praise and worship as well as in-depth spiritual growth teachings, soon began to eradicate the feelings of anxiety and uneasiness. People were excited about the freshness, sensed the momentum rising, and bought into the vision with great anticipation. It became apparent to me that the enthusiasm that emanated from the pulpit had reached the pews when people often said things like, "I've been a Christian for many years, but it feels like I have just become a new believer!" People were outspoken about their excitement of coming to church.

Our Challenge

Growth, however, always brings its unique challenges—and pain! It's a good kind of pain, but it is a pain nonetheless! One of the greatest challenges we soon faced was to balance the care of the existing members with accommodating the scores of many new people who were coming. I felt responsible for making sure all our people were taken care of and that no one was falling through the cracks. It happens so easily in a church, and in our case, with what the church had gone through, it had become a sensitive issue. On the one hand, people needed to know they counted, and on the other, they wanted their presence to be known, not to have fellow members think they had also left the church.

We were new in the church, which increased the challenge, as could be understood since we apparently did not know most of the people. We had little knowledge of who was new or who had been there for a long time. Neither did we know who had left and had now come back. Perhaps in a certain way, this may have been good; I'm not sure. It helped much that my wife and I, over our years of ministry, had always made sure that our people felt loved and accepted, regardless of who they were or from what background they came. So, to concentrate on it now came somewhat naturally.

These recurring challenges continued to make me extraordinarily apprehensive and concerned as a pastor, thinking there may be people who needed assistance, going through tough times, feeling lonely or discouraged, and then have nobody who knows the valley they are walking through in their lives. It concerned me that people may have thought they were not valued or needed and considered drifting away from the flock—and I may not even have known it, because I may never have missed them! But how in the world do you handle everyone? How can you possibly keep in touch with every family?

It was utterly impossible to employ enough staff to take care of all the pastoral demands of a growing congregation. By this time, we already had more staff members than the church had ever had in its history. But at the same time, being a student of church growth for many years, I knew there had to be a system or procedure that could meet the requirement and bring balance to the existing members and the new additions. Our team concluded that we had to find a logical approach to relating to people as quickly and efficiently as possible. The sooner you can make people feel they belong, the more successful you will be to retain and disciple them to become thoroughly committed members who can help you reach the lost.

Believing,
belonging, and
becoming

We also found in the process that with a high influx of new people, you often have numerous people coming in who are not yet entirely devoted followers of Christ, and instead of ignoring them, you incorporate them into the functions of the church. Obviously, I do not mean putting them into critical positions of ministry. But I wish I could tell you the scores of people who felt they *belonged* before they *believed*. And when they then believed, they became totally dedicated members of the church, joyfully involved in ministry.

Laying Down the Tracks

Through His incredible grace and mercy, the Lord gave me clear directions on how to steer the ship during this season. With so many people coming, and the atmosphere loaded with excitement, it was evident that we were experiencing considerable momentum. I felt the way to go at that moment was to get the people all on the same page as quickly as possible. As a foundation for creating spiritual unity, we developed a process of life-transforming discipleship—today known as the Growth Track—which helped immensely to integrate everyone into a learning environment. This process was indeed a revelation from heaven! It became the catalyst for building a healthy and vibrant church. I wrote manuals for every level and every class, and it released an incredible atmosphere of harmony.

When we launched this process, we had a whole week of a *teaching revival.* I taught our people two chapters per night for five nights and poured the *Foundations for Christian Living* into them. It was profound! I do not have the vocabulary even to begin to explain what it did. People's lives were changing because of the teachings, and the spiritual climate in the church rose almost overnight.

From there we developed the Wheel of Learning with more courses, which eventually became the Growth Track, mentioned above. Simply stated, it is a means of taking an individual from the point of connecting with the church to the end of, not only being a fully devoted follower of Christ but also faithfully involved in meaningful ministry. It is more than just teaching spiritual content—it is a process that takes people somewhere significant. Our process is designed to not only provide *information* but, even more so, to bring *transformation.* Sometimes church leaders offer excellent content but have no means attached to it. The result is that people become spiritually obese with all the appropriate spiritual food they receive but experience no involvement in the ministry of the church and therefore become lazy.

Unbelievable numbers of people attended these sessions, and it helped my wife and me to get much closer to a more substantial number of members in a short period than we would have otherwise. We ended the *teaching revival* with a massive fellowship celebration on Saturday evening and an incredible graduation ceremony on Sunday. The church members invited their friends and families to the event, which added significantly to the joyful occasion. People packed the church to overflowing. We gave each of the participants a beautiful graduation certificate which, to many, became a treasured article. It was a festive occasion that accomplished way more than we ever anticipated.

But There Had to be More

This first spiritual growth conference met a particular need and was highly successful and served its purpose well. Unbeknownst to us, spiritual growth conferences began to create a particular culture in our church which later became our identity. But we still needed more cohesiveness and more effective assimilation. The conference did not necessarily provide the glue that would connect people with each other, long term. There was no active community established yet, and the awkward feeling that was still haunting me was that at some point in time half of the church would not show up the next Sunday. I feared that the newness would wear off at some point, and if people were not then connected, they would move on. I guess the good thing about this feeling was that it kept driving me until I found the optimum solution. And thank God, I did!

After having established the course-direction for the church, during one of our team-building meetings (sometimes known as staff meetings), I expressed my concern and frustration. Attempting to share my heart spontaneously and express my thoughts clearly, I somehow began to *create* an image of what I felt was desperately needed although I had no real concept of what it was we were searching. As we evaluated the situation and shared our thoughts with each other, we agreed that we needed a system, not just a program, and probably not a quick fix either. We needed something that would become a way of providing care to the existing congregants and connect new members as they became part of the whole. It almost sounded impossible to achieve.

These informal but frank discussions continued for another week or two. And then we entered the *Care Revolution*, which catapulted us to levels we never thought possible. One member of my team had heard about a concept that was reasonably addressing the concern we had discussed and thought it might serve us well to take a little closer look. I am so glad Randal Smith remembered Dr. Melvin Steinbron. We eagerly invited him to visit our church—a great servant of God who in later years became my *mentor* for pastoral care. He enthusiastically introduced us to the revolutionary concept of preparing Lay People for Lay Pastoring. What now? Lay people doing pastoral care? That sounded like a dichotomy to me!

Mel had designed a system of congregational care while he had been on staff at College Hill Presbyterian Church in Cincinnati, Ohio, and with his team had proven the concept to be highly successful. His experience was tremendously helpful to us in grasping all the truths and principles he had formulated. Mel was both passionate and patient and took time to explain the model to us at length. It was abundantly clear that he knew the subject well and had worked through the many challenges they faced in their process. He had answers to most of our many questions and most graciously helped us get around our religious and traditional thinking. The principles Mel taught sounded straightforward, and yet they were profound.

> "Eureka!
> We have found it!"

We attentively listened to this exciting application of ministry and knew this was the answer! I felt like shouting, "Eureka! We have found it!" Today I can say that among all the other great things the Holy Spirit led us to do at Glad Tidings, this was the most influential and most prolific ministry we ever launched. If I had to lead a church today or plant a new one, this is where I would begin. Once people have bonded, it's so much easier to realize a church's vision through member-participation. Added to that, is the peace of mind a pastor experiences for knowing all members are being cared for in meaningful ways.

After Mel had done our first equipping seminar, with singular success, we launched our care ministry and saw with amazement how it was releasing unity, peace, and fulfillment beyond our own expectation. Our people were ecstatic and performed their newly acquired ministry skills with great enthusiasm. And then, when we got ready to train the next group of care leaders, we found it necessary to design easy-to-follow workbooks and training manuals derived from our experiences. Our implementation brought into being a ministry concept that met the needs of realistic congregational care to every person that called our church home. It changed our lives, our ministries, the dynamics of the church, and the attitudes of the members. It was absolutely incredible!

And those principles and philosophies we discovered, designed, and unfolded, are the things I want to share with you throughout this book. I am going to take you on this personal journey with me and give you all the keys, principles, and concepts of how you can join the *Care Revolution* and how you, too, can develop a network of care in your congregation. I realize that I will be sharing an abundance of material, but if you are like I am, then you would want to gain as much relevant background information on a subject before you begin sharing the concept with your leadership and congregation.

Our care concept has the potential of changing your congregation positively like few things you have ever done. Truth be known, most churches today do not have any reliable or operational framework of taking care of their people on a personal and dependable basis. In our systems of church development, we call this the *Care Track*.

And just to pull everything together, before we move on, let me recap:

Each church must have two tracks it runs on:

1. The *Growth Track*—which is life-transforming discipleship.
2. The *Care Track*—which is developing a community of care.

Now in this book, we are only addressing the *Care Track*, which we base on Jesus's words of *Love your neighbor as yourself . . .* And this introduces us to the *Care Revolution*, which has been proven to have the potential of renewing your church and, at the same time, releasing the pressure on your life as a pastor. It adds value to people, builds deep friendships, develops genuine relationships, and offers recognition, significance, and purpose to all who relate to the congregation. A healthy church like this cannot do other than grow!

Preparing for the Initial Revolution

Planning and preparation remain the essential keys to developing a ministry of any kind, but especially a concept as dynamic as a care ministry. It affects the entire congregation and influences many areas of ministry. It is imperative that all members, and especially all leaders, are familiar with the concept and understand the vision. That is why I took quality time to develop the process. At Glad Tidings, my first action step, after our pastoral team had sorted out the concept, was to share the vision with my board leadership and make sure they understood the entire application, including the benefits. I then set apart a whole month to explain the concept to the church. The first Sunday I mainly gave a brief overview, and over the following three Sundays preached a series of explicit messages that related to our notion of care. I still find today that spending time casting the vision is essential if you want to launch an active care ministry.

It's not
about adding
another program

The proper perspective of evaluating this ministry is to gain the understanding that it is not about adding another program. It is about affecting your church's DNA. You are going to cultivate a culture of care that is going to be so powerful that you will wonder why you hadn't done it many years ago. You are going to live out the reality that you care about what God cares about most—people! Jesus didn't die for a church building—He died for people. He didn't hang on the Cross for a program or good idea—He did so for people! Yes, frail, failing, imperfect people. People still are mere humans who need someone to be there for them; someone who can help them bear their burdens and love them regardless. "But when He saw the multitudes, He was moved with compassion for them, because they were weary and scattered, like sheep having no shepherd" (Matthew 9:36).

In our original discussions with Mel, I asked him with all sincerity, "Are you sure this will work?" I could not dare take a chance on something that could fail. As kind as he always was, he looked at me and said, "I do not doubt that it will work; firstly, because it is a proven concept, and secondly because it's in the Bible." Mel was right!

I could not
dare take
a chance.

After we had begun the process of equipping our people, the evidence of added value became evident almost immediately. People were highly encouraged when they realized they, too, could be involved in the ministry of care even though they had not received formal credentials. I do not know that I have ever seen such a level of enthusiasm in a church anywhere. It was evident that there were scores of people who felt a particular calling they could not fulfill in any other way than providing genuine care to others.

After we had commissioned our Care Pastors, we assigned family units to them and then released them into their ministry with eager anticipation. It did not take long for the atmosphere in the church to joyfully change and for people to respond in a more relaxed and loving manner. As a sweet lady told me before a Sunday morning service, "Pastor, in all my years in this church, I have never felt so loved and cared for as I do these days. Everybody seems to be talking to everybody lately. I can hardly wait to come to church!" She almost giggled with delight.

Another lady, on the other hand, confirmed my fears of the past. I was standing in the foyer after a Sunday morning service, shaking hands with people as they were leaving. I noticed a lady remain standing a few feet away from me. Somehow, I could tell she wanted to speak to me, so when most people had left, I made my way over to her. We exchanged a few cordial words with each other and then she said, "I have something on my heart I have to confess," she began. "Pastor, I didn't like you much when you came to our church at first." Wow, no pastor wants to hear that! At least I was glad about the *at first* but was unsure what was to follow.

> "Pastor,
> I didn't like you
> much . . ."

She went on to say, "The reason I felt that way is that I was in the hospital at the time and heard that you had visited another member there, but you never came by to see me." She was uncomfortable to tell me this story, but the slight smile around the corners of her mouth let me know there was a soft side of the story. "It made me feel so rejected and unworthy." Well, of course, being new, I had no idea she was there, and nobody had told me. "To be frank," she said, "I decided not to come back to church, but then I heard about all the good things that were going on here at Glad Tidings, and today, of course, I am so happy I didn't leave. And, what I want to say is that I can see how this caring ministry is going to help in so many ways. I think I want to become a Care Pastor myself!" And she did!

Unless we have a way to stay connected with people and follow up on them, they will continue to fall through the cracks, and sadly, often drift away from the church entirely.

Beyond the Walls

As our Care Pastors began to serve more and more proficiently and became more comfortable in hospital visits, personal relationships, and functioning per the fundamental concept, word got out into the community. The result was that our caring ministry opened the door for even more people than before to come to our church. It attracted people from every walk of life because our hearts were open, we cared, and nobody was judgmental. We adopted the slogan, and I joyfully announced it every Sunday morning: "Welcome to exciting Glad Tidings, where everybody is somebody, and Jesus Christ is Lord!"

There was now a network of care that was keeping the whole church together, and people were no longer falling through the cracks. When people needed help, there was always someone there for them. When they rejoiced, there were people to celebrate with them. The church became an actual family. It was not just another program; it was a spirit of genuine love and care that permeated the congregation. People were no longer only receiving care in times of crisis, but also during the non-crisis times of their lives.

I can tell you today that the *Care Ministry Network* is indeed poised to solidify a church and to provide the caliber of care as the Bible instructs us. But it has additionally been proven over and over that when such a culture of Christ's love prevails in a congregation, people from outside the church start coming from all over. And what was meant to be a ministry for the saints, in a roundabout way, became a tremendous evangelistic outreach to the community. I cannot quite explain how this happens; all I know is—it happens!

Fast Forward

Glad Tidings Church continued to grow over the years to the point where we had to build a 3500-seat auditorium and saw it filled to overflowing on several occasions. It was nothing strange to see people line up at four o'clock in the afternoon on a blazing, hot, humid, summer day in Louisiana, to get a good seat at our major events. Part of our young people's ministry was to serve the waiting people with bottles of cold water. Our youth pastor, Keith Bryan, also arranged for massive, industrial fans to cool off the people. The encouraging fact is that once people know you care and that what you are doing is about them, momentum kicks in and draws people from many miles away. When they connect with a loving congregation and experience the love of God, the obvious next step has always been for them to get involved in reaching others with the Good News of Jesus Christ.

My present-day ministry travels across the nation bring me in touch with many pastors and leaders. A vast number of them have known me for quite a while or have at least heard about our ministry. Thus, so many of them wanted to know how we were so fortunate to build such a large church in a relatively small city. Now honestly, I have never thought of myself as being a successful pastor because, in my mind, I have always just been doing what I thought all other pastors were doing. But the more I began to travel; the more pastors were asking the same thing.

These questions made me stop and look back at our journey from where we had come. In this process, I then found that the further I got away from the forest, the clearer I could begin to identify the trees and recognized which were the things that stood out as pillars of strength. The Care Ministry most assuredly shines like a bright beacon. And, as I said before, if I had to plant a new church today or revitalize an existing one, this is most assuredly where I would begin. Having a defined discipleship process along with new outreaches were some others, but again, that's not where we will be going in this discussion.

To my greatest astonishment, as I began to pay closer attention during our travels, I realized that, for the most part, intentional *caring* was a missing component in most of the churches in America, and most likely also in other regions of the world. And this is true regardless of the size of a church or even its denominational affiliation.

Having come to this realization, I then began to gradually help pastors and churches, one-on-one, to implement some of what we have learned and applied and saw the most favorable results. It became apparent that this care concept was not only an excellent tool for fast-growing churches to sustain their visitors and members, but also most useful in churches that are seeking ways of building community, retaining relationships with their established members, and providing a net, so everyone feels protected, secure, and loved. It's a practical method, regardless of the size of a church.

The Concept Is Transferable

It was apparently necessary to reassess and rethink our once-effective concept to ensure it fits the demands of present-day culture. Any idea should be reevaluated and modified from time to time, or else it will lose its significance. In the light, thereof, I took the time to rethink our entire care system and adapted the concept to be more viable in the twenty-first century. In the process, I rewrote our previous training manuals, produced some new ones, and designed some additional tools.

Today we can provide pastors and churches with everything they need to cast the vision, organize a training conference, and offer all the relevant training tools. After a weekend training event, we additionally make an e-book available to help pastors and churches launch the ministry and supply all supplemental material. We refer to it as the Implementation Guide. We never leave a pastor or church to struggle on their own.

Pilot Program

After I had completed manuals with the newly adopted concepts, I asked a few pastors and churches to conduct a pilot program over a period of a little more than a year. I wanted to know if the new concept would work and if it would be equally valid when others implement the idea. The results have blown me away! Not only did they describe the joy of so many more of their people involved in ministry and the momentum it triggered but were especially thrilled by the numerical and financial growth that took place.

One church added close to 150 people in one single year and ascribed 95 percent of their growth to the effectiveness of the *Care Revolution*. Some of the others had to go into multiple services, while yet another church recorded unprecedented attendance in their morning worship services.

> One church added
> close to 150 people

A pastor called me one Monday morning with excitement in his voice clearly to be heard, and said,

> "You won't believe it, but we had the most significant attendance yesterday morning than we have had in the past 25 years!"

"Wow!" I said, "What made that happen?"

> "It's the Care Ministry!" For a moment, I thought he was going say, "What else do you think, Dummy?" But he

continued politely instead by saying, "Our people say they feel they now have part of what's going on in church, and through our care ministry, they have now begun to reach out to people that have dropped out of attendance. There's excitement in the air, brother!"

These pastors all reported a fresh newness among their people. There was newfound joy and real enthusiasm which went beyond the mere emotional. It instinctively created an atmosphere of unity, spiritual dynamics, and other wondrous things through worship, prayer, discipleship, evangelism, etc.

People who know say that when natural sheep are at peace and feel cared for, their heads are down, they feel secure, are feeding, and grow numerically. They are not anxiously looking around in fear of some danger that may threaten their survival. The same happens when the flock in a congregation experiences this type of care—they feel safe and secure, are at peace, and in this healthy environment, expand evangelism efforts.

Not only did the people in each of these churches feel cared for and have their needs met, but the exciting thing was that much of the burden had lifted from the pastors' shoulders, who were now freed to do more things in ministry they had always longed to be able to do. The concept lifted their burdens which in itself was already worth the effort! It's exciting because, for the most part, many pastors otherwise are doing what they don't like, and don't like what they are doing.

We realized the concept was working, and the launch of the *Care Revolution* was the result! I know today that this idea is transferable and can most certainly work in a church of any size—and any denomination! After the pilot program, had delivered excellent results, we subsequently shared these hypotheses with many other pastors in a seminar setting with singular success. We came away knowing there was a massive vacuum in our churches and we need to fill it.

What I do want you to know, in conclusion, is that what this concept had done in our church, and what it accomplished in all these others, can be a reality in any church. These churches are not unique; they are no different from any other regular church. The answer is shifting congregational care to the members, who can function more efficiently in this area than a single pastor. "There are people like that in every church who have gifts for caring, capable of loving, available to 'be there' and perhaps even waiting to be called into this kind of ministry. Every observant pastor will be able to identify members of the congregation who are already caring for people."[5]

Seeing It for What It Is

The reason I believe this *Care Revolution* is gaining so much ground and getting the attention of so many pastors and leaders is that it's a buried biblical expectation that the Holy Spirit has resurrected. We have theoretically overlooked the proper meaning of this truth and have missed the power of its intention. To me, it is imperative to have readers understand that, what we are dealing with in the *Care Revolution*, is not merely another means of making our churches efficient, but rather the fulfillment of a commitment to Christ to take care of His sheep. This statement may be an excellent opportunity to introduce you to the *Great Commitment*—an exciting unfolding of great value with unbelievable divine reward. Discovering the revelation of the Great Commitment may be as much of an eye-opener to you as it has been to me.

---

5   Melvin J. Steinbron, *Can the Pastor do it Alone?* Regal Books, 1987, 29.

3

THE GREAT COMMITMENT

What I referred to as the *Greater Missing Link* in chapter one is more fully identified as the absence of what I call the *Great Commitment*. To only make a personal assertion that there is a link missing in churches may not in itself carry much weight. But when we find a command in Scripture, and we do not see the correlating application in our churches, then naturally, it becomes worthy of our attention. We should always affect ministry on the sound basis of a biblical model, or else it may become dangerous to the health of a church.

Although you will not find the words *Great Commitment* in the Bible,[6] it can readily be extracted from the words of Jesus Christ at

---

6   For clarity's sake, we need to mention that the *Great Commission,* as such, is also not referred to in the Bible. Both are used as identities for collected action.

the occasion when He answers the Pharisee's question relating to the *Great Commandment* (Matthew 22:35-40). Taking a closer look at Jesus's response helps us discover that we have misplaced this truth over the years. We have most certainly applied some of the required elements, but not the complete commitment.

The discovery of this truth has become the primary catalyst for me to continue preaching, teaching, and writing on this subject. It has become such a passion to me that these days I am devoting large blocks of my time to inspire pastors and churches to see the power of this revelation I call the *Great Commitment.*

A Profound Question

While Jesus was sharing His mission, and explaining the principles of the Kingdom on earth, people often confronted Him with severe issues of immense magnitude. It was especially true when, case in point, they challenged the existing religious system. His astonishing and revelatory answers astounded the so-called learned men of His day. But He did even more than that: His answers consistently conveyed distinct values to build on, truths and principles to consider, and deep thoughts to ponder. His responses went far beyond merely clarifying a question that was directed at Him.

It was during one of these occasions that the Pharisees chose the law as their subject to question Jesus. They did this because they knew if He got it wrong on this one, nobody would ever believe Him again. One of their lawyers asked, "Teacher, which is the greatest commandment in the law?" (Matthew 22:36)

In His response, Jesus then made one of the most profound statements imaginable, and I don't want you to miss this. With divine wisdom, Jesus answered him, "You shall love the Lord your

God with all your heart, with all your soul, and with all your mind. This is the first and greatest commandment" (Matthew 22:37-38). With the inquirer's interest peaked, Jesus went on to say, "And the second is like it: 'You shall love your neighbor as yourself'" (Matthew 22:39).

In His answer, Jesus stated that there is not one, but instead two commandments and that the two are *equal*. What Jesus was saying was an encapsulated version of the Ten Commandments as recorded in Exodus 20. Looking at it a little closer, we notice that the first five of the Ten Commandments refer to humanity's relationship with God, while the second five apply to our relationship with each other. Jesus made clear that the order God had given to humankind, through Moses on the mountain, still prevails and remains the guidelines for us to live by today. It is not a matter of holding on to the Law but rather a continued path by which to order our lives. Everything God has ever done has *order* attached to it. And in that order, you will always find a healthy balance, as is the case with the Ten Commandments which depicts our relationships with both God and humanity.

> These two
> commands are pegs

Many times, we tend to stop at the end of the two statements mentioned above that Jesus made and, in so doing, often miss a most insightful expression: On *these two commandments hang all the Law and the Prophets* (Matthew 22:30). Eugene Peterson, in *The Message Bible*, translates it as These *two commands are pegs . . .* (Matthew 22:30 MSG). Since the word *pegs* more explicitly indicate an object for things to be hung on or attached to, it sheds a little more light on our discussion.

Without trying to oversimplify the account, from Peterson's expression, we can freely excerpt from Jesus's statement that all and everything we do regarding ministry should somehow be attached to the following two essential expectations: (1) Love the Lord your God, and (2) love your neighbor. Every principle and direction should relate in some way to these two truths, which are, in fact, the foundation of the *Great Commandment*. These two elements ensure that we are providing the full continuum of all that is required to bring forth completeness in the body of Christ.

Three Principles

Out of Jesus's answer to the Pharisee-lawyer, I want to point out three paramount *beacons* that clarify the development of ministry in our churches. These are essential elements that influence our mission, vision, and core values. Considering these components will help us understand how we could be most effective in our execution of ministry.

We can best describe these three rudiments in the following three ways:

- *Firstly,* the Great **Commandment**
- *Secondly,* the Great **Commission**
- *Thirdly,* the less known Great **Commitment**

We readily identify well with the Great *Commandment* and are involved, in some way or another, with the Great *Commission*. At this stage, I would like to introduce you to a third component, which I identify as the Great *Commitment*. Most people are not familiar with this aspect and apparently have not paid much attention to its importance.

Not only do I want to focus your attention on discovering the value and purpose of the *Great Commitment*, but also help you make the connection between it and the *Care Revolution*.

Since it directly touches the nerve of developing healthy churches, most likely you are going to agree with me that the absence thereof may well be the missing link that has stifled the growth of many well-meaning churches. Today I am convinced that you just cannot grow a vigorous church without intentionally applying the *Great Commitment*. What is more important in this regard is not only knowing what the Great Commitment entails but also to understand how to practically implement the concept within the body of Christ that we have, until now, misplaced. Under the heading "The 3 C's of the Church's Mission" here below, I will more clearly unfold the meaning of the Great Commitment. It touches on a redefined paradigm in our churches.

As Findley Edge said, "Ministry is being done by the wrong people!" And he is correct. According to the Bible, it should be the members, under the direction of the pastors and other elders, who should be performing ministry in partnership with each other. One cannot do it without the other.

It is becoming more apparent that the Holy Spirit is driving this *Care Revolution*. Because of its relevance, it is spreading all over the entire country in churches everywhere and is now taking form in other nations as well.

The 3 C's of the Church's Mission

I am about to break open a fresh revelation of ministry to you. What I am about to uncover is the result of many unbelievable hours of study and Scripture reading. There is hardly anything available in books or articles that bring the whole of the subject into perspective as you will discover with me. It started on that day when some lawyers questioned Jesus with the motive of proving Him wrong, as we have referenced earlier. Taken from Jesus's response that the Great Commandment consists of two aspects which are equal (*First,* you must love God, and *secondly,* you must love people) we discover two clear rivers flowing from a life-giving source towards the vast expanse of the mighty ocean of life. As we identify these two flows, we will find the essential balance of ministry within the context of a local congregation.

We see these two qualities flow all throughout the New Testament. We identify one as the Great Commission; the directive Jesus gave us to make disciples of all nations (Matthew 28:19-20). The other is what we are identifying in this discussion as the Great Commitment; the directive the Lord gave us to take care of the sheep, as we see in John 21:15-17. The first instruction is to make disciples, and the second is to care for those who become disciples. For the sake of providing full ministry, our clear goal should always be to align these two principal streams in our churches. When we do the one at the neglect of the other, we deprive our churches of the health it needs to grow.

These two rivers, or streams, are my expression of the two expressed laws Jesus mentioned when He answered the question concerning the Great Commandment. Let's take a moment to look at it a little closer:

- "You shall love the Lord your God with all your heart, with all your soul, and with all your mind"—**Loving God.**
- "You shall love your neighbor as yourself"—**Loving People.**

I refer to these two facets (loving God and loving people) as *the 2-Tracks* of a healthy congregational process. As I mentioned in chapter two, the first track, the *Growth Track*, is life-transforming discipleship. The second track, the *Care Track,* is cultivating a culture of care in the congregation—but more about that later on.

As we discover more of "The 3 C's of the Church's Mission" and draw the circle closer, we can begin to identify the three top elements:

- First, our passage of Scripture describes what is known as the Great **Commandment**, from which flows
- Second, the Great **Commission** (Matthew 28:18-20)
- Third, the Great **Commitment** (John 21:15-17)

These three—the Great Commandment, the Great Commission, and the Great Commitment—are what I refer to as "The 3 C's of the Church's Mission." As we have noticed before, the Great Commandment consists of two defined components, from which we develop a healthy process of growth in a congregation. We will regard the Great Commission stream as an outflow of the *Loving God* element, while we consider the Great Commitment as the outflow of the *Loving People* element.

The following sketch will help you understand the 3 C's in correlation better:

THE GREAT COMMANDMENT

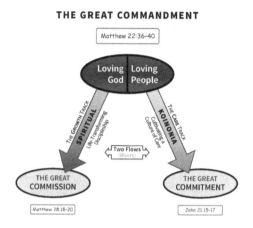

Great Commandmant

The Loving God element flows into the *Great **Commission*** and represents everything we do that develops the spirit being of humanity which results in us becoming more like Jesus. It includes evangelism, discipleship, prayer, praise, worship, spiritual gifts, sanctification, etc. We need not say much about this aspect since it has for the more significant part been adhered to over all the years as a vital function of the church.

The Loving People element flows into the *Great **Commitment*** and describes our obligation to care for the people God has entrusted to us as well as those around us. Jesus gave Peter a clear responsibility (John 21:15-17) to take care of His sheep, which later became the charge Peter gave to the Elders, which was finally passed on to the Church-at-large. We describe this as being *the Great Commitment* and has more to it than meets the eye.

Paul seems to have grasped the understanding and the importance of what the *Loving People* element truly means when he expresses it as follows:

Owe no one anything except to love one another, for he who loves another has fulfilled the law. For the commandments, You shall not commit adultery, You shall not murder, You shall not steal, You shall not bear false witness, You shall not covet, and if there is any other commandment, are all summed up in this saying, namely, 'You shall love your neighbor as yourself.' Love does no harm to a neighbor; <u>therefore, love is the fulfillment of the law</u> (Romans 13:8-10) (Underlining by author).

This reference makes us know that the expectation to love others is not an outdated or Old Testament law, but rather remains valid in the present-day ministry of the Church. When we abide by it, we are fulfilling the outflow of the prevailing Great Commandment Jesus expressed.

An Overall Understanding

To form an overall understanding of this concept, let's consider all three mentioned aspects one-by-one in an attempt to grasp how they fit jointly together and then unfold the power of the Great Commitment more fully:

1. The Great Commandment

The more we look at the profound statement of the *Great Commandment* and how it flows onwards into the two definite rivers, the more we will notice the importance of applying it to our churches and ministries. We even see the principles of *Loving God* and *Loving People* clearly demonstrated in the symbolism of the Cross of Calvary: The vertical pillar of the Cross denotes our relationship to God, while the horizontal beam signifies our relationship to humanity. When Jesus hung on the Cross, His body distinctly took on the form of the Cross, as He became the propitiation for our sin. His outstretched arms (in a horizontal position) were symbolically reaching out to humankind, while His body (in a vertical position) was symbolically reaching up towards God. In this posture, Jesus became the Atonement (*at-one-ment*) by which He reconciled sinful man with Holy God. It was in Him that it all came together, and it is still in Him that everything comes together.

When Jesus said we ought to love God and love people, He knew one day He had to set the example and physically demonstrate what that truly meant. He became the living example of the truth this commandment holds. He consecrated Himself to the Father while giving His precious life for people.

We could never have experienced the love of God if it was not for Jesus's sacrificial death. Likewise, it would have been impossible to understand loving others if it was not for Him who first demonstrated that kind of love by giving His life for His friends. We can see that love shown when Jesus explained the *Great Commandment* to them; it was more than just an answer. It was rather a vision statement of what was to come, coupled with the clarification that all we do in ministry should hinge on these two components.

2. The Great Commission

Before His ascension, Jesus gave us what we refer to today as the *Great Commission*—the mandate of our Lord for us to go out and spread the Good News. This charge should be every believer's driving force and remains an essential element in building the Church of the Living God. We find the *Great Commission* mainly recorded in Scripture passages such as Matthew 28:18-20 and Mark 16:15. Of importance is the fact that, although Jesus was addressing His disciples when He gave the Great Commission, He did not give it to them alone but, most certainly, also to the Church-at-large. It is such an official commission that we could likely even refer to it as the Church's job description or marching orders.

The Great Commission has three components:
1. *Making disciples*—which is evangelism
2. *Baptizing them*—which is affirmation
3. *Teaching them*—which is discipleship

Although I classify the Great Commission here in three separate steps, I do need to mention that per the Greek grammatical construction, the Great Commission is basically to *make disciples*. That, in turn, unfolds into two components: baptizing and teaching. It may not make much difference in our genre how we depict the process in this instance, provided we remain obligated to winning them, baptizing them, and teaching them the principles of the Word of God.

> Every local church
> should have a
> defined process

Every local church should have an established *process* of spiritual development to be faithful to the Great Commission. Our mission is not only to lead people to Christ but, also, to incorporate them into the Body as a result of *baptism*—the latter being much more significant than most people realize. But the process should not end there either.

After we have baptized people as new converts, they should have the opportunity to follow a *Life-Transforming Discipleship Track* as provided by the local congregation. Through this process, people should be guided and trained to grow in Christ and systematically proceed until they are fully involved in some form of ministry in the church.

The discipleship we have in mind requires us to not only provide *information* but even more so, *transformation.* If we merely base our discipleship-teaching on transferring information, it will ultimately lead to obese Christians—overfed believers who have never put the principles into practice. Our discipleship goal should always be to see people transformed into the image of Christ and should include a defined process whereby they become faithfully involved in ministry. *Process* is the buzzword here. Unless we have such a track in our churches, our people will remain unfulfilled and never reach their full potential.

However vital this subject may be, it is not within the scope of this book to fully develop the thought of discipleship. I merely mentioned it here for you to fully grasp the illustration of the two rivers that flow from the *Great Commandment,* but even more so to substantiate that I do not disparage the importance of the Great Commission. I have developed material separate from this book regarding applying the discipleship process—*The Growth Track.* In keeping with the theme of this writing, our concentration will be on the next feature which deals with *loving people*:

3. The Great Commitment

The flow of the *Great **Commission*** (Loving God) throughout the New Testament is well known, and the Church has, to a great extent, applied itself well over past centuries in fulfilling this charge.

The aspect of the *Great* **Commitment** (Loving People), on the other hand, is not that well known. We relate to John 13:34 as the origin of this premise when Jesus said, "A new commandment I give to you, that you love one another; as I have loved you, that you also love one another" (John 13:34).

We recognize these same words in the Great Commandment statement we use as the basis of our 3C Mission of the Church (Matthew 22:35-40), but with the added description of "as I have loved you, that you also love one another" (John 13:34). This instruction describes more clearly how we should "love your neighbor as yourself" (Matthew 22:39) and makes us realize how important this charge is to Jesus.

It is the *implementation* of this statement—"love your neighbor as yourself"—that has become the great missing link in most churches. It's not so much the statement, but even more so the application of it in a practical sense that we have neglected. The reason for this could be that we may not have grasped the full impact of this expectation as we continued to minister to people around us. I believe in many ways we have assumed that just being kind and sweet to people, joining hands with them in prayer, and hugging them during Sunday morning worship, is all that is required to comply for loving your neighbor. Reality has proven, however, that people today earnestly desire to develop meaningful friendships and foster genuine relationships. To them, having the sense of belonging is a high commodity because it demonstrates to them that the church has accepted them and thereby offered them the opportunity to fulfill their life's purpose. This understanding creates the stability needed to build a healthy church.

Life has sadly become such that most people no longer care about the personal needs of others. It's almost as though a spirit of selfishness has taken over—even in our congregations. We never stop long enough to ask the question, "Who in this room needs my help?" And because we are not paying attention, we miss the apparent needs of people around us. We have developed a tendency to rush into the church and rush out again as fast as we came. Some have fallen into the habit of entering late and leaving early. But, in the process, we have overlooked the crying needs of people who have come desperately looking for hope in a cruel and cold world. They have tried everything else in life, believing they could find the answer by attending a church as their final resort. Graciously, through the ministry of the Holy Spirit, hopefully, many find their solution in Christ, but they never discover the friends they had hoped to meet.

Paul, writing with an enthused passion to the church in Philippi, said about Timothy, "I have nobody else with a genuine interest in your well-being. All the others seem to be wrapped up in their own affairs and do not really care (for the business of Jesus Christ)" (Philippians 2:20 PHILLIPS). Being "wrapped up in their own affairs" sadly describes where many people are today. The tremendous pressure of the world we're living in has caused us to lose concern for our fellow church members. And as a result, we must encourage our people to shift their focus from themselves to others intentionally. God created us humans to connect with each other. "You must learn to be considerate of one another, cultivating a life in common" (1 Corinthians 1:10b MSG).

God created humankind in His image

Humanity is a unique species of being. According to the Bible, God created humankind in His image as a *trifold being* consisting of spirit, soul, and body (Hebrews 4:12). We understand that the spirit of man is that part attached to God; the soul part comprises our mind, will, and emotions; while the body is that part attached to the world around us. While we are alive, these three things are inseparable.

Developing firm believers requires us to bear this human configuration in mind. We are responsible for ministering to the wholeness of humankind. Often in our process of teaching people, we concentrate on developing them spiritually but tend to overlook their needs personally, emotionally, and physically. This void may be one of the main reasons so many people never completely reach their spiritual goals. We may have unwittingly concentrated only on spiritual development at the neglect of the other two important aspects of our members. If we do not address the full spectrum, we should not be surprised when many times our ministry efforts are not as effective as we had hoped they would be.

While spiritual development is of utmost importance, we should realize that when we do not meet a person's basic human needs, the body may not give any physical indication of deprivation immediately. But the individual will most assuredly feel anxious and tense, which most often results in negative behavior or the display of a bad attitude. People usually cannot respond with good grace to spiritual values if we do not meet their *physical* needs. In most cases, it stifles the spiritual growth in an individual's life and severely curtails our efforts to develop people as active followers of Christ entirely.

These things help us understand that we have an obligation to minister to the wholeness of humankind and not only concentrate on the spiritual values. In their assumption that meeting the human needs of people does not fall within the mission of the local church, many have taken on the position of believing they should not spend time, energy, and resources on doing so. This neglect has caused a severe imbalance in the church which resulted in many hurting people drifting away.

The way we respond to people's needs determines how they react to spiritual development. It is when we neglect this aspect of human behavior that people feel disconnected and not cared for and is the reason I call it the missing link. Unless we pay attention to this principle, we will forever struggle to build healthy churches. For that reason, later in this book, I will devote an entire chapter on discussing the five basic human needs of humankind, entitled, "Why People Act the Way They do." God created us with these necessities, from which we can never separate ourselves no matter who we are or where we find ourselves.

The Care Revolution Connection

The Great Commitment (loving people) has primarily to do with taking care of the sheep that God has entrusted to us. The way we extend tender loving care to our neighbor is with the help of the *Care Revolution,* which is our present-day expression of the *Great Commitment.* We base this directive primarily on the mandate Jesus gave to Peter in John 21. Subsequently, Peter then urged the leaders of the Church in 1 Peter 5:2-4 to likewise implement this charge. Of course, many other passages of Scripture relate to this subject, and we will deal with some of them later.

In developing the case for the *Great Commission* and the *Great Commitment,* we need to re-emphasize that when Jesus gave these charges, He did not direct it at the disciples only, but certainly to the entire Church. Both the *Great Commission* and the *Great Commitment* are essential in developing healthy churches; they carry the same weight and are equally important. They flow directly out of the *Great Commandment*. The *Care Revolution* purposes to inspire the significance of the *Great Commitment* to bring balance to both flows in the Church today. Just as much as we equip people to win the lost, make disciples, and reach the world, we should likewise equip those who are gifted and called to care for Christ's followers to fulfill their calling.

The Two Flows Are Not Sterile

In our discussion of the Great Commandment, we indicated two definite rivers that flow out of it—*loving God/loving people*. We should, however, be careful that we do not observe these two flows as being sterile to each other. I am saying this because these two streams have definite points of intersection and overlap which support rather than oppose each other. As we develop the attitude of building healthy churches, we should endeavor to equalize these two streams. Neither should be done at the neglect of the other.

If we would concentrate exclusively on the *loving God* aspect of the New Testament by evangelizing the lost and making disciples, we could come to the faulty conclusion that the Christians' energies should be solely channeled to those outside the Church. It would seem the *Great Commission* is the Church's only mission. If, on the other hand, we would concentrate only on the *loving God* aspect of the New Testament, and thereby concentrate entirely on caring for people, shepherding the flock, and giving attention primarily to the household of faith, we can conversely come to the faulty conclusion that our energies, as Christians, should be spent only on believers at the exclusion of those outside the Church. It would then seem the *Great Commitment* is the singular mission of the Church.

To maintain a healthy balance in our churches, we should emphasize both these commands. That is the reason the Holy Spirit gives different gifts to different people. I am saying this, so we can understand that, although we have defined the two aspects of the Great Commandment, we should not compartmentalize all we do so strictly into categories. This would restrict the free flow of the Holy Spirit and hamper our effectiveness in the ministry. Both could and should function together. Jesus demonstrates this clearly when we see Him healing the sick and feeding the hungry while, at the same time, teaching about the principles of the Kingdom.

James Emery White summarizes it well when he says; "He mandated concern for the widow and orphan, the homeless and naked, the imprisoned and hungry while speaking of the bread of life and a home in heaven. If Jesus, so the church; we should be interested in both conversion and the common good too." [7]

The Origin of the Great Commitment

We can trace the source of the *Great Commitment* all the way back to the commitment Jesus asked of Peter in John 21:15-17, which finally became the charge he gave to the Church in 1 Peter 5:1-4. Building on the foundation of the *Great Commitment* to establish the premise of the *Care Revolution,* it may serve us well to take a closer look at the relevance of this profound responsibility Jesus asked of Peter. This exhilarating expose will enlarge our understanding of the Great Commitment in profound ways.

---

7   James Emery White, *The Rise of the Nones: Understanding and Reaching the Religiously Unaffiliated* (Grand Rapids, MI: Baker Books, 2014), 102.

When Peter exhorted the elders in 1 Peter 5:1-4 to take up the *Great Commitment*, it was not another impulsive thought that dropped into his heart at the spur of the moment. There was a distinct journey that started a long time before that occurrence. It is paramount for us to understand this progression, so we can grasp the weight of what the *Great Commitment* means and how we arrive at a new paradigm for pastoral care.

4

A NEW
PARADIGM

Through the ages, whenever God has a significant assignment He desires to accomplish, He always first seeks for a man—a person He could entrust with the task. In the case of the *Great Commitment*, this responsibility unmistakably fell on the shoulders of the Apostle Peter who played a leading role in its fulfillment. The way this incident unfolds in Peter's life is a fantastic revelation and will help us understand that this entire notion is not about a good idea or just a modern-day solution for the Church. It is, instead, Christ's model of ensuring adequate care for the sheep He loves.

When Peter made the profound statement, as we have it recorded today in 1 Peter 5:1-4, it was not a free hanging thought or a sudden invasion of brilliance, but rather the culmination of a journey he had taken after a definite commitment he had made to Christ. This pathway led Peter to the significant moment of delivering the charge, or persuasion, first to the elders of his day, and ultimately to the body of Christ at large:

> To the elders among you, I appeal as a fellow elder and a witness of Christ's sufferings who also will share in the glory to be revealed: Be shepherds of God's flock that is under your care, watching over them—not because you must, but because you are willing, as God wants you to be; not pursuing dishonest gain, but eager to serve; not lording it over those entrusted to you, but being examples to the flock. And when the Chief Shepherd appears, you will receive the crown of glory that will never fade away (1 Peter 5:1-4 NIV).

There is so much more to this statement than initially meets the eye. It contains not only an explicit instruction but even more so, a glorious and exclusive promise of high reward.

The Story Has a Good Beginning

To gain the full perspective of this commitment, we need to go back to the day when Jesus called Simon Peter as a fisherman from his daily chores and instructed him to follow Him. What is so fascinating is that at the time when Jesus called him, Simon Peter was mending nets after the previous catch in preparation for the next. *To repair a fisherman's net* in the Greek is the word *katartismos*, which I only want you to take note of right now. I will pick up on this thought again in chapter eleven and bring you back to this fascinating observation.

Peter was a fascinating character. He was extraordinarily impulsive and habitually outspoken. He always seemed to act before he thought. Whatever was in his mind came out of his mouth without considering the consequences. When something didn't suit his fancy, he corrected it—immediately! Without thinking! But he was a close follower of Jesus and probably had more insight than many would have ascribed to him.

1. Peter's Great Confession (Matthew 16: 13—20)

On a particular day, nearing the end of His life on earth and being alone with His disciples, Jesus chose this private occasion to reveal to them what His true life-purpose for coming to this world was. Remember, most people at the time still thought He was going to overthrow the Roman Empire and set up His kingdom. Even the disciples were under that impression. However, the time had now come for Jesus to bring them to the understanding that establishing an earthly kingdom was not His intention—at least not at that point. Instead, His mission was to build a Church—an *ecclesia* or *koinonia* of people. It would be a kingdom of far greater magnitude than what people may have anticipated.

To create the atmosphere for this astounding revelation, Jesus chose this intimate moment (Matthew 16:13-20) to ask them the now-familiar question, "Whom do men say that I, the Son of Man, am?" (Matthew 16:13). Sometimes we say we don't care what people think or say about us, but Jesus did. Perhaps we should, too. Most likely His question was meant to test the impact of His ministry to determine whether ordinary people knew the actual reason for His coming and who He in fact was. Christ never said who He was and instead chose His works to identify His mission and ministry. The disciples responded and said, "Some say you are John the Baptist; some, Elijah, and others, Jeremiah, or one of the prophets" (Matthew 16:14). Although these may have been honorable opinions, from the context, it appears that was not, in fact, the most important thing Jesus wanted to know.

Apparently, Jesus did not react outwardly to their statements, but then discretely drew the circle a little closer and asked them pointedly, "But who do you say that I am?" (Matthew 16:15). It may be a fair assumption to say that, evidently, Jesus wanted the disciples first to realize who He indeed was before He revealed to them the real purpose of His earthly assignment. It was necessary to Him that they have precise knowledge of His true nature because He knew the entire weight of His mission was going to rest on their shoulders eventually.

It would be the responsibility of the apostles and prophets to build the Church, and much would depend on how discernably they knew Jesus's identity. Their impression of how they saw Him would affect their efforts and especially the way they would lay the foundation of the Christian Church. So, in asking this probing question, Jesus was evaluating the moment of when to reveal to them the great mission of His Church. The moment was crucial, the atmosphere tense. *But who do you say that I am?* There may have been a moment of concentrated silence, and then, without flinching, Peter intuitively responded and said, "You are the Christ, the Son of the living God!" (Matthew 16:16).

It is possible that Peter had known this truth for a while but waited for the appropriate moment to disclose the revelation, or perhaps it was an unexpected prophetic moment he experienced; we're not sure. He may not even clearly have understood all he was saying, but his confession came out of a heart of simple trust that Jesus was the Christ, the Son of the living God. Peter was unmistakably the first of the disciples to understand who Jesus was. In his spirit, he saw a bright, heavenly "snapshot" of Christ, the Anointed One, and realized that His mission was a higher calling. He had a prophetic glimpse into the future nobody else had and understood something no-one else did.

With John 1:42 in mind, Jesus was likely not amazed at Peter's bold statement and readily responded by speaking great blessing over him, "Blessed are you, Simon Bar-Jonah, for flesh and blood has not revealed this to you, but My Father who is in heaven" (Matthew 16:17). Peter's proclamation was a profound and blissful revelation from a heart of clear conviction that blasted forth a truth that eventually became the foundation of the Church. What a momentous day it must have been for Peter when Jesus turned to him and said, "I also say to you that you are Peter, and on this rock, I will build My church, and the gates of Hades shall not prevail against it" (Matthew 16:18). Using my personal paraphrase in context, Jesus was likely saying, "Not only have you received a revelation from My Father of who I am, but now I want to reveal the way through which you will be part of the fulfillment of the entire mission of building My Church."

There are different theological views of Jesus's statement "on this rock; I will build My church . . ." I certainly do not want to make this a point of dispute, and I also want to be careful that my remarks do not sound as though I want to deify Peter. It is the author's opinion that Jesus did not imply that He was going to build His Church on Peter, or even on Peter's revelation, but rather on the divine revelation of who *He* was (and is)—the Son of the living God. It becomes even more interesting when we take a closer look at this conversation.

After Peter's response, Jesus no longer referred to him as "Simon, son of Jonah (or son of John)." Instead, Jesus said, "And I also say unto you that you are **Peter**" (Petros) which means little rock, or a stone, or a fragment of the big rock. Note that Jesus said, "You are Peter." In this, Jesus did not so much describe *whom* he was, but rather *what* he was. We realize that, especially in Bible times, people's names identified more of their person, occupation, character, heritage, etc., than anything else. Considering that truth, I feel safe to say Jesus had a particular function in mind He was going to assign to Simon that would match his new name. What his new name, or personal identity *meant*, is what is significant.

Taking a closer look at all this, we realize that if we regard Jesus as the Big Rock (*Petra*) or the Chief Cornerstone, then it appears Peter (the little rock) was the one who was assigned to be an immediate extension of Jesus Christ—a chip off the Big Rock. We will see more of this unfold shortly. In his assignment, Peter would be instrumental in the building of the Church and the mission thereof. His voice would become an echo through the annals of time, declaring the heart of the One from whom he had received a divine revelation of the Father Himself.

Jesus expanded His commission to Peter by saying, "And I will give you the keys of the kingdom of heaven, and whatever you bind on earth will be bound in heaven, and whatever you loose on earth will be loosed in heaven" (Matthew 16:19). Through these words, the King of Glory and Head of the Church bestowed upon Peter a remarkable delegation of authority as an acknowledgment of his brave and honest confession, and most likely also as an emblem of unity. Afterward, this power was also bestowed upon the other apostles (Matthew 18:18) and later passed on to all believers.

A remarkable
delegation of authority

Although Jesus promised spiritual authority to Peter on that occasion, Peter did not see that manifestation until the Day of Pentecost after the Holy Spirit had descended upon them in the Upper Room. It is no wonder that it was again Peter who took the lead and announced the revelation of what had happened among the followers of Christ in the Upper Room and explained the prophetic relevance of Christ's divine mission. Peter was also the first man who ever opened the door of the Church to both Jew and Gentile. He was selected as one of the three, with James and John, to be in the inner circle of the disciples. He was with Jesus at the Transfiguration. He is the one who wanted to build three huts on that important site immediately. Peter, through his impulsive nature always seemed to display excellent leadership skills.

A Divine
Caution

Later, when Jesus was on His way to the Cross, He warned the disciples that they would be offended because of Him and that He would become the fulfillment of the prophecy, "I will strike the Shepherd, and the sheep of the flock will be scattered. But after I have been raised, I will go before you to Galilee" (Matthew 26:31-32).

Note: The word "sheep" here is probably referencing the disciples, but also refers to the followers of Christ at-large. "Galilee" was known for its shepherd fields, and this whole mention points to pastoral connotation. Do not miss the significance of this prophetic affirmation because later in Peter's restoration, the sheep come into play and the *Great Commitment* we are talking about finds significant meaning.

2. Peter's Great Denial (Luke 22: 54-61)

As we follow the steps of development with Peter in Matthew 26, we are struck again by his spontaneous statement when he says, "Even if all are made to stumble because of You, I will never be made to stumble" (Matthew 26:33). Jesus said to him, "Assuredly, I say to you that this night before the rooster crows, you will deny Me three times" (Matthew 26:34). And still, Peter persisted, "Even if I have to die with You, I will not deny You" (Matthew 26:35).

Again, this statement reveals how close Peter felt to Jesus and how ready he always was to protect Him. Before the crucifixion, as another example, when Jesus went into the garden to pray in anguish, it was again Peter who was within a stone's throw of Him—so close that he could hear every word of pain and agony from the Master's lips. Peter heard Jesus praying to the Father, asking Him for the cup to pass from Him. He could not have missed the sorrowful anguish. Later in the Garden of Gethsemane when they came to arrest Jesus, one of the disciples stepped forward and drew his sword and sliced off the ear of the high priest's servant. But look a little closer; it's Peter—again impulsive Peter! He was all out to defend his Master.

Jesus turned around and probably said something like, "Peter, put away your sword, that's not the way we do it!" I can imagine feisty Peter saying, "If he doesn't watch out, I'll chop off the other one, also!" But that's not in the Bible! Luke only records that Jesus touched the soldier's ear and healed it, but my imagination wants to believe Jesus bent down and picked up the bleeding ear from the ground, dusted it off, and stuck it back on the soldier's head. But again, that's not quite the way they wrote it.

A prediction
fulfilled

But then the moment came when they arrested Jesus, and the painful journey to the Cross began. Fear overtook the disciples, and they all fled, including Peter. He, however, then continued to follow Jesus from a distance and watched His every move. He just could not stay away. As the night proceeded, he went into the palace of the high priest and sat down with the servants around the fire to warm himself. I am sure, in that hectic moment, there must have been great turmoil in his life, with thoughts pounding his mind, probably even analyzing all the shocking incidents that have occurred over the past few hours. He may also have questioned the validity of Jesus being the Messiah and wondered about all the values He had taught them. It was at this intense moment that a young lady recognized him as one of Jesus's followers, but he vehemently denied it.

> Great turmoil
>
> in his life

Then another maid saw him and said to those who stood by; This *is one of them* (Mark 14:69). But he denied it once again. A few moments later those who stood by said to Peter, "Surely you are one of them; for you are a Galilean, and your speech shows it" (Mark 14:70). This time Peter even chooses to cuss and swear a little (verse 71) to hide his identity and says, "I do not know this Man of whom you speak!" (Mark 14:71) And then suddenly a cock crowed loudly, and Peter abruptly remembered the words of Jesus, "Assuredly, I say to you that this night before the rooster crows, you will deny Me three times" (Matthew 26:34). Like a gushing waterfall, anguish washed over him as he began to weep profusely. The naked reality of the moment had suddenly dawned on him, and as a man awakening from a deep sleep of an anguish-filled nightmare, he realized the horror of what he had just done.

In that moment of distress, he wrapped his garment tightly and ran as fast as his feet could carry him into the darkness of the night headed towards an unknown destiny. Coming somewhat to his senses, he slowed down and with his heart pounding in his chest and his lungs burning, decided to make his way to the Temple Court, hoping he could see Jesus one more time. His soul-cry was "If only I could ask for His forgiveness!"

When Peter gets there, he is just in time to see them lead Jesus away from Caiaphas to the Hall of Judgment and in a remarkable moment, his eyes meet those of his Master (Luke 22:61). And when he looks into those eyes, he does not see anger or rejection, but rather an attitude of forgiveness, understanding, and the most significant expression of love one could ever imagine. He would never forget the deep impressions of those moments of the most intimate encounter with the One who has compassion beyond human comprehension.

The days that followed must have been days of agony for Peter. He was the one who had received the divine revelation of who Jesus was, the man who somehow understood something no-one else did, defender of his Master as few others, but now stumbling through the streets of Jerusalem, realizing the traitor he had become. He felt the profound loss of the close relationship he once enjoyed with Jesus, but now understandably feeling disgustingly uncertain about the friendship. It is no wonder that the message of Christ being raised from the dead a few days later had the effect on him that it did.

The uncertainty must have hounded him like an untamed wolf, and the often-experienced silence in the company of the other disciples justifiably caused him even more uneasiness. This agony filled his days with pain, regret, and remorse for not having remained with Jesus to the end. He was anxious to get the misery of the dark and restless nights behind him but did not know how. Not having the opportunity to ask Jesus's forgiveness filled his life with torment.

We can understand why, on that beautiful resurrection morning, Peter did not stop outside the grave as John did, but ran right into the now open tomb, desperately yearning to have his relationship restored with his Master, his Best Friend, the One he loved so much. He had to know for sure that Christ had risen because if indeed He had, it meant that he could potentially be reconciled to Him and have another chance in life and experience a new beginning. But it was not yet the moment of restitution.

3. Peter's Great Commitment

One day followed after the other until finally the moment of Peter's restoration came and was possibly more important than most people realize. John 21:1-17 describes to us the occurrence of the long-awaited instance when, after His crucifixion and subsequent resurrection, Jesus met again with the disciples in a personal setting on the shore of the Sea of Tiberius. According to John, this was the third time Jesus showed Himself to them after having been raised from the dead. After they had eaten, the atmosphere changed to become an intimate and revealing moment, especially for Peter. Jesus, the great Restorer of broken lives, hopes, and dreams, appeared and chose this setting to reinstate Peter to his divine calling. "For the gifts and the calling of God are irrevocable" (Romans 11:29). Not only was this apostle of Christ going to be restored, but in the same process receive a charge that would remain through the ages and become an overall clarion call to the Church.

This entire encounter gives hope to every minister who had ever failed, in whatever manner you could imagine, that Christ stands ready to restore every single one of His followers who has fallen, to complete righteousness, and simultaneously give them a new assignment of high magnitude. If you have ever failed in some area of your life, you are not a failure. Failure is not a person it's an event. When God restores, He multiplies!

The Love Confrontation

At a decisive moment, during this critical gathering, Jesus turned to Simon Peter and said, "Simon, son of Jonah, do you love Me?" (John 21:15) This question at first seems unassuming, asked with the intent of evoking conversation. But in reality, there was much more to this question than one would casually perceive.

Since Jesus focused on the subject of *love,* let's first take a brief look at the word *love* in general terms. For the most part, we can differentiate the word *love* in the New Testament by observing the context in which we use the word. But let's simply consider these following terms:

- *Eros*—which has the meaning of erotic or sexual love. It is not necessarily always a sensual word and merely means a desire toward another person with the intention of getting something back from the relationship. It is a *fleshly* love which could also be described as selfish love.
- *Phileo (or philia)*—which we customarily accept as the friendship kind of love. It's the kind of love we have for people in general—better explained as fellowship. It could also be referred to as brotherly love.
- *Storge*—this is the kind of love we have for our family. It is deeper than friendship-love and usually creates a feeling

of security and a sense of belonging. That sort of love builds strong ties.

- *Agape*—which is known as the unconditional love of divine origin. *Agape* is selfless love and does not arise from a need within a person, but from a need within another. One who loves at the *Agape*-level does so expecting nothing in return. It seeks no reward. It is the God-kind of spontaneous love which the Holy Spirit develops in us towards others.

Considering these words, we know when Jesus asked Peter (or Simon) this question, "Do you love me?" Jesus was not referring to *Eros*—so we do not even have to consider that expression in our discussion. However, let's continue to take a closer look at this provocative question. It is interesting to note the closing words of the question Jesus posed to Peter when He said, "Do you love Me more than these?" What could that mean? Well, it could, *first*, have indicated that Jesus wanted to know if Peter loved Him more than the other disciples did. *Secondly*, it could have meant in return that Jesus wanted to see if Peter loved Him more than he loved the other disciples. Most likely He was referring to a higher kind of love than universal human love. *Thirdly*, it could have even meant that Jesus wanted to know if Peter loved Him more than his earthly possessions, occupation, and surroundings. Jesus was looking for a closer confession of love—a *more than these* kind of love.

Undoubtedly, Jesus wanted to establish whether Peter loved Him in a way that was more than the typical human love, which is merely brotherly love. He was not seeking a response that would satisfy pure love rationally. Neither was Jesus aiming for what we customarily find in a family relationship. He was looking for an *Agape* love response from Peter. *Agapao (Agape)* love, meaning the God-kind of love we describe more fully as genuine, spontaneous, zealous, superlative, cherished, unselfish, incomparable, love; the kind of love we can only experience in a spiritual context.

The Threefold Confession

This entire encounter was a tense moment. Jesus was getting ready to pronounce a significant charge to Peter which required unequivocal love beyond any shadow of a doubt. It had to be love on a much higher and real level than that which we typically find among people.

At first, Peter responds almost casually, "Yes, Lord, You know that I love You" (John 21:15). And then with a divine projection (don't miss this), Jesus requested a particular commitment from him. This application was not something like, Go and perform miracles, heal the sick, open prison doors, or raise the dead. Jesus merely required of Peter: "Feed My lambs" (John 21:15).

Then Jesus asked him again, a second time, "Simon, son of Jonah, do you love Me?" (John 21:16) He said to Jesus, "Yes, Lord, You know that I love You" (John 21:16). This time Jesus does not add "more than these" to the question. But when Peter answers in the affirmative, once again, Jesus does not give him some huge assignment, but instead only repeats the appeal to take on this specific commitment. He does not command him to go and rent the Jerusalem Coliseum and conduct a massive crusade and do great things in ministry. He just requires him to, "Tend My sheep" (John 21:16).

Jesus said to him the third time, "Simon, son of Jonah, do you love Me?" (John 21:17) "Peter was grieved because He said to him the third time, 'Do you love Me?'" (John 21:17) But you see, Peter denied Jesus three times, so he had to repeat this confession three times for Jesus to restore his apostolic calling. "And Peter said to Him, Lord, You know all things; You know that I love You" (John 21:17).

Saying that Jesus knew all things might have been the confession Jesus was seeking. Peter now realized that the love Christ was asking him about was way higher than only *liking* or loving. It referred more to a statement of final surrender. And again, Jesus does not give Peter some dynamic, earth-moving, mind-boggling mission. He once again merely charges him to, "Feed, My sheep" (John 21:17).

> The confession
> Jesus was
> looking for

The sincere confession Peter made in John 21 qualified him to receive the high charge of taking care of God's Flock and substantiates the necessity of such an important gathering. Christ committed Peter to care for His lambs and His sheep, who were all in different levels of development. This whole scenario naturally occurred after the Resurrection. Jesus was now preparing to go to heaven, but before doing so was gravely concerned that *the flock,* He had given His life for, would receive adequate care. When Jesus, therefore, forgave and restored Peter, He entrusted him with the most cherished pearl He had on earth—His Flock (the Church!). I am not sure we always understand the significance of this moment when Jesus, the Rock, shifted the weight of the responsibility of caring for the sheep onto the shoulders of Peter, the little rock.

Follow the progression:

1.   "Feed My lambs . . ." Refers primarily to nurturing and watching over new believers in Christ who need more intense love and care. Christ's concern is that the new lambs are not left uncared for, but receive instructions and teaching based on the basics of the Christian walk and become part of the flock (1 Corinthians 3:1,2).

2.   "Tend My sheep . . ." Contains the action word *tend*, which carries with it the notion of being actively involved. It refers to the ongoing practice of pastoral care and spiritual development of mature believers. It describes a process of making sure that they advance in their walk with Christ. "That we should no longer be children, tossed to and fro and carried about with every wind of doctrine . . ." (Ephesians 4:14).

3.   "Feed My sheep . . ." is a general reference to a continuous process of nurturing the sheep on spiritual food (the Word) so they can grow, become established, and be involved in ministry. This expectation can best be described in the words of Paul when he stated, in the company of the other disciples:

> Till we all come to the unity of the faith and of the knowledge of the Son of God, to a perfect man, to the measure of the stature of the fullness of Christ (Ephesians 4:13).

His very breath and blood flow through us,
nourishing us so that we will grow up healthy in
God, robust in love (Ephesians 4:16 MSG).

Don't Miss This

What is also gripping, is the unspoken qualification that took
place at this crucial moment. Before Jesus released Peter into the
Great Commitment of caring for the sheep (loving people), He *first*
established his love for Him (loving God) by asking Peter three times
whether he loved Him. It almost sounds like, what we would today
call, a job interview Jesus was conducting with Peter. It was only after
Jesus was satisfied that Peter loved Him the way he should, that He was
willing to give him the charge of taking care of the flock. The evident
reason for this is that Jesus had such a caring concern for His flock
that He was not willing to entrust their care to anyone but those who
genuinely love Him first.

It's when they love Him sincerely that people find joy in their
labors to care for His sheep. It's their love for Jesus that compels them
to continue in their caring for others even when they face difficulties,
discouragement, and resistance. It's loving Jesus that motivates
continued service and not the acceptance or applause of people. *Loving
God* leads to *loving people*, and through loving people, loving God
becomes evident. *How can you say you love God but hate your brother?*

Seeing It in Perspective

Here is the man who had the mighty, heavenly revelation of who
Jesus was. Here is the man who Jesus marked as the *little rock* which
was to be the extension of the *Big Rock* and the first one to receive the
delegated spiritual authority from the Head of the Church. Here is

the disciple who later preached the first message under the anointing of the Holy Spirit on the Day of Pentecost and 3,000 people became believers. Here is the man who, after Pentecost, received the heavenly vision of breaking with tradition and going beyond the restriction of legalism and became the one that opened the door of the Church to both the Jews and the Gentiles. And yet the Great Commitment Jesus asks of this influential leader at his restoration moment was just: *Take care of My sheep!* That is huge!

Although we are heavily concentrating on caring for the flock regarding the local church, we should not discount the fact that the charge certainly also includes making provision for the sheep yet to come. The love we are talking about, as well as the caring we are advocating, should go beyond the walls of our churches or else it becomes a selfish love that serves no purpose.

Not to Peter Alone

The charge Christ gave to Peter was not given to him alone. Just as He did in the case of the Great Commission, Jesus gave the Great Commitment charge to all the disciples and, ultimately, to the Church-at-large. "He charged them all, not only to be fishers of men by the conversion of sinners but feeders of the flock, by the edification of saints."[8]

We can see the evidence of the importance of this charge in the fact that even the Apostle Paul picks up its prominence. He says, "Therefore, take heed to yourselves and to all the flock, among which the Holy Spirit has made you overseers, to shepherd the church of

---

8   Matthew Henry, *Matthew Henry's Complete Commentary*, Volume 5 (McLean, Virginia: MacDonald Publishing Company), 1232

God, which He purchased with His own blood" (Acts 20:28). Shifting the responsibility of caring for the flock to the church-at-large has become a new paradigm and is fast becoming the driving force to establish healthy congregations in the church of the . The way we do congregational care these days will determine a successful outcome for the church of the future.

All this biblical background and history is essential, so we understand that the Great *Commitment* is no less than the Great *Commission*. They are BOTH a part of the Great *Commandment*. The Great Commitment indicates "Taking Care of the Flock," which is better known as "Shepherding the Flock." In our supposition, we refer to it as the *Care Revolution* and in the local church application as the *Care Ministry Network*.

"Caring follows evangelism in the spiritual order just as nurturing follows birth in the biological order." (Mel Steinbron)

4. The Great Charge (1Peter 5:2-3)

Persuaded by the significance of this charge and the powerful affirmation as a background, Peter urges the Church to commit to "Shepherd the flock of God which is among you . . . Not by compulsion but willingly, not for dishonest gain but eagerly; nor as being lords over those entrusted to you but being examples to the flock" (1 Peter 5:2-3).

We realize that some could reason that this charge relates primarily to the role of the vocational pastor. But we should not lose sight again of the fact that the shepherd, as part of the five-fold equipping gifts to the Church (Ephesians 4:11-13), has an obligation, not only to shepherd the flock but also to train and develop the members likewise to function in their role of caring for one another. All who are Christ's have the commitment to care for the sheep, which are His, and His only ". . . members should have the same care for one another" (1 Corinthians 12:25).

5. The Great Reward

The Great Commitment is so important to God (the matter of taking care of the flock) that Peter emphatically brings to our attention that those who are faithful to shepherding the flock, ". . . When the Chief Shepherd appears, (will) receive the crown of glory that does not fade away" (1 Peter 5:4). This reward, called the *Crown of Glory*, is reserved exclusively for those who will remain faithful in taking care of the flock. Those dedicated to this cause will receive this crown from no one else but the *Chief Shepherd* Himself. It is the real reward of those who cared for the sheep, shielded them from the attacks of the enemy, the deception of other people, and the pain of life.

If nothing else underscores the utmost importance of caring for God's people, this fact indeed does. Think of it—an exceptional crown earmarked for particular individuals who have done a unique ministry. That makes us realize: The Great Commitment is crucial, and we cannot and should not ignore this element.

Reality check: When people receive Christ as Savior and become part of our churches, they have the right to expect to be loved, cared for, nurtured, prayed for, and encouraged. They have a right to pastoral care. The Great Commitment guarantees this right, and we need to take up the charge.

5

WHY HAVE
A CARE MINISTRY?

The reasonable question some may ask is, "Why should we be so anxious about focusing our attention on providing care in this season of the Church? What has changed?" That is a vital question and needs particular consideration since we prefer not to do something just because it sounds good, but because it is essential. So, let's stop, take inventory of our activities, and contemplate the needed application of providing congregational care.

Considering Church history and present-day realities, it becomes evident that we are in an *interim age,* not being sure whether we should hold on to the past or take active steps into the future. The fact is: The Church mostly cannot remain where it is now. Conventional structures are disassembling; membership is declining, and so are the finances. Our culture, in general, is uninterested, unsympathetic, or benignly intolerant. Our communities do not think the Church is relevant and does not support its cause.

In this interim age (the period between what the Church was and what it is becoming), church-development strategies differ significantly. Some churches are trying to recapture the past. Their goal is: Do what we have always done, just do it bigger and better. Some are holding steady. Their hope is: The curve somehow will turn back upward again. Others are shifting gears. Their risk is: We'll cast our lot with the Scriptures and successful church models.[9]

As we get ready for the next great move of God, it may serve us well to take progressive and reformist steps ahead to stabilize and invigorate our churches. If we never evaluate the level of ministry we provide and the results we are getting, our congregations will continue to struggle and even continue to regress. There are few things as valuable as self-evaluation—if done honestly.

Despite the many great things happening in many churches across the world, the truth remains that most churches are facing unbelievable challenges, have stagnated, or are in severe decline. No wonder unregenerate people are asking, "Where is the glue to reassemble the degeneration and the disarray?" It's almost like the young lady who frantically cried out one day in desperation, "the only thing that is holding me together is my hairspray!"

It's Time for Honesty

If we are serious about revitalizing the Church and bringing freshness to its relevance, I am convinced that we should stop blaming someone (or something) else for the position we find ourselves. It's not

9   Melvin J. Steinbron, *The Lay Driven Church* (Ventura: Regal Books, 1997)

going to help us much to continue finding fault with our denominational systems or criticizing its leadership, or the lack thereof. It is honestly time to take a moment to consider where we have come from, evaluate where we are, and then fervently bring innovative direction to a bright new tomorrow. We all understand that we can do nothing without the Lord. But truthfully, as the saying goes, if it's going to be, it's up to me.

> Without Him,
> we cannot.
> Without us,
> He will not.
> St. Francis of Assisi

It is the *epitome of stupidity* for a person to continue to do the same thing over and over and yet expect different results. When are we going to learn in church circles that it is time to get out of the rut—or the proverbial *box*—and get something done? As it is said: "If you **want** something you've never had, you have to **do** something you've never done!"

The Reality

It is my full intention to not only help you identify the problem and then offer a solution– but instead go beyond and let you know of the appropriate resources available to you—so you can implement the solution. I don't know about you, but, quite frankly, I have become tired and frustrated listening to speakers and teachers telling us *what* to do and even *how* to do it but never provide or at least point us to the tools *with which we can accomplish* the task. Don't just tell me I should build a bridge from where I am to where I need to go—I get that. Help me with the vehicle to get there.

That is what I have in mind! Hopefully, you will get just as excited about the concept as so many others have, and when you get ready to build the bridge, you will discover that we have already done all the work for you. All you will have to do is get behind the steering wheel of the bus and steer your people toward their determined destiny.

I will begin by describing the background of the local church's dilemma, show the biblical basis of the solution, lay the foundation for a system that works, and thoroughly explain this useful and proven concept to you. Unfortunately, in ministry, we often attempt to rush to the solution at the expense of actually evaluating the way we have come. We quickly get excited about what may potentially work and implement it before we have calculated the outcome.

We are forever looking for a quick fix, which usually never works. The truth is that unless we discover what caused the stalemate and learn from it, we will never be able to reach our dreams of tomorrow. As it is said, if we forget our history, we will tend to make the same mistakes again.

> If we forget our history,
> we will make the same
> mistakes again!

A Quick Snapshot

People today are looking to the Church for interaction and personal attention more than ever before. The vast expansion of the electronic age has caused people to become reclusive and, in the process, created a relational void. I don't know how long it has been since I have seen such a search for real relationships among people as we know it today. Look around you on Sunday, and you will see many church members have even become more and more distant from each other, and yet they desire the closeness they once knew.

Church members often feel the leaders don't hear their cries, don't help to heal their hurts, and do not give proper attention to their personal and family problems. Others feel the church does not assist them sensibly in their social, relational, and employment struggles. The bottom line is that most people feel distant from their church and its leadership and as a result often feel abused. Attending church on a Sunday is great, but that alone does not provide the cohesiveness that is required.

To our amazement, when we started focusing our church on caring for people, we found to our dismay that often our people were not regularly visited and prayed within hospitals—or at least not systematically. Individuals in nursing homes and other aged and infirm people felt neglected, while yet others thought they did not receive the attention they deserved concerning spiritual matters. All of this was happening primarily because, in most cases, the ministry was being left to a select few people to do.

And it's not that our folk had no concern for their fellow church members; it's more a matter of them not knowing how to reach out to others resolutely. People seem to come to church and then unassumingly leave without sincerely showing interest in what's happening in the lives of other people. But then it almost looks like a paradox! While they are longing for a relationship, they become reclusive in their attitude.

Our church was certainly not unfriendly. But what we discovered was that our people were often gathering in groups, seemingly lost in their delightful conversation but oblivious to those who were desperately seeking connection. These were typically individuals in leadership or those more prominent in the operation of the church. But the quiet, withdrawn, and less-known members and visitors many times felt ignored and wondered if anyone even knew of their existence. They walked in, and they walked out, and nobody seemed to care. This action usually causes a distant feeling by people, which creates the vacuum in relationships.

The truth of the matter is that those who are substantially engaged in ministry, especially on higher levels of leadership, for the most part, don't sense the reality of relational depravity. If they need attention, care, or support, it's usually freely available. I have found over-and-over that those people who are noticeable in the church or have been in leadership a long time, or even members forever, usually say they don't need someone to care for them. "We don't need someone to be there for us," they say. "We have a pastor if we need one." Prominent as these people are, they may be correct when they say they don't need additional attention, but unfortunately, it creates the impression that nobody else needs care or attention.

These leaders find their fellowship, love, and acceptance in the long-term relationships they have built with each other over the years. However, this is traditional thinking has led the church to stagnation. In their minds, the congregation is being taken care of, and they need do no more. But those who are further away from the core are frequently left in the cold, many times struggling on their own and seemingly never receive any meaningful attention. To them, the church as a body has become useless.

After I had done an in-depth presentation of the workings of a ministry of care at a growing congregation in the

Dallas-area, a senior member of the church came over to me and said,

> "I so appreciate this concept you are bringing to our church. I have been part of this congregation in leadership for a long time and have always wondered if we are adequately staying in touch with everyone and making sure we are tending to them."

She went on to say, "They have recently discharged me from the hospital, and I must say that my church and pastor took care of me well. I learned to appreciate my spiritual family." Her tear-filled eyes were saying much more than she could express.

"But strangely enough," she continued, "I was lying in my hospital bed, thinking of the concept you are sharing with us. I was wondering if all the people in the church were also receiving the same kind of attention." She apparently had a heartfelt passion for people as she continued her thought process, "What about those who are not as well-known as I am? I don't think they do!"

She said she started asking other members about the situation and, quite frankly, did not like what she was hearing from her *loving* church. People came up with all kinds of excuses, but the bottom line was that all people were not receiving the same level of care she did.

"I am saying all of that to underscore that your teaching comes as an answer to my prayer. I cannot believe all the confirmation you are bringing. Why haven't we always done it this way?"

The more we consider these things, the more we will realize how many of our people are going unnoticed—feeling distant and uncared for by their church. If they are not *in* with the in-crowd, they are out. It is quite often the quiet and reserved people that do not get the attention they should.

Can we honestly afford to continue this way? Are we secretly just hoping it will get better? Do we think the needs of people will disappear, or that they don't expect our attention? Or do we assume people will understand that times have changed and that we are all busy, and then just get over it?

The basic answer to these questions is: No, it will never change! No, they will never understand! People are people, and their human needs will never change. There is a biblical expectation for us to care for those God has entrusted to us. Reality beckons us to answer the question: If we are not taking care of those God has already sent us, why should He send us anymore?

Seeing People for Who They Are

Our dilemma lies in the fact that many people come to our churches, but just as many also leave. We advertise, we market, we promote, we put on *Big Days*, and the people come. But we do not retain enough of our visitors, and sometimes, as Pastor Rick Warren said, "It seems as though we are pastoring a parade."

Attracting a crowd is not that difficult but keeping them is! You can do all kinds of things to get people to come, but if you don't have a system to retain them, your labors will be futile. *Big Days* work, well-known guest speakers and celebrities could help attract people from the community, musicals can open the door, offering each person who shows up a twenty-dollar bill will guarantee you a crowd, but if you do not have a process of keeping them, you are wasting your time and resources.

Some years ago, I read of a denomination that did some research on people that had left their churches and did not know the reason for their actions. I cannot remember the exact percentage, but I do remember them reporting that the most significant portion of these people said they received no contact whatsoever from their church after they had left. A significant number stated that they would have at least appreciated a conscious effort from their pastor or even a church member before they decided to separate from the church permanently. But nobody called or followed up.

And if the truth were known, it is not that pastors and churches do not care; it is instead that they have no system or ministry plan for retaining these people and consequently have no workable method of rescuing members when they do fall through the cracks. For that reason, we need a new paradigm. Pastors often just hope the people who left will come back. But that is a myth, and we know it.

People usually leave because the church does not meet their expectations or because they were not able to establish close enough relationships. On the other hand, new attendees come, for the most part, to receive the love, attention, and fellowship that the church has become known for, but are many times disillusioned when they realize that the care and concern they had hoped to find is not there. They quickly discover religion, but then battle to find relationships. And if new members do not make close friends within six months, they will begin to drift off again in search of another church or fellowship. That is why we need a system.

For the most part, we are not tending well to God's flock and, unwittingly, creating an atmosphere of unrest and insecurity. The people are anxious, they're not feeding well, the fruit of evangelism has become minimal, and those who are supposed to support the church financially are holding back in their giving because their souls are not satisfied. That's when they slip out through the holes in the fence to seek another shepherd who may potentially take care of them. And I know, our mission should be to have people be satisfied with Jesus more than anything or anyone else, but if people experience a vacuum of some sorts, they find it difficult to connect to the spiritual.

Everyday Realities

A once faithful family in a respectable church dropped out of attendance after their son died of AIDS. Nobody seemed to care, and nobody was there for the family. The congregation handled them as if they had fallen from grace. After a long absence, someone asked them one day, "But why did you leave the church?" With pain in their voices, they answered, "We did not leave the church; the church left us."

Wow! What an indictment. That certainly makes you think. But these are not isolated cases—the incidences and circumstances may change, but it's happening in almost all of our churches week after week. But it's impossible for pastors to connect with every family in a way where they can be attended to when a crisis occurs.

Another young man who had not attended church for a long time once said, "We stopped going to church when my parents were divorced. The church just ignored them and never reached out to them. I have just not personally had the courage to get back in!"

One of the many reasons this happens is because most people seemingly do not know what to say or how to handle those who are hurting or going through a personal crisis. This fact is an excellent example of the missing link we are talking about and why our people need to be trained and developed for reaching out to others. There must be an intentional system of care in our congregations or else this will continue to happen over and over.

Hurting People All Around Us

A classic example of this took place in a pace-setting church when one of the families went through the traumatic experience of the sudden death of their first-born grandson. Their daughter and son-in-law were also members of the congregation, and as a result, everyone knew about her expecting their first baby. The whole church rejoiced in the prospect of this great adventure for the entire family.

Because of anticipated complications, the mother had her baby boy in a larger city a few hours away. The joy of having their first baby was suddenly dampened by his death only a few hours later.

The first Sunday after this tragedy, the whole family returned to their church with understandable and yet unbelievable brokenness. They looked forward to connecting with the family of God, knowing they would find solace with their longtime friends and peers. But to their shock, amazement, and incredible pain, they found that people were ignoring them and suddenly disappearing into nearby restrooms or offices when they saw them coming.

It confused them and hurt them more deeply than words could ever explain. They thought they would find love and comfort, longing for the embrace of those that had known them for many years, but instead experienced rejection and avoidance.

The next Sunday after the morning service, the grandparents came to see the pastor. They were apparently hurting sincerely, and with tears in their eyes said, "Pastor, we do not understand what is going on. Did we do something wrong? Did we offend someone? Why are people ignoring us?"

They explained how people were responding and how, from their side, they had tried to reach out to people, but to no avail. With tear-filled eyes, they were lovingly seeking to express how they felt without being judgmental. They were not angry, but understandably confounded and deeply hurt.

The pastor began to talk them through this painful journey wisely and assured them they had done nothing wrong, He explained that even church folk, for the most part, do not know how to handle people who walk through deep valleys of pain and loss. He clarified that the reason people were seemingly avoiding them was probably not a matter of rejecting them, but that they instead loved them so much that they were afraid they might use the wrong words or ask the wrong questions. They did not want to hurt them any more than was already the case. People honestly many times just do not know what to say!

But that is precisely the reason we should change our way of thinking. Should we not have made *caring* a priority in the body of Christ? Should we not have equipped our people to handle crisis moments of fellow believers? Does the Bible not say, "if one member suffers, all the members suffer with it?" (1 Corinthians 12:26). Should we then not have developed a system or network that intentionally reaches out to hurting people?

You would think that the followers of Christ are trained to be more understanding and know what to do. But they're not! There is an enormous missing link in our churches, and most of the time nobody knows about it. Unless somebody starts a *revolution*, people are going to continue hurting and falling through the cracks. A new paradigm for congregational care—that's what is needed!

In his book, *Core Values,* Dr. George O. Wood relates this heart-rending story. He writes:

I think of an unassuming sixteen-year-old girl who attended our church a couple of times. I'll call her Amy. Amy hung herself in her bedroom. I was asked to serve at the funeral. I'll never forget that day.

Amy's suicide haunted me because I realized in looking back that our congregation probably did not do enough when she came into our midst to actually reach out to her . . . Amy had been a calm face in the crowd. We didn't sense her despair.

She was going through a very distressing time in her life. I realized just how fragmented her life had become when I did the graveside service. At the end of that service, I watched as Amy's family walked to their cars. The grandmother on her cane walked to her car. The mother on the arm of her latest boyfriend walked to her car. The father with his new wife walked to his car. The older sister, alone, walked to her car.

Four members of that nuclear family left that funeral and went their separate ways. I realized that Amy, in her final months, just got lost in the process. There was no one to love her, and no one to care for her. And our church missed that opportunity.

That will always haunt me.[10]

When we read accounts like these, we realize the pain and the frustration of caring pastors who discover time-and-again that they can never touch all the people who relate to their congregation and efficiently care for each of their members if they have no-one to help.

The Psalmist seems to capture the cries of the people well when he says; "There is none who takes notice of me . . . no man cares for me" (Psalm 142:4).

The man at the pool of Bethesda, in John chapter five, lamented that he had "nobody to help him" into the pool when the angel stirred the water and, therefore, continued to suffer in his infirmity. People in our churches are eagerly looking around for someone to help them overcome whatever obstacles they are facing, but seemingly, nobody shows up for them.

However, I don't want to create the wrong impression: people are not coming to church primarily looking for *warm fuzzies* or *pat-my-back* tender care. It is community they are after. They need to connect with other people and build relationships. They desperately want to feel they are part of the whole and are important enough to get the

10   George O. Wood, *Core Values* (Springfield: Gospel Publishing House, 2007), 18.

attention they require. Many people's needs are not personal, but to instead have the opportunity to minister.

Even psychologists are saying that 70% of people's contentment and gratification in life comes from joyful, congruent, and wholesome relationships. There is a reason the Bible says we should not forsake the assembling of the saints—and it's not to provide an audience for the pastor to preach to or a crowd to give in the offering. It is to create an environment for edification and an atmosphere for personal interaction among the members to foster relationships.

> And let us consider one another to stir up love and good works, not forsaking the assembling of ourselves together, as is the manner of some, but exhorting (encouraging) one another, and so much the more as you see the Day approaching (Hebrews 10:24-25 *(Parenthesis added)*.

Our Many Programs May Have Hurt Our Progress

As pastors, we are driven by our enthusiasm to add more and more programs to our churches, often hoping it would bring the results we were anticipating. But, unfortunately, it never actually provides the answer, and we have been going around the mountain time and time again with no tangible results. We deal more with this in the chapter where we discuss "Why People Act the Way They Do." It primarily deals with the basic human needs all people experience.

What needs to be said at this juncture, though, is that there is absolutely no way that the members of a church can give the attention that is required to care for all their fellow members when we keep everyone so busy all the time. In most churches, you cannot drop a pin on the calendar without hitting at least three things that are scheduled to occupy the over-burdened, faithful, and loyal people.

Realizing this may create an excellent opportunity for pastors and leaders to consider simplifying their church programs and re-evaluating whether everything they had begun over the years is still relevant or even necessary. It is a proven fact that effective churches today are those that have taken a serious look at the multiplicity of their activities and made the process of church-life simple.

In this fast-paced world, we are living in, people on all levels of life are desperately looking for ways to simplify their already complicated lives, and if we're not careful, they will begin to cut back on their church involvement. That is why we need to design a workable process primarily. We are going to have to start choosing priorities because our people are tired and burned out, and we must earnestly find ways to steer their energies in the right direction.

> Many of our churches have become cluttered. So, cluttered, that people have a difficult time encountering the straightforward and powerful message of Christ. So cluttered, that many people are busy **doing** church instead of **being** the church.[11]

> The clutter can often make things in a church look okay, even impressive. The busyness is usually a great disguise for the lack of life. The complexity is a great cover-up. Churches can sometimes be fancy coffins.[12]

---

11   Thom S. Rainer and Eric Geiger, *Simple Church* (Nashville: Broadman & Holman Publishers, 2006, Page 19.

12   Ibid, page 20

Several of the complex church leaders we talked with admitted their busy churches were void of life . . . Often significant amounts of activity do not produce life change.[13]

Healthy Community

For as long as we are alive, people will always be facing issues and will still need someone to be there for them. There is always somebody who is facing some crisis or trauma, admitted to the hospital, experiencing painful marital or family discord, the litany of lust-driven behaviors, financial disasters, loss of employment, and the list goes on. But then sadly, for the most part, they discover that there is no one to hold them up, pray for them, or extend some kindness. The tragedy is that nobody knows what they are going through in life.

The ongoing struggles most humans face present a significant challenge to the Church in its attempt to build healthy communities of care and compassion. We just cannot continue to allow people to battle alone. The Gospel makes it clear that caring for others is at the heart of Christ's message. His message is not only about salvation but also about hope, comfort, and deliverance for those who find themselves marginalized, demoralized, and heartbroken.

A broken-hearted mother said it like this one day,
"After our daughter died from a severe illness, we walked through the valley alone. During her extended illness and even her death, no-one from the church, including the leaders, ever contacted us."

---

13   Ibid, page 20

And I understand—I do! So many people go to the hospital, or are ill, or face some trauma, but never inform the pastor or call the church office. It is evident that pastors cannot attend to a crisis if they are not aware of it. People assume somebody will call the church, but most of the time nobody does, and they fall through the cracks. And the church, even more so the pastor gets the blame. When asked why she didn't call the pastor when she went to the hospital, an apparently upset lady said, "Well, he was supposed to know!" Really? I know pastors are expected to know everything, but they are not superhuman beings.

But what if we had a way whereby we could connect every member of the congregation to someone in the church who has been trained to correctly give attention to their fellow brothers and sisters, or to at least become a channel to inform their pastor? Now that's a thought!

What if we had a network through which we were close enough to our people whereby we could know what they are going through quickly? What, if we could somehow surround a grieving family with comfort and care without them feeling they have become an added burden? Often, it's not even what people say that matters, it's just having someone being there—someone to hold a hand or wipe the brow of a sick person. Loving people—that is the qualification.

Frustrated Pastors

We realize in this equation that it is most definitely not only the members who are frustrated; it's also the pastors. I do not know of any pastor that would nonchalantly say that he or she couldn't care less about their people's well-being. In the real world, you will find pastors who are devoted and committed to their people and are genuinely concerned about their welfare.

There are many pastors, if not most, that go to bed at night with grave anxiety when they pull out a note in their pocket and realize they had missed going to see a church member in the hospital or slipped up on some other emergency. The pressure of the day made them lose track of time, and their overloaded schedule simply got the best of them. Sleep then does not come quickly, and thoughts of other missed connections flood their minds.

"I'll do better tomorrow," they say. But *tomorrow* never comes; the calendar continues to dominate a pastor's time, and the next evening is as painful as the night before—only the names, faces, and circumstances have changed. Most pastors are tired to the bone, but it should not be this way.

We Need a New Paradigm on Both Sides

We are evidently facing a challenge that comes from two distinctly different directions. First, there are the members who feel they are not receiving the care they should. And then secondly, there are the pastors who are gravely concerned about not being able to adequately meet all the needs of their congregants—for many reasons.

When pastors and members alike live out unscriptural and unrealistic expectations for ministry, we usually see the consequences revealed in a negative atmosphere of tension and dissatisfaction, which often results in stagnation and even severe decline.

Many church members feel distant from their pastors and presume that they no longer matter. They believe that the ministry has become so professional and specialized that their pastors don't have time for them and don't care about what they are facing in life. They assume they are just names on a membership roll.

Pastors, on the other hand, are exhausted because they are often expected to act like Superman, and some even sometimes try to live up to it. But do they have any other choice? They feel compelled to be everything to everybody all the time. This demand is a sure recipe for burnout to any sincerely devoted pastor.

Too many needs go unmet when the caring responsibilities of a congregation are left entirely to the vocational pastors. The task is of course overwhelming. And while *some* may receive adequate care, *most* do not. The tragedy is that if there is not a structured procedure of caring for people, many church members erroneously assume someone is indeed meeting the need. Without a system, however, we do not have ways to know who is receiving attention or who are feeling neglect. The adage fits well here: "Everybody's business is nobody's business."[14]

The answer may be for the Church to focus on building relationships that last. It is entirely possible that we have shifted our attention to events rather than people. I am a firm believer that Sunday morning services are the most significant entry points any congregation has. Therefore, it makes good sense that we spend a lot of time and energy to do it right. But I have wondered for a long time if we are not missing the mark because sometimes it appears our efforts are invested in providing a *show* (said with respect) to attract a crowd, but never actually reach the people and developing meaningful community.

Pastor Geoff Surratt seems to share this thought with accuracy:

I miss the church we left when we moved from South Carolina. I don't really miss the services (I can watch those

---

14   Henry Webb, *Deacons: Servant Models in the Church* (Nashville: Broadman & Holman Publishers, 2001), 77.

online). What I really miss is the community. We invested 14 years into the community of that church, and we have yet to find the Oikos we left behind. Life without community is a lonely business.

I think the mistake we make as church planters is that we try to plant a service. We hire a band, we rent a school, and we put on a show. There's nothing evil or wrong about the show, but there is no one in your city sitting at home on Sunday morning thinking, "Man, I wish there were a great showdown at the middle school cafetorium. If there were, I'd be there. And I'd give my life to Jesus if the show were excellent."

There are, however, a lot of people in your city thinking, "Man, I wish I could find community. Life is lonely, and I'd love to feel connected. If I could belong, feel like I'm a valuable part of a team, I'd consider giving my life to Jesus." They wouldn't express it that way, but that is the longing at the bottom of their hearts. They aren't finding that community at work or on Facebook or at the gym. If they show up for your weekend show, it's only because they think they might find community.

Where have you experienced community? Maybe it was on a sports team or around the table at a family reunion or on a short-term mission trip. Why did you experience community there? What experiences enhanced that feeling? How was the dynamics of that community? That is what your city is desperate for.

As church planters, we need to step back from the equipment, the band, and the sermon to figure out how we can stop planting services and start planting Gospel-centered community.[15]

Pastor Geoff said that well and emphasizes again people's desperate search for community. I believe the key to growing healthy churches today is found in the effective ways we create for people to develop meaningful relationships. The music may not be what they prefer, the programs may not be that hot, the facilities may not be that cool, funds may be limited, and even the preaching may be somewhat lacking, but once people connect through community, they will hardly ever leave a church. It is proven that "a caring church draws people where Christian love is demonstrated through attitudes and actions."[16]

The Crisis and the Need

It is crucial that we lead our churches to be love-filled communities. It's love that reaches people; you don't debate people into the Kingdom of Heaven, you love them into the Kingdom of Heaven. You will be amazed to see the difference it makes in someone's life when you simply reach out to them and have them understand they are valuable and needed in the church.

Paul says to the church in Philippi, "Each of you should look not only to your own interest but also the interest of others" (Philippians 2:35).

---

15   Geoff Surratt, blog on October 1, 2012 *(Used with permission)*.

16   Ibid., Webb, page 81

Pastor Rick Warren says, "I believe that God is just waiting for a church that will love people unconditionally. He can use that kind of church to spark a spiritual awakening in your city that all the forces of hell couldn't stop. It would change the climate of your community for Christ. Nothing can stop a loving church."

But let's maintain a correct perspective: a loving church is more than people talking, laughing, praying, and worshipping together. It goes way beyond that. It goes even beyond shaking someone's hand during fellowship time on a Sunday morning or being friendly to them. It's not what we do on a Sunday that's important, but rather what happens between Sundays that makes the difference.

The crisis we face in our churches today is that society views the Church as being out of touch and no longer meets their required needs. As a body of believers, we have become self-centered and unaware of those who worship with us, whether they be regular attendees or guests. We say that we care, but our actions often fall far short. Our model seldom matches our mission. We have in many ways adopted a culture of seclusion which does not allow people into our private bubble. This attitude has caused hurting people to hurt even more, which has caused multitudes sadly to avoid the church in their search for recovery.

The need is an authentic system of congregational care that intentionally connects all our members to each other, and in the process, have them experience a sense of belonging, are valued, accepted, and feel needed. We need a proven coordination of care which allows church members to partner with their pastor to provide significant attention to one another, thus preventing people from falling through the cracks or slipping through the back door. This "coordination" is vital because meaningful care will never happen on its own. We should diffuse the notion that we indeed provide necessary care and begin to face the reality that most of our people feel uncared for and neglected.

6

IF IT AIN'T BROKE, BREAK IT

We just don't seem to be able to help it. We have designed our activities based on our created core values, missions, and visions to the point where we have come up with cute slogans which, in many cases, don't even mean much to us and often don't match what we are doing, or ought to be doing. Our statements don't always match our vision, while our activities don't relate to our mission either.

At times, it appears we have created some of these mission statements to condone our inability to efficiently keep the people we are reaping. If we don't keep them, we say, "Well, that's not what we're about." For instance, just the other day I read a statement of an up-and-coming church here in the United States that says, "Our mission is *reaching* people, not *keeping* people." Really? That sounds catchy, but you must wonder what happens to the people.

I fully realize our ultimate focus should never be to see how many members we can accumulate or merely chase numbers in our churches

(I detest that), but rather on building His Church. But my question is if you are *reaching* people, but not *keeping* people, then who is *nurturing* those people? If you *reap* them but don't *keep* them, how do you *grow* them? And if you don't grow them, who is going to help you reach more? And where does discipleship come into play? That's like giving birth to babies and leaving them on the sidewalk hoping that someone will find them and take care of them.

Recently I heard a leader make the following statement at a conference: "As a pastor, you should focus on the people you want to reach, instead of the ones you're trying to keep. If you do so, you will find, to your greatest delight, that when you don't keep them, there will be no-one ever to gripe or complain. They never say the sound is too loud, or the AC too cold; the songs too contemporary, or the preaching too long. It's the ones you keep that gripe and complain," he said. I at first hoped that was a tongue-in-cheek comment. But it wasn't.

If We Are Serious About a New Paradigm

I fully understand that it's enormously frustrating to deal with micro-thinking conformists who have become set in their ways of holding on to what has always been instead of fulfilling the church's mission and reaching towards the goal and do what they have never done. If we are serious about changing the paradigm, then we have to begin by training and developing people to get involved in ministry with us and break the mold we have been holding onto forever. The more people we get involved, the more the atmosphere will change, and the more the atmosphere changes, the more vibrant the church will become.

The best way to have people connect with a congregation is by building relationships with them and having them feel they belong and are needed—whether they are new believers or new members. We can never do this at a distance; we have to learn how to get close to people and be involved in their lives. And yes, this can be easier said than done. As an example, we can never let new believers struggle on their own. Once we have won them to Christ, we have the responsibility of bringing them to a place where they can be nurtured and discipled. And, like it or not, as it is in the natural, babies can be messy. They throw up on you. They don't always act cool and don't always smell good. They keep you awake at night and often place high demands on you. But someone needs to be there who are willing to provide the necessary attention and help people work through this phase. Once you have helped people successfully walk through their first steps, they will be ready to make their commitment and be prepared to grow spiritually.

Andy Stanley brings an excellent perspective when he says, "You cannot grow spiritually if you're not connected relationally." Andy is correct; it takes a spiritual family, who are attached to each other, that causes all to grow in Christ. Growth only happens when we see the branches connected to the vine. Being attached to the body of Christ is what makes a person experience the life and nutrition that flows through the entire system. We should link people to each other while we ensure that everyone remains connected to Christ (the Vine). That has always been God's plan. These connections must be intentional, strategic, and meaningful. That will require us to develop a strategic model of training through which we can release our people to become active in establishing these connections.

We must have a
the process of development
in the church

I have always believed we should have a complete process of development in the church. From my standpoint, we should win people to Christ and then nurture and develop them in meaningful ways to expand the Kingdom. The more we can *keep,* the more we can *reap.* That is how a church increases its influence, and that is how it defies the works of the devil.

Here again, the buzzword is *balance.* We should have both the reaping and the keeping in place. But there is something we should not leave out of the equation: Our attempt to *keep people* could and should never be an end in itself. If we desire only to keep all we reap, the church will become ingrown and eventually die, and that's probably not what we want. Our mission should be to *win* people and *keep* them long enough to train them so they in return can go out and *reap* others.

Our goal should never be to keep people only to appease them and cater to their every need. If a church does not have a set method of developing and advancing their members, the church has become ingrown, headed for stagnation and ultimate death. Those are the churches that believe the pastor is a hireling and has the sole responsibility for doing ministry. It is in such an atmosphere where discontentment rules and strife becomes the mission. Our goal should always be to develop people spiritually, integrate them relationally, and equip them intentionally for ministry.

> Our goal should always be to grow people spiritually, integrate them relationally, and equip them intentionally for ministry.

The only reason we should retain people should primarily be to disciple them so we can together then ultimately make more disciples. Our aim should be to continually reach new, disconnected people, whoever they may be. Is it possible that we can link part of our problem to the fact that while we earnestly desire new babies to be born into the Kingdom, we never prepare adequately to care for them? Are we continually looking to add more new members, but have no means of connecting them or, worse still, of caring for them? And, by the way, caring for people is as much a part of discipleship as equipping people for ministry.

> It's not so much about
> growing our churches larger;
> it is a matter of developing them healthier

Fundamentally, our focus should not be on growing our churches *larger*, but instead developing them *healthier*. After all, Jesus never told us to build a crowd. He called us to build a Church. I know you must attract a crowd before you can build a church, but reality has shown that it's only a healthy church that can grow.

These days a strong emphasis is placed on discipleship, which I applaud. That is a significant part of our mission. But my perspective is that before we are competent in our outreaches and discipleship, we have first to make sure the church is healthy. A church body that does not provide adequate care to its members and where the members do not love each other in meaningful ways is, in fact, a dysfunctional family. Such a church cannot adequately see positive results of spiritual growth through their discipleship efforts. Even the fruit of evangelism is usually minimal. We have to start by first making the church healthy and building unity and cohesion in the congregation. Paul says that the members should have equal care for each other (1 Corinthians 12:25).

We have five healthy grandsons, and neither their parents nor we make them grow. Because they are healthy, they develop by themselves. They just need to be fed and cared for; growth happens naturally. This same principle rings true for the church as well. If it's healthy, it's natural for it to grow. All we should do is provide spiritual nutrition and create a healthy environment by caring for them.

The Bible helps us understand something about the health of a church when it says,

> You can develop a healthy, robust community that lives right
> with God and enjoys its results only if you do the hard work
> of getting along with each other (James 3:18 MSG).

When the Church becomes the Church, displays the compassion of Christ, and takes care of one another, we will become the community people are looking for in this season. We will then not only reach people; we will retain them.

> As each part does its special work, it helps the other parts
> grow so that the whole body is healthy and growing . . .
> (Ephesians 4:16b NLT).

> The focus of my letter wasn't on punishing the offender but
> on getting you to take responsibility for the health of the
> church (2 Corinthians 2:9 MSG).

We do acknowledge that although growth happens naturally, it doesn't happen automatically. Natural development means that someone must provide the nutrition, and someone should provide the care. If someone does not feed or nurture a baby, growth will not take place and death will be the result. For any physical body to be healthy, there is of necessity a required responsibility to maintain its well-being. In every living being, there must be a system of wholesome care in place. This principle is also applicable when it comes to the living organism called the Church. It requires a healthy balance of Christian love, genuine care, and balanced sustenance. It takes more than just a simple application. Having said all of what we have mentioned above, it stands to reason that we should likewise integrate care it into our discipleship system, and in return, integrate discipleship into our care system.

So, if your church's mission does not allow you to keep those you reap and you don't provide care for those who God sent, then it's time to break the mold. *If it ain't broke, break it!*

A Shift in Our Focus

Simple question: Is your church where you want it to be? Is your attendance where you know it could be? Are you reaching your goals? Has there been ample growth and expansion over the past few years? If not, then why not? It could be that your focus is on the thing. In our desire to continuously accumulate more people, we have inadvertently continued to miss the link that will genuinely help us reach the exponential growth we are after. The result has been that many times our efforts have resulted in disappointing outcomes and, in some instances, even proven to be futile.

After all, their toil and labor, overworked pastors and committed church members are exhausted and often profoundly discouraged because the *fruit* of their labors is frequently minuscule. They have worked hard and spent many hours in preparation, but there's little to show. It's not a matter of people not coming; it's a matter of people not staying.

To be able to change this scenario efficiently, we are going to have to re-focus our attention and re-evaluate the human resources God has given us. We just cannot continue to stretch our people to the max, expecting them to give more of their time and forgo more of their family gatherings, and then not have them see any positive results. As pastors, we cannot continue this way either. We have learned that that is the shortcut to burnout.

Most people are loyal and committed to their church and will bend over backward in loving devotion in assisting their pastor and sacrifice much for the cause of Christ. But there comes a time when there is no return on their investment, which causes people to get discouraged and begin to back off and back out. Often it results in people leaving the church altogether.

People always tend to follow a success story. They will overlook a breakdown here and there, but not a history of failure. If they continue to put tremendous efforts forward, sacrifice time and energy, and see no growth in the church, they lose heart and give up hope. That is why there is so much apathy in the church. There must be a better way of building a church and seeing more people added to the Kingdom. Could it be that our focus has inadvertently been on the wrong people? I recently read a book written by Larry Osborne that captures this thought succinctly when he says:

> I hate to admit it . . . I wasn't dialed in on tending the flock
> God had entrusted to me. Instead, to be brutally honest, I was

using the people I already had to reach the people I wanted to reach. They weren't sheep to be cared for; they were tools to be utilized. And while I doted on every new person who came through the front door, more and more were walking out the back door.

I know that sounds crass, unspiritual, and pretty lame for a pastor to admit. But it's true. Sadly, true. And what's worse, I'm not alone.

The decision to focus on the people I already had, helped to close the back door."[17]

I think Pastor Larry hits the nail on the head and touches a sensitive nerve in his confession. The truth is that this has become the trend in so many of our well-intended churches. It almost seems as though we all need some Holy Spirit wake-up call to help us again see the importance of caring for the people God has entrusted to us. In my opinion, Larry's statement puts the spotlight on the *missing link* we have discussed previously. If you would read his book further, you will discover how this change of heart helped them become an influential, life-giving church, with many people being saved as a result. Having a system in place to assimilate new believers, became the key to making them a healthy church.

The experiences that Pastor Larry and North Coast Church (and many others) had makes us ask the probing question: If we are not taking care of those God has already given us, why should He send us anymore?

---

17   Larry Osborne, *Sticky Church* (Grand Rapids: Zondervan), 26,27.

If we are not
taking care of those
God has already given us,
why should He send us anymore?

Closing the Back Door

We fully realize that no church in this whole world can keep everyone that walks through its front door. Our overarching challenge, however, is that we are losing them unintentionally just as fast through the back door. It's okay for people to move on, but it's not cool if they keep slipping through the cracks because we don't have a system to retain them. So, then the obvious question that arises is, "How do we close the back door? And how do we care for all the people God has given us?" And following right behind this, we ask, "Does caring for people now mean disregard winning the lost, or terminate our discipleship program?" These are the questions, plus much more, that we are going to address.

Knowing the life of a pastor, we understand that with overloaded schedules and packed calendars, pastors on their own cannot provide the adequate care and attention their people need and deserve. This vacuum is one of the primary reasons pastors are highly frustrated and genuinely concerned. Their challenge is that, for the most part, they do not know how to overcome that. Pastors often go to bed at night, and as they think about the day behind them, feel as though they have accomplished nothing. It's not a matter of them not having been busy; it's instead a matter of not having been able to meet all the demands of ministry.

But what I am going to share with you goes way beyond only that! Together we are going to look at how we got here, consider the need, and then come up with the biblical and practical solution. We'll look in-depth at building churches that last and are vigorously healthy—vigorous enough to fulfill the *Great Commission* and impact their community. In the following pages, we'll explore how to do that.

We'll discover the powerful concepts, systems, structures, and applications that make it useful. I will share with you proven values and priorities and provide you with a working model with which you can release a *revolution* in your church. It will be guaranteed, not become another *flash-in-the-pan* program. This system promises to affect your church's DNA positively and put you on the pathway of developing fulfilled members and enjoy joy-filled years of ministry. Just a word of caution: Please do not consider this concept as just adding another program. Instead, think of it as a positive culture change in your church.

Building Community

While the thought of closing the back-door is exhilarating and providing a safety net, so no one falls through the cracks, is most exciting—and I will be referring to these quite often—those are only some of the *side benefits* of the *Care Revolution.* Retaining people without an intentional process of nurturing them is void of purpose. There is a saying that goes something like this: "If we catch the fish and don't know how to fry the fish, we are wasting our time!" (In our context, it would mean that if we gain the people, but we do not nurture the people, our efforts are futile.)

The hypothesis of my book is not so much zeroed in on what the concept can *do* for us as much as it describes how it will help the local church *become* what it should be. The first Reformation focused on what the church believed; this second Reformation will focus on what it does. It is our *becoming* that will influence our *doing,* which in turn provides the results we are looking for most. I am setting my focus on building community and developing meaningful, biblical relationships in all its aspects. Together we will dig deep and discover the incredible depths of what will happen in a local congregation when we sincerely begin to minister to the wholeness of humankind and not solely concentrate on one or two facets, as most are doing.

We don't need
another Band-Aid

In church circles, we are often guilty of handling our challenges by only trying to fix it with a simple Band-Aid. We don't seem to want to take the time to dissect the problem, and most often just look for a quick fix. Is it any wonder that so many challenging situations that we have not dealt with have become like cancer in the body with unimaginable pain and hurt in its aftermath?

Most churches are inclined to search for the latest and greatest ways to attract more people from the outside. They spend most of their energy and resources on marketing and developing fantastic programs, but are frustrated because the people who come, do not stay. It is likely that we have our focus on the wrong aspects and it's not meeting the needs people have in these days.

Passion is one
of the strongest
motivators

We are driven to increase weekly attendance and strive to expand the crowds continually, but often do not realize that the strength of building a church is by first connecting people one-by-one with each other through meaningful relationships. One of the things we may have somehow lost in our transitions is *passion*. We have spent much energy, resources, and time by providing so many other things—flashing lights, blacked out walls, roaring sound systems, cutting-edge worship songs, and the list goes on—but in the process lost what matters—passion!

The more efficient we are in developing compassion through a meaningful community in our churches, the more effective we will be in retaining people. Passion is the main reason people still come to church instead of them watching using live-streaming on their phones, or the internet. People crave passion, period! We must zero in on the benefits of this essential aspect in our churches if we are going to build healthy and growing congregations.

People can never feel sincere passion through any form of electronic media. Unless we exude passion, people are going to continue to drift away from attending church and start experiencing their worship electronically. The latter is ideal for evangelism and shut-ins but is not beneficial for local church effectiveness. Herein lies the key to the church of the future: meaningful, intentional passion of the Christ-kind. People will never experience this action by any other means but through personal interaction with genuine, caring people. Unpretentious passion is the way to attract and retain visitors. But it won't happen by itself. We are going to have to work on cultivating a culture in our churches that is conducive to that atmosphere. That is where the *Care Revolution* comes in.

Breaking the Religious Code

A paradigm shift is what is needed. This change will require us to let go of some of the things we have held on for dear life and begin to generate the kind of atmosphere people are craving. If we don't, the numbers of *Nones* and *Dones* will continue to soar.

The challenges we face as the church are enormous and has become varied. Sometimes we are even confronted by different cultures in different geographic areas, especially if they are part of a robust religious persuasion where even our outreaches and campaigns could become non-effective. That does not mean the community does not attend or are not excited about what we call our outreach events. They often visit in large numbers. But in so many cases, to them, it has become just another means of entertainment. After we spend all our energies and abilities, we realize there is no evident growth in the congregation. The only positive thing that could be said is that it brought awareness of the church to the community. So, it's not all in vain.

The most efficient way to breaking the sacred code and reaching a community such as this is through their family and friends within our churches. Begin by fostering meaningful cohesion among the church members. This bonding is of vital importance because people have often become elusive and are relative strangers to each other within their congregations. They never seem to connect with their fellow members. At best, they shake hands with those across the aisle, and only when asked to do so.

We should lead church members into becoming a true family who exhibits unpretentious relationships and honestly care for one another. This action will call for a meaningful system of congregational care that has as its purpose to grow the church healthy enough to reach outside of the walls of the church. Evangelism starts in the church and then enters the community. The love of God must flow down the aisles of our churches before it will flow down the streets of our cities.

The love of God
must flow down the aisles
of our churches
before it will flow down
the streets of our cities!

Moving Ahead

Assuming a church already has a process of discipleship, once cohesion begins to realize through genuine care, it's time to start equipping people for evangelism and other meaningful ministry using useful training tools. It is futile for a pastor to challenge his or her people to reach others with the Good News before they have first experienced the love of the family of God. As believers, they already know what *loving God* is all about; what they now need is to experience *loving people*. Larry Osborne says, ". . . Happy sheep are incurable word-of-mouth marketers."[18]

Being a pastor for many years, in a religious community, I can tell you that the above pattern was one of the dominant ways of growing our church to become a mega-church in a relatively small city. When we concentrated on those God had given us, developed them personally and spiritually, word hit the community, and people came in droves looking for what they were longing for in their lives. But what's more is that our members now had experienced the passion we desired and dared to approach their family and friends, wanting them to experience the atmosphere of a loving church with genuinely caring people, serving an indisputable loving God.

---

18   Ibid. Osborne, page 31

One of our most significant challenges these days may be the fact that we continue to add new programs and ministries, but none of them are helping people connect, which severely hampers our efforts of building community. People need to be needed, and if they do not feel connected, they will never attach themselves to a church. It's probably not about people wanting everything to be about them. It's, instead, the sense of knowing they are accepted while, at the same time, knowing they will be able to play a meaningful role in the functioning of the Body. People are tired of coming to watch the show with the same individuals on the planks, over and over. They are frustrated, highly frustrated, watching everyone else play the game while they never get the opportunity to handle the ball. We gratefully recognize there's a change in the spiritual atmosphere these days and it's mobilizing people to get out of their seats and get their hands dirty. This atmosphere is an opportune time for us to recognize the unusual gifts of the people God has given us and begin to utilize them in purposeful ministry.

The Winning Recipe

To bring total balance in the church, it may serve us well to move away from an *industry mindset* with all its trappings, and preferably find ways whereby our people can experience the presence of God in a new, fresh way in our services. Our earnest goal these days should be to present means for people to change from being spectators to becoming participants, not only in our ministry but also in our worship.

I am convinced that when we again have people encounter God in a personal way, many of our challenges will disappear. We are going to have to move our gatherings from entertainment to true worship. Once people sense a genuine Presence of God, it will result in them enthusiastically conveying to the community the powerful moments of God moving in spectacular ways. There is absolutely no other way to have the Church become relevant again in a changing world.

Many times, churches do not have to do too much to ignite the passion of His Presence but will be amazed if they would help their people take small steps toward a personal encounter with God. When that happens, people will come from all over.

But when the people come, we should have a way to connect them to the Body. If we could have people understand that they can become part of this exciting group of people called the Church, that they could connect with each other in sensible ways and become part of this winning team, there is no telling where such a church will go. This mindset will require more than a friendly handshake during fellowship time and a gift at the *Connect Center.*

Here is the winning recipe—it may sound simple, but I know it works:

1. Cultivate an Atmosphere for the Presence of God
2. Cultivate a Culture of Care for the people of God.

Blessed to be a blessing . . . is what the Word teaches us. After people encountered God, we need to help them join with each other sensibly. It is when they become part of the body of Christ that people begin to realize that each one of them is needed and that the one cannot function without the other. Developing them spiritually and taking care of them personally then becomes the channels of blessing which produce peace, unity, and safety.

Small Groups

Many churches today affect personal ministry by utilizing some form of small group. These groups are tremendous and indeed meet the needs of many people. It serves a marvelous purpose in building relationships and developing spiritual growth. What may be necessary for many of these small groups seems to be intentional care, and more pointedly, a system of care whereby they retain ongoing support to their group members. If we're not careful, we can end up in the same scenario in our small groups as we see in our Sunday gatherings where we love each other, pray for each other, and encourage one another, but when the meeting is over, we leave everyone on their own. The solution to this in our small groups is for someone in the group to take on the responsibility of staying in touch with each member individually to provide the ongoing care that is needed. It takes more than fellowship, Bible study, and occasional get-togethers to ensure we are providing the level of care we are pursuing. The process we have designed for congregational care promotes five definite points of contact, and we highly recommend that churches with small group ministry incorporate these principles, or most of them, to cover all their bases.

There is another significant aspect that needs consideration regarding small group ministry, and that is that data suggests that most churches have an average of 30 percent involvement of their members in small groups, at most—(there are some explicit exceptions). This stat then means that approximately 70 percent of our members are potentially not receiving the same personal care and attention as those within the groups, and therefore often feel neglected—even less valuable. This reality underscores the necessity of having a network of care in place in spite of there being a small group ministry in the congregation. It is important to note that having small groups as well as a system of care does not oppose each other. They both have tremendous value, and each serves an essential purpose and when blended, become a tremendous blessing to any church.

Don't Stir the Water

When we create an atmosphere of love and care in our churches, people will feel much more accepted and be eager to receive ministry from us. You can be with scores of people in a church and still feel alone and disconnected if you don't experience real community. We must realize that it's not only relevant what happens during our single event on Sunday, but even more important what happens between Sundays that matters.

The idea of community comes from the root word *koinonia*, which is better known as fellowship. It means that all believers are as committed to each other as they are to Christ. It's in developing genuine relationships of this kind that new life begins to flow through the church. We should purpose to have each person who attends our churches sense that they belong, are accepted, and can become partners in the ministry of the church.

> All believers are
> as committed to each
> other as they are to Christ

Sometimes individuals are so deep into the water of life that only the ends of their noses are sticking out, and they are desperately saying, "Please, no one stir the water, don't cause any more waves,"—fearing that the slightest ripple will overtake and drown them. You and I know that people find their answer only in Jesus Christ. And make no mistake, my friend, when you teach on these so-called "felt needs," you are not taking anything away from the message. Instead, you are helping people find a pathway to overcome their struggles in life and lead them to experience forgiveness and healing.

When a *culture of care* and connection prevails in a church, we will all be much more sensitive to link with those around us. When the person sitting beside you is dealing with a medical crisis that's leading to a faith crisis, then they don't care how many angels can dance on the head of a pin. They need someone they can relate to who can help them connect with the real Source of Life. A dying person should never be allowed to die without someone being with him or her. No one should ever have to face the first night alone after the burial of a loved one, and neither should an individual be left alone in the evening after their divorce.

When people face the crisis of life, and everybody will at some point, we must have a system in place in our churches that will provide the loving support all need. That is how we take care of the sheep Jesus cares about and makes us realize again that it requires more than the pastors alone to provide this level of support. It stands to reason that a church that offers this kind of intentional care has no alternative other than to be healthy, to grow, and become the instruments the Lord desires.

At the outset, an approach of this magnitude may seem close to impossible to execute and could cause us to wonder if it's even possible. The exciting news is that it's already being done and could be implemented by any church of any size, regardless of denomination. You don't have to be an exceptional church to accomplish this either. The key lies in employing a proven system, thoroughly training and equipping church members, and releasing God's people to fulfill their calling. The Bible has the answer, and the Holy Spirit has given us insight as to how we can accomplish *loving God and loving people* utilizing a straightforward application of using the people God has already given us.

It's a Proven Model That's Lacking

Many congregations already have most of the components it takes to develop a healthy church. What is missing in most cases is an official system that pulls it together. All the pieces of a jigsaw puzzle scattered on a table have little meaning when left by itself. It's only a collection of odd-shaped pieces that, on their own, almost seem awkward. But when each piece is placed into its correct spot and connected to the right parts, we see the complete picture, and then it makes sense.

> Many churches
> already have most
> of the components

Intentionally placing people in the correct positions of ministry to function in a caring role will dramatically help us build community that we so desperately need in our churches. Looking at the analogy of a bus, it's not only important to know who is driving the bus but also to know who should be on the bus and that those on the bus are sitting in the right seats. This application requires a meaningful, workable system and a well-designed process. That is what we have meticulously developed over some years and are now presenting to you through this book. The *Care Revolution* is the most practical and biblical way of solidifying a congregation and making sure we provide adequate care to all our members.

The benefits of this system go beyond description and allow us to apply the expectations of the Scripture in meaningful ways. Our concentration is on encouraging members to serve one another, to build community, and to be involved in caring, prayer, and personal interaction with each other. These are the things that have become essential to growing a church and retaining the people. Through the *Care Revolution* system, we provide the ability for church leaders to develop a consistent and meaningful method for people to experience and share *loving your neighbor as yourself* . . . Taking these aspects into consideration will let you understand more and more why we are saying *an indispensable revolution has begun*—a revolution of care.

In the following chapter, I will introduce you to the *Care Revolution Concept* from which we will develop the local church's care ministry network. There are some pertinent things that we should and should not do for the proposed care system to function adequately. I will make sure we address all these things.

7

THE CARE REVOLUTION REVELATION

To grow a church numerically and lead it to become healthy does not only require us to preach good sermons but also necessitates us developing good systems. Just as the human body has different systems to make it function, so too the body of Christ. We fully understand that the Church is not a system, but it needs systems to be able to operate healthily. The Bible instructs us to "do all things decently and in order . . ." (1 Corinthians 14:40).

The notion of systems is not unfamiliar to most pastors. Many churches have systems in place for evangelism, discipleship, assimilation, leadership, stewardship, and more. But few, if any, have a suitable system of congregational care. At best, they are functioning along the lines of the traditional model they inherited, and we now know it's not working.

In the absence of a suitable care system, we will always attempt to make things up as we move forward and in so doing never fully achieve what we set out to accomplish in the first place. Needs will remain unmet, and people will stay unfulfilled. The *Care Revolution* system provides the answer to the crying need of delivering authentic care to all the members of a congregation. It is not only a slogan or a mere concept, and neither is it another added-on program. Instead, it conveys the idea of cultivating a culture of care within every congregation based on Scriptural principles. The critical perspective of equipping church members to execute this caring ministry is what sets the *Care Revolution* apart from most other pastoral care systems. Through this plan, we connect people through creating healthy relationships and developing much-needed community.

Caring is part
of the Church's Mission.

As we begin to unfold the premise of caring one for another, I want to say at the outset that I do not believe, neither do I advocate, that caring is necessarily the highest calling of the Church. I do not see it as the fix-all either. The Church has a five-fold mission, and *caring* is only one part of the overall assignment. I am highlighting the aspect of care primarily because I see it as one of the most neglected and misunderstood components of our calling. If we can successfully incorporate meaningful care into our already functioning systems, you can only imagine where it will take any devoted church. Saying this does not mean that the other aspects of our mission are less critical because that is not the case.

My plea for a relative community, authentic care, and connection approach has as its catalyst the fact that we will never execute much of the Church's mission if the church family is unhealthy and even, in some ways, dysfunctional. I am convinced, and I say it often, a sick church (where congregational care is not happening intentionally and authentically) will never be able to fulfill the Great Commission substantially. An unhealthy body, in the natural, lacks the energy and ability to accomplish its obligation; so, it is with a church. That is one of the main reasons many churches never sprout. If pastors and churches could figure out how to efficiently handle the issue of pastoral care, their churches would become healthy and grow.

The *Care Revolution* does not promote its principles with the intention of leading a church to become self-centered or spend all their energies on meeting people's needs. Its purpose is furthermore not to create *fuzzy feelings* where people hold hands and sing *Kum ba yah* all the time either. It instead aims to connect believers in a Christ-like community to develop healthy relationships by which means they can fulfill the Great Commission. It's not a matter of promoting an attitude among church members of *what can you do for me* but is instead set to develop an atmosphere of belonging and acceptance where church members desire to become engaged in Christ's mission for His Church. Through establishing their value in the Kingdom of God, incorporating them in meaningful ministry, and allowing them to utilize their God-given gifts, sets the scene for people to become all God wants them to be.

The Power of the Care Revolution

As we move closer to unveiling our system of care, let me first clarify that the *Care Revolution* is the *overall description* of the entire concept of caring for people in our churches and community. Out of it flows a local church application and implementation which we refer to as the *Care Ministry Network*. In a capsulated form, the *Care Revolution* deals with the overall subject of cultivating a culture of care in the defined absence of community within the body of Christ.

- The *Care Revolution* affects a church's culture, which enables members to have a spirit, personality, or character of care, one for another—not mechanically, but intentionally. Cultivating this biblical culture of attention in a congregation becomes the catalyst that inspires church members to reach out to others with friendship and concern and treat their fellow believers with brotherly love. That is how connection takes place and how we form a community.

- The *Care Revolution* speaks to the basic needs all humanity has, with an emphasis on a Christian perspective. It touches on the neglect of the Priesthood of All Believers and brings into focus the reality of equipping the saints for the work of the ministry. We determine the health of a church by how we engage the members with each other and the Mission of the Church.

- The *Care Revolution* further introduces the little-known Great Commitment, and how that is important to our churches today. To arrive at a sound conclusion, the *Care Revolution* also touches on the crisis and the need that brought us to this dilemma and then comes up with a proven system that enables churches to develop a network of care.

- The *Care Revolution* captures some of Church history and undergirds each stated principle with the sound basis of the Word of God. It also underscores the importance of the pastor's leadership and influence as well as helpful ways to solicit member involvement as an essential part of the entire theme.

My intention is for you to have a solid background and a firm foundation of the overall synopsis of care, community, and connection. I am convinced that this background information will help you understand not only *what* we should be doing but also emphasize *why* we should be providing care at this level.

> If we don't understand "why," then "what" is not important!

It is a proven fact that if we don't understand *why* then *what* doesn't matter. *Why* holds within it the purpose or the reason for doing something. *Why* is like the kernel of the seed. It contains within it the tremendous power of the potential future. If we understand the purpose of why we do something, then it becomes fulfilling to do what is necessary.

The good news is that we have done all the hard work for pastors, leaders, and congregations, and have completed all the necessary groundwork. Everything you will need to initiate and maintain a culture of care with your leaders and to cast the vision to your congregation is entirely available. The essence of material even includes sermon outlines for use by the pastor as well as teaching guides to equip church members. We furthermore provide implementation guides to help pastors and leaders develop the concept step-by-step.

We have prepared e-books to make sure it is easy to implement the idea no matter where you may find yourself. The first step is to grasp the fundamental concept and become knowledgeable about the subject of care as applied biblically.

It's More Than a Program—It's About a Culture

It is stated often throughout this book that the *Care Revolution* is not an addendum to all we are already doing. Neither is it merely a vision statement; it instead deals with affecting the personality of the church and is the reason we talk about *cultivating a culture of care.* Seeing it from this viewpoint determines not only the way we think but even more so *who* we are. The culture of a church is its most potent dynamic and determines how the members will respond to the vision of the church and its leadership. It's paramount to realize that it's also a church's culture that will either attract or deter visitors. Culture decides atmosphere. And this is important because certain things thrive in a particular atmosphere while other things die in the same environment. For that reason, we encourage pastors, leaders, and influencers to thoroughly grasp the elements of the care concept to gain the most benefits from it.

Known as the
Caring Place

So, instead of only dealing with adding another program, we are calling for a culture adjustment—the tweaking of a congregation's personality. Instead of another plan where only some are affected, we are dealing with a concept that affects everyone. It is not so much about *doing* as it is about *being.* Our objective should be for our churches to become known as *The Caring Place* among the population in which we live.

You see, vision and strategy typically deal with goals, results, and amenities. But when we talk about *culture*, we are talking about the people—the membership. Jesus died for *people*, not for our vision, our goal, or our strategy. Neither did He die for our buildings or facilities. It's about people, and when we effectively cultivate a culture of care, we will soon realize we could potentially even exist without many of the other installed programs. Neglect the care culture, and the buildings, amenities, and strategy become vain. As a congregation, we do not live only to fulfill our established plans; we live to reach and transform people.

We need to understand that the subject of pastoral care carries with it the necessity of genuine passion. You can *give* without loving, but you cannot *love* without giving. To be successful in our quest to provide adequate care to our people, there should first be *passion*. Our vision should be an outflow thereof. I believe that a vision statement should be the verbal articulation of our heartfelt conviction. If you can *feel it,* you will be able to *see it*, and if you can see it, you will be able to articulate it, which will result in being able to *reach it.*

It's Not Always Easy

I fully understand that it's not always easy to make a cultural shift in a church—not even a culture of care. But when this change has taken place, and it has developed a personality of love and acceptance, people are energized by it and are enthusiastic about their participation. This ministry breeds high loyalty and releases unbelievable unity. People are at peace, and the atmosphere becomes conducive for visitors to come—and stay!

The profile of a church's culture can only be adequately defined (and changed) when it originates from the lead pastor and church leadership. Culture change can never happen from the bottom up. It should flow from the top down. It is the enthusiasm, integrity, and competence that mostly the pastor provides that shapes the culture and determines the successful outcome. That's the reason we reference the role of the pastor in launching this ministry so frequently in discussing care and community.

To summarize what we have stated above we can see that we are not talking about an added-on program but instead addressing a personality change of a congregation. Once people have accepted the culture of love and acceptance and are serious about caring for one another, it becomes the church's culture, and healthy relationships become a natural outflow. People then no longer think of a system, but instead spontaneously respond with a caring heart. At that stage, the church will have a warm incubator of love, taking care of the new believers in Christ, while at the same time providing a safe harbor for all its members.

The Pastor Cannot Do It Alone

Congregational care, if done as it should, can never and should never be supplied by the pastor alone. Even a multi-staff church cannot ultimately meet that need. It's not practical; neither is it Scriptural. It is nothing short of pride for any one person to think that he or she could single-handedly do all the work of the ministry. It is the responsibility of the entire congregation. Look around you and see all the failing churches and fallen pastors. Christ indeed did not have that in mind for His Church.

And He Himself gave some to be apostles, some prophets, some evangelists, and <u>some pastors</u> and teachers, <u>for the equipping of</u>

the saints for the work of ministry, for the edifying of the body of Christ . . . (Ephesians 4:11-12, Emphasis added).

These verses make it clear that those who the Lord calls into the fivefold ministry have a responsibility to not only serve in their office but to also equip the *saints* (church members) for their work of ministry. That means that pastors should not only shepherd their flock but also develop the church members to become involved in the work of pastoral care. *"Pastoral"* in this sense does not intend to describe a position or office, but instead function. It is a term expressing the care of sheep in a fold. Jesus often referred to His followers as *sheep* and collectively as a *flock.*

Our *Care Revolution Concept* conveys the message of caring for the flock and can only be applied efficiently by developing a workable system. It has proven to be most successful in many churches and has become the catalyst for exciting expansion. *Caring* becomes the glue that connects people to the local congregation. Programs *attract* people, but they do not *connect* people.

> Programs attract people,
> but they do not
> connect people.

We describe our care concept as *congregational care* which we apply through identifying a sizable number of members who are willing and able to be trained, equipped, and then commissioned for the task. The exciting aspect of this all is that church members are the ones who become the instruments for the revolution to take place. This mindset may well mean that we should change our thinking of how we execute pastoral care futuristically.

The contagious churches of the next century will be different from the traditional churches of today. One revolutionary difference will revolve around pastoral care. The exciting prospect is that everyone in the congregation will receive regular pastoral care from a gifted and trained layperson. – Dr. Jim Garlow

A statement like this underscores the position we hold in decreeing the necessity of developing a sensible system of care in our churches. If everyone in the congregation is supposed to receive care, then it only stands to reason that we can no longer provide pastoral care in the traditional way we have typically done in the past. Dr. Garlow says it best when he states that the solution is to provide "care from a gifted and trained layperson."

The challenge becomes factual when we realize that most people expect their pastors to visit all the sick, officiate at every wedding, preach at every funeral, attend every church meeting, counsel the members, prepare cutting-edge sermons, be a competent leader, plus a whole host of other things. Attempting to do all this is already more than a plate full, but if the pastor then still has to visit every member, he or she becomes incapable of doing what is essential. And what's worse is that the church will never be healthy and grow. And the irony of it all is that the more the pastors attempt to be everything to everyone, the more the church members expect it of them. It creates a vicious cycle that ultimately becomes the reason for burnout, short tenures of pastors, stagnation of churches, and even worse, churches becoming ingrown, ending up in stagnation.

If a church desires to grow, the members are going to have to let go of the antiquated expectation that their pastor will be available for every need and every hospital visit, every celebration, and every catastrophe. Our mindset is going to have to change. The pastoral care model most Bible colleges promote, and congregations hold on to is unreasonable and impractical and should be corrected immediately. It's not working, and it's unscriptural.

So, do not make the mistake of equating the *Care Revolution* concept with the traditional pastoral care notion we have become accustomed to in the church-world. That is emphatically *not* what it is. The obvious answer for providing the right kind of pastoral care is to identify, train, and develop church members to become partners with their pastor to take care of the flock, so they can nurture all who are part of the membership. In this way, we meet the ministry demands and adequately care for the members.

What we will introduce you to will provide a system that will provide ongoing, essential care to the *total* membership. We need to present this kind of ministry whether members face a crisis or not. This attention is of vital importance, because when people feel neglected they begin to disconnect, which in turn makes it easier to drop out – first out of ministry, then from financial support, and eventually from attendance.

> People disengage
> before they disappear.

Ask thousands of people across America (and other western countries) and they will tell you that disengagement started when they felt that no one cared, and they no longer felt needed. Once people disconnect, they lose their energy-participation, which becomes the first indication they're on their way out. It is a fact that people disengage before they disappear. *Caring* executed appropriately becomes the safety net that makes sure people don't fall through the cracks. It implies that we intentionally connect each member to someone in the congregation which makes it close to impossible to slip through the cracks or disappear. People want to know someone cares. And it doesn't always have to be the pastor.

A Network of Care

The absence of a functional system that cares for people inevitably brings us to a crucial point of decision. We can go ahead, ignore the problem, continue as we always have, and then bear the apparent consequences. Or we can make a quality decision to adapt our thinking and design innovative ways to embrace our people by providing a system of care. The obvious answer will be to let go of our traditional mindset and reach for a practical and scriptural model of giving attention.

The *Care Revolution Concept,* in so many ways, provides the answer to the significant challenge we face regarding the provision, bonding and nurturing that is so desperately needed. It solves so many problems and fills so many gaps that you, too, will ask what so many have already asked: It's so simple; how did we miss this? Or as one pastor of a significant church said, "I wish I had thought of this first!" Another pastor in his late fifties said, "I wish I had known about this twenty years ago!"

Pastor Carey Nieuwhof says, "The best answer I know of for pastoral care . . . is to teach people to care for each other in groups. I'm convinced that if we change how we do pastoral care, we will reach more people. And in the process, we'd care for people much better than we do now."[19]

It is incredible to note how the cry for change in the application of pastoral care is rising from all over. The present twenty-first century generation has become reclusive and desperately lonely. Searching for significance, people often approach our churches, but regrettably do not always find the kind of relationships they are seeking. That is why Carey suggests that "if we change how we do pastoral care, we will reach more people." And just like Jim Garlow, he states that we should "care for each other"—implying that church members should provide the care.

As unbelievable as it may sound, we have never made any serious attempts to change the redundant and useless pastoral care model we have been employing for many years. It appears many have taken on the position that there is no other way. But there is! But in all reality, we are going to have to begin by letting go of our archaic way of doing pastoral care, start thinking real-world and become more innovative in our approach regarding congregational care.

It's Not Too Late

Since Christ has not yet returned, we thankfully know that it's not too late to adjust our congregational care perspective. I assure you that those churches who are not going to adapt to a new care paradigm in some way are going to remain in stagnation and ultimately face decline. Through their efforts, the attendance may somewhat grow, but before too long they return to the autopilot of where they had been before. We are going to have to reset the dial.

---

19   Read Carey Nieuwhof's entire article "How Pastoral Care Stunts the Growth of Most Churches" at http://www.churchleaders.com/pastors/pastor-articles/267069-how-pastoral-care-stunts-the-growth-of-most-churches.html

Again, looking for a quick fix is not going to solve the problem. It hasn't worked in the past, and it won't work now. I am saying that because, through this concept, I indeed do not have something in mind as merely suggesting that the pastor gather a group of people to help with a blitz-visitation over a weekend to just call on people or arranging a home prayer campaign. It is an ongoing and proven system of authentic care with lasting results.

If all I wanted to share with you was a basic concept, I feel sure we could have done it in much fewer pages than I have covered in this book. Instead, it is my intention to share with you the background and supportive information of what becomes significant in dealing with people in a congregational setting. It is entirely possible that we have potentially seen people, or even more so ministry, purely from an overall *spiritual* perspective alone, and in so doing neglected to realize that people are people, who are all just human with necessities in life. If we do not know what makes people function, we will never be successful in our overall ministry efforts.

For that reason, I am going to share with you the background of all of this, the missing link we have discussed in a previous chapter that is becoming more and more apparent in most churches, the real fundamental needs people have, and help you understand what helps people to engage in a church. I also want to state the biblical basis of my persuasion and touch on the history of how we got here (so we don't repeat the same mistakes).

A Closer Look

At this point, I want to introduce you to the actual workings of the *Care Revolution* as it pertains to its functioning in the local congregation. This primer is not meant to be a full description of the concept but is instead a glimpse into the structure and composition of the overall function of the ministry. In this model, church members are recruited to partner with their pastor to provide authentic and consistent care to one another. They receive thorough training and are equipped to provide the nurturing that adequately supports the community of believers. They are trained to exemplify a lifestyle of loving people unconditionally and ensuring healthy relationships to develop.

Out of the above statement alone, we can begin to dissect some of the related elements of what we are saying. *First*, we recognize that if we want to be successful in sustaining and developing a church to its full potential, it will take more than the pastor(s) to do it efficiently. Thus, we *secondly* clearly recognize the importance of developing church members to be involved in this enormous task of ensuring that all members receive care on a constant basis. An added benefit to this concept is the crucial feature of providing care also to those who serve as care providers. The key to it all is a healthy partnership. Paul says that the "members should care for one another" (1 Corinthians 12:25).

The Revolution and the Local Church

Although I alluded to it briefly before, I want to again, for clarity's sake, explain the difference in terminology between two different aspects. The *Care Revolution* describes the overall movement of cultivating a culture of care within the body of Christ. In the local church, on the other hand, the application is identified as the *Care Ministry Network.* The effectiveness of the entire *Care Revolution* concept (caring for one another) finds its fullest expression through implementation in the local congregation.

Caring for one another is undoubtedly not meant only to be a cold philosophical statement, and neither should *loving God* or *loving people* become a cute slogan on a church website. We should "earth" these truths and release them among God's people by applying them in real-life situations. That is the only way it will find true meaning.

Definition

We have spent considerable time on laying the foundation, developing philosophies, and establishing principles for the necessities of caring for people; we should now begin to develop a mental picture of the actual structure of the care system. The best way we can get this off the ground is by beginning with a clear-cut definition. Here it is:

> The *Care Ministry Network* is an authentic and proven system of congregational care that enables God's people to care for one another on a regular basis.

There is much more to this definition than meets the eye at first, and we will, therefore, break it down further as we move along. At first glance, we notice that church members (God's people) are the ones involved in the implementation of this process. Wisdom lets us understand that members should not be released to care for one another unless we had thoroughly trained and equipped them for the task. Releasing them without preparation will be a disaster and will hurt more than it will help. Preparing church members for the task requires the necessity of *equippers* to be available for that purpose. That is where the credentialed ministers (the pastors) come into focus. Ephesians 4:11suggests that the pastor should *equip the saints for the work of caring.*

You will notice in the definition that we refer to the concept as a *system.* This description says that it's not an added-on program, but rather a full-fledged, robust ministry that could potentially change a church's

DNA by establishing a *culture* of care. Therefore, caring for one another in a meaningful way is done using a purposefully applied system, and assuredly not assuming a mindset that it will happen by itself. Church people already love (and care) for each other, but if there is no system designed to channel their efforts, it won't have any significance and will serve no purpose. Systems require intentionality, which puts all our efforts into action. It is this *intentionality* that makes all the difference between a church being friendly, and a church that cares.

The People Involved

The effectiveness of the *Care Ministry Network* lies within the involvement of church members who execute the ministry. It is when we put this dynamic into place that we see enthusiasm detonated among the believers. And believe me, there are scores of people in every congregation who have the giftedness, ability, and even the desire to provide the care that is required. All they need is a pastor who has the vision and a church that provides the opportunity for them to be trained and become involved in the ministry. When you take a closer look, you are likely to find people in your congregation who are already caring for others in one way or another because it's who they are. We, as pastors and leaders, are most likely the ones that have been the lids that have kept our people down and away from breaking out and doing ministry the way they should. The *Care Ministry Network* is the instrument that will provide all of this and more.

The Scriptures do not restrict *caring* to vocational pastors only. Many church members have a similar passion for people, and experience has proven that they can become instrumental in providing congregational care. In addition to this, we also realize that releasing people to fulfill their God-given gifts becomes the most noticeable spark to reignite any church. I want to underscore the fact that church members are well able to "pastor" one another.

> Mel Steinbron says, "Peter was not an installed pastor, yet Jesus told him, 'Tend my sheep' (John 21:16). True, he had been with Jesus for nearly four years, but many church members have been 'with Him' longer than that."

> He goes on to say, "The elders to whom Peter gave this charge, 'Tend the flock of God that is in your charge' (1Pet. 5:2), were not people with seminary degrees."[20]

The key to growing churches healthier and more abundant lies entirely within the hidden power of developing our church members for the work of the ministry. Thankfully, the days of superstars are over. The Holy Spirit is again powerfully and energetically emphasizing the importance of the Priesthood of All Believers—the truth that *every believer is a minister.* This mindset is what is going to define the Church of the future. The care system is a ministry *by* the believers *to* the believers. It does not run on the feet of the clergy but the feet of the laity (*Laos*—the people).

> The Church should
> not run on the feet
> of the clergy, but
> on the feet of the laity.

---

20   Melvin J. Steinbron, *Can the Pastor Do It Alone?* (Eugene: Wipf and Stock Publishers, 1987), 29

Most people are so busy these days that they do not have any additional time to attend another meeting or event at church. If they give you a night, they will take away another night from attending some other scheduled occasion. The *Care Ministry Network,* therefore, is thoughtfully designed in a way whereby members at large (of course not the Care Pastors themselves) are not expected to attend another added event that takes them out of their homes. Instead, we take the ministry to the people. It is not designed to be an outreach ministry as such, but instead provides a network of care to solidify the functions of the congregation. Taken present day culture into consideration, the more we can take ministry to the people, the more effective we will be in making our churches effective.

The system provides the means of caring for the church members— the flock—the household of faith. It is not intended to initially draw people in from the peripheral closer to the inner circle. Our emphasis is rather on developing church members to take on the task of providing essential care to their peers and in so doing, cultivate an atmosphere of a healthy community that will result in the body reaching beyond the walls of the church building. Even though our care *system* concentrates on the members, our Christian *love* is extended way beyond the four walls of the church building. We can and should never lose sight of those who are not yet part of the flock.

In a practical sense, we recognize that there are always some who would, for some reason or another, never take on formal membership of a local church. They are faithful in their attendance, moral support, and finances. We refer to them as *adherents,* gladly embrace them in the care system, and provide them with all the benefits of the ministry.

Our motive is to connect with people and develop their worth. Connecting people to the church is, of course, imperative, because if people don't join, they will never stay. In our church, it had come to the point that when people connected with our congregation, it became almost impossible for them to disconnect again. It was almost to the point where people had to say, "If you contact me one more time I'm going to have to call the FBI!" No, just kidding. It wasn't quite like that! But we had a proven system of connecting people, and once you have a system in place with a core of trained people, it's just difficult for folks to get lost in the shuffle of life.

The truth is that when you have created a loving and caring atmosphere, nobody *wants* to leave. The reason for this is that in most churches the sense of belonging, along with the desire for acceptance, has become such a rare commodity that if any congregation creates a loving environment, people flock to it. Churches that become serious in their efforts of cultivating true community will have people standing in line to be part of it.

The Structure

You have had the opportunity to see the definition and learned more of the insights of the concept. It may be appropriate now to briefly look at the recommended *structure* we have designed to make congregational care function appropriately. This system has already helped many churches. In this chapter, we will not fully explain all the intricate details of the training aspects, but simply provide a foretaste of the application for a proven care network. We more fully explain additional essential details, principles, and in-depth applications in our *Training Kit for Churches.*[21] That is where you will also find the equipping

---

21 These materials are all available from Care Ministry Network International (CMNi), PO Box 5788, Frisco, TX 75035. *www.spiritwind.org*

manuals, worker's qualifications, job descriptions for each level, etc. It also includes the implementation manual and many other helpful tools to ensure a successful outcome of a workable care ministry. For the remainder of this chapter, we are going to become a little more procedural as we explain how we configure and structure the ministry.

Levels of Leadership

To have the system function efficiently, we need to develop a functional organization with precise designations of levels of leadership. These guidelines will be helpful as you initiate your care system. In any well-organized body, you will always find the following:

1. Levels of leadership,
2. Lines of authority, and
3. Avenues of communication.

Through these levels of leadership, we establish the understanding for everyone involved to know whom they are *accountable* to, and whom they are *responsible* for. We have purposely incorporated these valuable precepts into our care ministry. A third aspect is also for everyone in the ministry to know whom you are in a *relationship* with— who are your peers? All of this means there must be a vertical *up-line,* a vertical *downline,* as well as a horizontal *peer-line.* Once you see this leadership perspective, it will help you in so many areas of your church organization as a whole—not only for care ministry.

Now just to put you at ease, don't get hung up on the titles we will be introducing you to in this chapter. If you don't, for instance, like the designation of *Care Pastor*, or whatever, then change it to what makes you happy and what you think will be most agreeable to your church. The same applies to all other ministry role-descriptions in the care organization. If you have any other descriptions in mind, that's fine—as long as your terminology makes sense. Names and titles are not what matters here. What is important is the *concept*. I have just chosen to go with the *labels* we have found most descriptive for our application since we should somehow identify specific roles.

Five Levels of the Care Ministry Network

The *Care Ministry Network* functions on *five* individually designed levels of care. Each of these levels has a specific role, which makes the entire ministry fit jointly together to ensure that we provide care to all—including those who are involved in the ministry-process.

Further on we will present you with an *Organizational Chart* that will help you have a clearer visual of how the levels of leadership are designed and how everything fits together. Here are the five primary levels for you to become acquainted with:

1. Care Director
2. Care Leadership Team
3. Care Shepherds
4. Care Pastors
5. Flocks

1. The Care Director leads the *Care Ministry Network* and has a leadership team that assists him/her in the execution of the entire ministry. In most churches, the Director is a servant-leader which does not have to be a staff position. But larger churches (1,000-plus) usually prefer a full-time person to head the operation. Having a responsible person to lead this ministry is vitally important, whether volunteer or salaried. Somebody must take the lead and be in charge—and it should not be the pastor. It is highly recommended that the Care Director not be involved in leading any other ministry. His/her involvement in the care ministry requires devotion and commitment. The Director is directly accountable to the Lead Pastor and also cares for the Leadership Team.

2. The Care Leadership Team functions alongside the Care Director and assists in leading the entire ministry and helps to put together meetings, seminars, and conferences. This team is made up of the Director and approximately four members out of the congregation. Each member of the Leadership Team provides care to three Care Shepherds (depending on the size of a church). During the beginning stage of the ministry, it is many times necessary to initially utilize some of the Care Pastors or Shepherds to function in a dual role.

3. Care Shepherds (some churches utilize their Elders for this role) provide leadership and supervision to five Care Pastors each. Care Shepherds are accountable to the Care Director and are also responsible for caring for five Care Pastors. Care Shepherds receive advanced leadership training to equip them further.

4. Care Pastors (in some churches functioning in the role of Deacons) provide ongoing care to five family units, called a Flock. The Leadership Team assigns these flocks to Care Pastors at the recommendation of the Lead Pastor. They function according to a five-point contact strategy, mentioned below. Care Pastors form the crux of this ministry and relate directly to their respective Care Shepherds. We thoroughly train these people in a *Care Pastors Training Conference* where they receive relevant training guides and instruction.

5. Flocks consist of approximately five family units that will be predetermined and assigned.

A family unit may consist of:
a.   A couple (husband/wife).
b.   Father, mother, and children in the home,
c.   A single parent and children in the house, or
d.   A single person, living on his or her own.

Organizational Chart of the Care Ministry

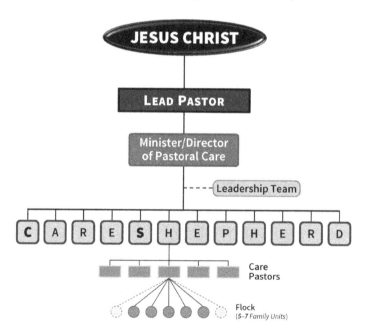

Five Points of Contact

The effectiveness of the *Care Ministry Network* lies within the implementation of five definite points of contact. All involved in this ministry, on all levels, should apply this five-point strategy.

Care Pastors are specifically trained and developed to make these five contacts with each of their family units in a prescribed way. In our *Training Kit for Churches*, we explain these five points of contact in detail and describe how they are applied. These are the core aspects of the *Care Ministry Network* and the *glue* that brings the entire ministry together. It provides the safety net that prevents people from falling through the cracks or being forgotten among the numbers. You just cannot operate a functional care system without these crucial points of contact.

It's because these five points of contact are so crucial that specialized training is necessary—and we are emphatic about this. If Care Pastors are not well trained to implement these five points, I can assure you, the entire ministry is doomed to collapse. Ill-prepared Care Pastors will be frustrated in their labors, and the effectiveness of the whole will be negatively affected. You certainly don't want to do that. Once people feel they have failed in ministry, it becomes challenging to get them involved again.

Please resolve here at the outset that when the time comes, you will thoroughly train and develop your Care Pastors before releasing them. In addition to equipping your people in a training conference for several hours with a proven curriculum, there must be ongoing training and development, and we will guide you in that also. The name of the game is in-depth training.

Caution

A kind word of caution: Pastors are smart, and most of them are early adaptors who usually get any given idea quickly. They could easily be tempted to implement a model such as this prematurely. If, however, you stop here and try to apply this concept to the little you have now already discovered, you will do yourself and your people a great injustice. I promise you; I know of some individuals who have taken the information I have given thus far and took off, implementing it without having the complete understanding of the concept and without the training material. They tried, and they failed—miserably! You don't have to, but, why would you? What you have in your hands to this point is just a foundation of the complete structure which is yet to come. This book is intended to give pastors and leaders a thorough understanding of the necessity and especially the value of a new paradigm for pastoral care. Once you have these concepts in your heart and mind, the required training will make sense.

8

IT'S NOT ONLY
A CONCEPT—IT WORKS

Whenever someone introduces a new idea, our first response is usually, *does it work?* That is a crucial question because nobody wants to waste their time, energy, or resources on something they cannot prove useful. In ministry, especially, we cannot afford to take our people down a pathway just to find the concept a disaster or end up with the proverbial pie in the sky.

Many people don't like change, but for the most part, I do. But the transition is usually never easy, because in its wake it holds some definite uncertainty, and it's this unknown that causes us to fear or become anxious. Our natural instinct then results in us choosing to avoid venturing into the unfamiliar or drives us to search for something tangible which will ensure a positive outcome. But we all realize that change is unavoidable.

202 | THE CARE REVOLUTION

Without change, there is no innovation, creativity, or incentive for improvement. Those who initiate change will have a better opportunity to manage the change that is inevitable.[22]

Everything that is alive, changes. That is also true in the life of a church. Even nature teaches us that seasons change, and it's all for a good reason. Without seasons changing, there will never be life and growth. Some things have to die in one season so that other things can sprout forth in another.

One encouraging change that is taking place in the church-world today is an apparent emergence among church members to actively be part of the activities of their churches. They no longer want to watch ministry; they want to do ministry. In the past, people were satisfied to hear the stories of what God was doing, but these days people want to be hands-on in the workings of ministry. They are willing to be equipped and trained and ready to roll up their sleeves. It is causing more excitement in our churches than one could ever imagine. And what's more encouraging than anything else is the rise of commitment and dedication that has come with this movement.

What's happening now is not a new phenomenon; it is instead a reappearance of how the church functioned during the time of the formation of the early church. It was never meant for ministry to be provided by vocational ministers only. As we look at the ministry of Jesus, we see the explicit model of how He trained the disciples and passed His ministry on to them. He prepared them by equipping them,

---

22   William Pollard https://www.brainyquote.com/quotes/quotes/w/williampol163245.html?src=t_change

teaching them, and then releasing them. We see the same pattern in the life of Paul who disciples Timothy and then instructs him to pass it on to other reliable and qualified believers (2 Timothy 2:2). Passing the ministry on to believers is a divine process that provides the dynamic life of any church. Remove this process, and spiritual death becomes unavoidable.

Pastors today realize they can no longer afford to do church as usual. The demands on them have become too overwhelming, and the attention people desire, have together, made it impossible for ministry to be handled by the clergy alone. It beckons us to focus our attention more sharply on developing relationships, embracing people, and building community in a new and fresh way. This reality calls for renewed efforts from all of us to prepare God's people for works of service. Our efforts will result in ministry flowing from within our sanctuaries to the depths of the marketplace where one of the greatest, next moves of God is going to take place.

A Workable Concept

Naturally, when more people become involved, more people are going to flow into our congregations. For that reason, we have to prepare to nurture those who will be coming and make sure they sense the love of God and experience the care of their newfound family. Out of this healthy environment, more equipped people can then emerge to reach more individuals with the Good News. This process requires a workable, practical, proven, and reliable system.

What is so amazing is to discover how many believers have, among other gifts, received God's gift of mercy to care for one another. They may just never have had the opportunity to employ these gracious gifts. This truth evokes the responsibility of pastors and leaders to earnestly focus their attention on developing, equipping, and training their people to be efficient in nurturing their fellow church members. If we are, however, going to involve our church members to partner with us in the work of ministry we have to make sure that the concept we introduce is reliable and workable and would stand the test of time. We do not have the time, neither can we afford the waste of energy and resources on things that will not produce the expected fruit.

When it comes to the *Care Ministry Network*, after many years of implementing it, added to the experiences of several other churches, it has proven to have stood the test of time and that the system in its entirety is applicable. The point I am driving at in this chapter is that I am not only conveying a concept in this book but also confirming that the *Care Ministry Network* is a workable and practical solution for any church of any size. So, if you would ask me if this concept indeed works and if people can do it, I can confidently say, "Yes, it can! Church members all over are doing it realistically and efficiently."

This Is How I Found Out

It happened late one Saturday afternoon after my wife, Anne, and I left a wedding ceremony. It turned out to be a joyous occasion, and everybody seemed to have had an exciting time. The sun was beginning to set in the West as we made our way to our car. We left before most other people did because for us the day was not quite over yet. Sometimes, as pastors, we are forced to pack more into a single day than we should. But I guess that's the life of a minister. Or is it?

It had already been a hectic week, and we both would have treasured some quiet time, so we could be ready for the challenges every Sunday holds. But as soon as I sat down to crank the car's engine, I noticed there was a message on my car phone that apparently must have come in during the ceremony we had just left. Everybody did not have this number, so I instinctively realized that it must be an emergency. I dialed in immediately to retrieve the voice message that was left for me. It was my Minister of Pastoral Care, Glen Beier. His message was brief and to the point, but I could hear the anxiety in his voice.

> Pastor, this is Brother Glen. I am on my way to the Rapides Medical Center in Alexandria (Louisiana). Ron and Brenda York (not their real names) have been in a severe car accident, and she is apparently not doing well. I know you are officiating at the wedding, but please call me when you can.

We never leave these kinds of calls for later. I called Glen immediately, but he did not answer—and today I am happy that he didn't. You will soon see why. I proceeded to call the hospital instead. As the telephone rang, many thoughts were rushing through my mind. When did this happen? How many hours could have gone by since the accident? How long had it been since Glen called? How serious is it? Shouldn't I just take off and make the two-hour trip? Are they still even there?

I hoped that this phone call would answer my questions or at least some of them. Although it probably did not take that long, it seemed like ages before the operator answered the phone. I explained the reason for my call, and they quickly connected me to the emergency room.

Emergency Room. May I help you?
The voice of the nurse in charge was understandably rushed and professional, yet kind.

Yes, ma'am. I understand there is a couple in your emergency
room that has been in a severe car accident," I stated. "Their
last name is York" (not their real last name). "May I possibly
speak with one of the family or somebody that is there for
them, please?"

She paused for a moment and then kindly asked,

"Sir, are you a member of the York family?"
"No, ma'am, I am not. But I am the family's pastor."

Her response to my statement was probably not what I had
expected. Sometimes revelations come our way when we least expect
it, and through means, we would never have thought possible.

"For goodness' sake," she said, "how many pastors do these
people have?" And without waiting for my reply, she
proceeded by saying, "A couple showed up and stated that
they were their pastors. We allowed them to go in. A little
while later, another couple came and said they were also
their pastors, and we allowed them in too. A little while ago,
I hesitantly let a third couple go in who also claimed they
were their pastors. Now you are telling me that **you** are their
pastor! How many pastors do they have, Sir?"

For a moment, I was stunned by her almost frustrated and
forthright response when it suddenly dawned on me what was going
on. Fortunately, I had enough presence of mind to realize an explanation
would not help her understand why so many "pastors" had shown up.

I smiled and said to her, "Okay. That's fine, ma'am. I understand. Please just do me a favor and ask one of 'those pastors' to give me a call as soon as they can."

I left her my name and number and hung up the phone. I sat quietly in the car pondering the conversation I just had. While the uncertainty of the York family's situation still had my mind captured, another thought began to steer my thinking in another direction.

Have we just experienced a powerful and practical demonstration of our care system? Could these *pastors* all have been Care Pastors? Is it even possible that they had all responded? I was suddenly drawn back to earth when my ringing phone interrupted my gushing thoughts. Glen was again on the line.

"Pastor, this is Brother Glen" (He always opened his phone conversations this way).

"Everything is under control, but I am sad to have to tell you that Brenda did not make it. Ron is okay and courageous."

I abruptly interrupted Glen by saying, "I'm leaving right now and will see you as soon as I can get there . . ." But he broke into my impulsive reaction and said, "No, you don't have to do that, pastor. All of us are ready to come home. Ron is also on his way back. We are getting ready to leave right now. We will call you when we get there."

And then Glen added the answer to my wondering: "Pastor, pardon me for rolling this in here, but in a nutshell, let me quickly say, you will be happy to know that our Care Pastors have been with the family for most of the afternoon and have helped them through this challenge."

He went on to explain the steps they had taken. After he had given me the rest of the information and I gave him some brief instructions, we hung up. I shared the heartbreaking news with Anne, and with my chin resting in the palm of my hand, I tried to work through this sudden loss of a church member—a faithful one, I may add, and my inability to not have been there. The thought of our care team, on the other hand, being so diligent, flooded my mind and filled my heart with sincere gratitude. It became clear to me that our care system was working.

Of course, I waited for them in their driveway when they arrived.

The Rest of the Story

What had happened was that the York's Care Pastor in one way or another got word about them having been in a car wreck and that an ambulance had rushed them to the hospital. He and his wife took off and, on their way, there, called their Care Shepherd who, in turn, felt it necessary to go also. While the Care Shepherd and his wife were still on their way, they received word that Brenda had passed away and, consequently, called Pastor Glen (who also served as the Director over all Care Pastors and Care Shepherds). He and his wife, Debbie, apparently, then also made their way to the hospital, and called me, on their way there. That explains why the nurse wanted to know how many pastors these people had.

But as for me, I was left troubled in my soul for the moment. I would so have loved to be there with the family. I liked this loyal couple. But at the same time, I realized a person could only be at one place at a time. Anne and I drove off quietly with another million thoughts still rushing through my mind.

What had just taken place over the past 30 minutes or so was playing over and over in my mind. While still feeling the pain of one of our church families, there was simultaneously a deep gratefulness in my heart for what we have learned out of it all. It cost an actual crisis for us to appreciate the reality that church members can indeed be developed to care for each other and can do so efficiently. Today as I write this, it almost sounds staged. But I promise you, this is how it works, and the same things are happening over and over in churches across America. Once people taste the joy of true ministry-involvement, they will never be the same, and their dedication to the work of God will increase substantially.

Caring People
Caring for
People

Now that I am helping pastors and churches across the nation, and also in South Africa, to function in authentic care, I am receiving reports like this all the time. They are joyfully telling me that when they arrive at hospitals to see their members, the response is often, "Oh, this is exciting, our Care Pastor has already also been here!" Those are the times when you almost wonder if you are even still needed as a pastor. But at the same time, the exuberant joy of knowing *people are caring for people* gives you hope for many other things in ministry. Of course, that does not mean the clergy no longer sees people in the hospital, because Care Pastors do not replace the pastors, they represent them.

Other Pastors Also Have Great Stories

A pastor personally shared a dramatic occurrence in his church with me. They had the traumatic experience of having to face the loss of three teenage boys out of their congregation who died as a result of a tragic wreck. There was no foul play, no drugs, or even alcohol involved in the entire incident. Their sudden death shook the church and local community to the core. It was not a large town, and the residents consequently knew the church well. Their peers recognized the boys as football heroes of their high school, which meant that everybody in the little town was potentially going to attend the funeral services. Adding to this already imminent crisis, two other influential members of the congregation also passed on during this same time, which meant they had five funerals within four days.

> The pastor said to me, "If this church did not have a Care Ministry Network we would have been crushed and may not have survived." He went on to say, "Hundreds and hundreds of people came to each wake and likewise to the funeral services. We fed them all. Our Care Pastors combined their family groups and took care of the broken and weeping families on a daily basis."

> I could sense the deep emotion of a loving pastor as he spoke. With tear-filled eyes, he said, "As much as I love all these dear folk, there was no way I could have been with them as long, and as many times, as I would have wanted to, and as focused as I usually operate. I did all I could, but my wife and I could only do that much."

I could still hear the stress in his voice as he said, "Knowing a large segment of the community was going to show up for each of the five funerals, I felt obligated to preach a new sermon at each of these services. That certainly made the challenge more difficult. But thank God, I was able to go to bed at night knowing at least that the Care Pastors were there. I heard later that some of them stayed, sometimes into the early morning hours."

He looked me straight in the eye, with his assistant pastor affirming every word, and emphatically said, "I want to say again, without our Care Ministry, this church would not have survived, and I am not sure if I would have been here today to tell this story!"

Once you have the *Care Ministry Network* in place, you will wonder how you functioned without it in the past and still lasted. It is a valid ministry with surprising results. I recently received another exciting report from a church that has a progressive Care Ministry in place:

During the recent storm, Harvey, much of our city flooded. Many of our members suffered great loss, with some losing all they ever possessed. We implemented the Care Ministry System in our congregation almost three years ago. During Harvey, our Care Leaders stayed in touch with their members and kept us, the church leadership, informed as to everyone's condition.

One of our Care Leaders became extremely concerned for one of their families who was stranded while the water kept rising until it was waist deep. This family consisted of an elderly lady, with Alzheimer's, and four other members. There was no way for them to get out, and rescuers did not seem to know they needed help. The Group Leaders kept phone contact with the family and let us know of their plight. We were finally able to reach a Harris County Sheriff friend who got the attention of a rescue team with a boat, and they were plucked out of their flooded home. Their Leaders stayed with them, continued to minister to them, and helped get them into a hotel.

Another Leader on the other side of town was alerted to the fact that one of his families of four was critically stranded in their home. Their cars were already underwater as the water continued to rise in their home. Their Group Leader decided to step in and drove to the scene as close as he could and then waded through the tainted flood water for many blocks to reach his family-group. He got there just in time. He personally carried one of the kids and some belongings, while the dad and mom were then able to carry the other child along with whatever little possessions they could manage. Their house and what was left in it was completely lost, but their lives were spared. Gabe took them home with him, where they stayed with his family until they could get another place to live. Robert and Millie Gitau will never forget what their Care Leaders did for them. We could go on and on to tell you more about the courageous deeds of our devoted Care Leaders.

As a pastor, you will sense freedom and profound gratitude knowing your people are sharing in a ministry of hope, love, and compassion. The Care Pastors will feel fulfilled and needed. The members, on the other hand, feel cared for, valued, and safe, knowing there is someone for them at all times. Knowing that every member of the congregation is being taken care of, brings incredible comfort and assurance to pastors. It is absolutely impossible for all members of a growing congregation to be directly in touch with the pastor, but it is imperative for them to be in touch with someone. The additional, notorious benefit of the Care Ministry is that it significantly shuts the proverbial *back door* of any church.

I promise you; this is so simple, and yet so profound that you are also going to say, "Why didn't I think of it?" My only prayer at this point is that you won't only read this book and then place it on the shelf next to the many others collecting dust, but instead decide to act and join the *revolution*. One year from today you are going to be so glad you did.

A Rural Church

The *Care Ministry Network* does not only function well in times of hardships as we have seen at the church above but equally as good when everything is going well. It works in the major cities and also in rural communities. Here is a report I received from such a country church:

> The Care Ministry Network has been a tremendous blessing to our church in numerous ways. It has given us a plan and a strategy that allows us to have ongoing/long-term care for every member of our congregation. Also, it has given each

Care Pastor a great sense of responsibility and ownership as they help to tend the flock, not to mention it has helped the congregation to feel they are cared for and loved. The Care Ministry Network has taken a huge burden off of the shoulders of the staff knowing that each member is receiving more than just crisis care. This system is a tool that every church needs to implement.

A Growing Church

This report, on the other hand, comes from a growing church that needed a system to reach all their people:

We have been using the Care Ministry Network model for our pastoral care for about eighteen months. It has been amazing how God has helped us to efficiently care for the people of our church as we have implemented this excellent care model. We have continued to add new care ministers and deepen the training for the ones we have. For the first time, we see active body ministry, and our people sense genuine care. As a pastor, I cannot express how it has helped to lighten the load and allow me to give my attention to other pressing matters. I honestly believe there has never been a time in the sixteen-year history of our church when our people have received better care. Thank you, Dr. Bosman, for introducing us to and training us in the Care Ministry Network.

A Metropolitan Area

The following report comes from a church in a more metropolitan area:

I believe in the Care Ministry Network! Our church has experienced a 40% growth in attendance since its inception. Much of this increase I attribute to the implementation of this ministry. Our people are getting cared for at a level that we previously were unable to offer them.

The Care Ministry Network has opened up a new avenue of serving for some in the church who have not had the opportunity before in any other area of ministry. As some people are providing care and others are receiving care, they become more dedicated and become a more integral part of the church body.

I highly recommend Dr. John Bosman and the Care Ministry Network to any church of any size. This ministry is proven and effective. To us at The Grace Place, this is not a program: it is a part of our DNA. With this network in motion, we indeed are *caring people caring for people.*

A Church in a Changing Community

I am Jana Meeks. My husband, Randy, and I pastor Lindale Church in Houston, Texas. I am the Care Ministry Director for our church. We began our Care Group Ministry in March of 2015. It has been a HUGE blessing to us and highly successful in connecting the members to the church body. We have sixteen groups of varying sizes and each has their own unique and particular personality. What the members all have in common is a sincere and heartfelt knowledge that they are all loved and necessary to the church and to each other. As pastors, we have seen a vastly improved avenue of information regarding the health and crisis situation in our church. Our people don't fall through the cracks or become lost in the shuffle. Critical information that sometimes eluded us in the past now has a direct and clear path through our Group Leaders. It just works!

After having seen it implemented across the country, it has now become evident that the excitement of the care ministry has become contagious. Reports that are coming in are exhilarating and encouraging. It has convinced me that we have hit a vein!

A Video Report

One of the churches produced some video recordings of the results of their *Care Ministry*. One of the testimonies was from a couple in their congregation that said they had heard of the *Care Ministry Network* but didn't pay too much attention to it. They were doubtful about whether they would like to give care or even receive care. They held this perspective until a doctor diagnosed the husband with cancer. For some reason, he and his wife had to stay at the hospital in a city quite a distance from their home.

As I watched this DVD, I could see how his eyes filled with tears time and again as his wife patted his hand and he said, "I had no idea that this is what the Care Ministry Network entailed. Pastor, this is an excellent ministry. Our Care Pastors showed up the first day I was admitted and came over to see me so many times I cannot even remember. They prayed as people would, who love me."

With tears now freely flowing down his cheeks, he went on to say; "I never expected this attitude. Some of the families in our group prepared meals, others brought food, while yet others helped us with our kids. What we experienced goes way beyond description."

Those are the moments when we realize we are His hands extended and that through us, people can experience the love of God.

When Calamity Strikes

In another church, a couple who had been members for many years frankly told their Care Pastors that they did not need them and suggested that instead, they spend their time on some other people who may need their attention.

But not too long after that, one of their close family members died unexpectedly. And to everyone's amazement, they did not call the pastor, but remembered about the Care Pastors and called them instead. Sometimes people think they don't need care until they need it.

Pause the Wedding

Another remarkable event occurred in a church where a young girl, let's call her Kathy, for now, fell hopelessly in love with another Christian young man shortly after she graduated from high school. They dated only for a short time before Jenny announced their intention of getting engaged and, to the astonishment of everyone, also divulged that they were going to get married soon thereafter.

Jenny's parents were some of those who did not think they needed a Care Pastor. They emphatically said they were a happy and stable family, and for all intents and purposes, they were. But now, ever so suddenly they realized they needed somebody, and being too embarrassed to turn to their pastor, remembered about their Care Pastor. Fortunately, Jenny respected the younger Care Pastor-couple and was willing to listen to their advice.

They lovingly pointed out the risks and dangers and helped her understand that neither she nor the young man was ready for such a massive commitment. They also included the young man in the process and offered to help them both through their journey. It worked out marvelously, as the Care Pastors were instrumental in rescuing two lives before it was too late. It was not the pastor, but an equipped couple in the church who had the gift of mercy with the desire of shepherding, who saved them from an impending disaster and a treacherous cliff.

We may never know how many people attending our churches, go through life with struggles, questions, and fears, who are reluctant to speak to the pastor, but will be more than willing to share their burden with a fellow believer. By saying this, we certainly do not mean that we exclude the credentialed staff because they most definitely have a significant role to play. What I am echoing is for church members to be included to serve all the members of the congregation, because the pastors just cannot do it alone. When I think of it this way, I realize the great opportunity a pastor has to pour into the lives of his or her congregants by training them and developing them to provide ministry way beyond the reach of his or her ability. This action should be one of the greatest joys of any pastor.

All people need attention at some point in time, and when they do, there should be capable and prepared individuals in every church to assist their brothers and sisters. But here again is the key for Care Pastors: Learn to build relationships with people before some calamity or tragedy strikes in their lives. Doing so creates the opportunity to be trusted when the tough moments do show up.

Make Your People the Champions

When I started zeroing in on training and equipping our people for ministry, I immediately stopped referring to the results of my hospital visits or any of my other ministry efforts. I instead found the success stories of those in the congregation and used them as examples during my preaching or teaching. It worked wonders! Sometimes I would purposely begin a story, and midway change the attention to whoever was involved in the practical outcome of a ministry. It would sound something like this:

> "This week Sister Bracken was in the hospital with a high temperature and excruciating pain, but the doctors had no idea what was going on. Her family called us and let us know. That was the beginning of a massive miracle . . . But why am I telling you the story? Brother Edgar, you come up here and tell us what happened."

Brother Edgar comes up and begins to relate the miracle:

> "You see, Sister Bracken was ill. When I walked into the room, she was in so much pain that she almost did not recognize me. I realized I had just to trust God and began to pray with every ounce of faith I could muster immediately. And then it happened. But hey, why should I tell you? Sister Bracken is in church this morning. So, dear lady, come and tell us what God did for you!"

Feeling somewhat shy she comes up and says,

"Brother Edgar is correct; I was ill. I thought I was about to die. But when he placed his hand on my head, I felt the healing power of Jesus flow through my body. The next moment everything became clear and the pain melted away like the morning mist before the rising sun, and here I am today!"

The church was on their feet cheering and clapping, and I was standing back, just smiling from ear to ear. I knew, the next time one of them would be in the hospital, they're not going to call me! They're going to call brother Edgar! He was the one that prayed that powerful prayer!

Once you have trained your people, you must release them. Will they make mistakes? Sure! But who doesn't? To be honest, I would rather err on the side of trusting my people too much than depriving them of valuable ministry and then not see the church become healthy, as it should.

And here is something else I want you to take into consideration. Even if you feel that you, as a pastor, can adequately handle all the care required in your congregation, you should still consider training your people. I am saying this because there are most assuredly people in your church who have the gift of mercy and have subsequently been called to care for others. If you do not identify, equip, and engage them, people will remain unfulfilled and, sometimes even leave to find a suitable place for ministry.

These Are Not Super Churches

The people who are so enthusiastically involved in caring for one another are no different from the members you have in your church. They are rational human beings. The difference is that they have caught the vision from their pastor and made themselves available to be trained and equipped to help care for the flock—and they are thrilled.

There are scores of people in your church who are capable of taking up this responsibility if given the opportunity—gracious individuals with the gifts and talents who stand ready to help bring stability and peace to the congregation through the ministry of care. But they will only become involved if the pastor and church's vision is broad enough to include them and develop them to be able ministers.

A pastor visiting our church said to me one day, "I can also build a great church like this if I had the people you have!" I thought he was joking, but no, he was serious. I looked at him and said, "My friend, I didn't find hundreds of equipped people sitting in a big room waiting for me to show up. I had to find them, train them, and release them. You can, too!"

What church members desperately need are leaders with vision and a heart to equip them, develop them, and involve them in meaningful ministry. Our people are more capable than we may think they are. Cast the vision, help them identify their gifts, then train and release them. You are going to be surprised, and your church is going to be blessed!

But There's So Much More

In the following chapter, I am going to deal with "Why People Act the Way They Do." We are going to touch on basic human needs, the necessities of life all people have. It is most likely one of the most neglected elements in most of our churches and the reason we do not become effective. We continue to run around in circles and never know the reason. Ignorance of understanding people's behavior could possibly be one of the reasons we have so many frustrated members and short-tenure pastors. If we don't know what makes people act the way they do, we will never be able to advance them in their personal as well as their spiritual growth, resulting in so many unpleasant atmospheres in our churches.

I know what it's like: We are always in a hurry to fast-forward to get to the bottom line. But spend some time and get the foundational stuff under your feet first. It will help you greatly as you advance in preparing yourself for the *Care Revolution.* I honestly believe your perspective of ministry will increase as you gain insights that have already surprised many other pastors and leaders. The chapter will help you understand why people act and behave the way they do. And please bear in mind, working with people means we never get the job done. It's always a work in progress.

9

WHY PEOPLE ACT
THE WAY THEY DO

Present-day, life-giving churches are willing to consider — and do consider — all aspects of human behavior toward accomplishing their mission. That does not mean they are compromising the Great Commission or lowering ethical or moral standards. It does mean deliberating and engaging those things that make people respond and function positively.

We accept that the Church is not a building, denomination, or an organization, but rather a living organism consisting of people. Our shared efforts, however, often seem to be on anything and everything but people. In many local churches, it appears as if it has become more about popularity, personalities, programs, and procedures — instead of people. For churches to be relevant in a hurting world, we must focus our efforts, once again, on successfully reaching people in their everyday life-circumstances. As Christians, our bottom line responsibility remains to reach people for the Kingdom of God and then to develop them to become all they can be for the sake of Christ.

While the Bible often refers to believers as *saints, it* does not mean they are perfect and certainly does not say that they have stopped being *human*. What it positively *does* say is that the power of Christ has changed them and they have been born again. They are under new management, live by a new set of rules, have a new destiny, and live with an excitingly different life-assignment. But they are still human, and the necessities of life remain. They still face the pressures of life, experience hurt, pain, hunger, thirst, loneliness, and all necessities of life in the same manner as do all other people. An active ministry should, therefore, include both the spiritual as well as the human needs of individuals if they desire to be effective. We just cannot provide the one without the other. When we understand where people find themselves on their need-levels, we will better grasp why people act the way they do under different circumstances.

God created
humankind in
His Image

Humankind is a unique species of being and obviously different from all other creation. The Bible says that God created man in His image as a *trifold being* consisting of spirit, soul, and body (Hebrews 4:12). We understand (i) the spirit of man to be that part which connects to God; (ii) the soul part includes our mind, will, and emotions; while (iii) the body is that part which relates to the world around us. For as long we are alive, these three things are inseparable and uniquely interconnected.

When a person faces a challenge in one area of his or her life, it affects the other areas also. Developing mature believers requires us to bear this human configuration in mind. We are responsible for ministering to the wholeness of humankind—spirit, soul, and body. If we do not address this full continuum, we should not then be surprised when many times our ministry efforts are not as effectual as we had hoped they would be.

We fully realize the importance of developing believers spiritually. But we must understand that when we do not meet a person's basic human needs, the body may not give any physical indication of deprivation immediately, but the individual will most assuredly feel anxious and tense, which most often results in negative behavior or the display of a bad attitude. People usually cannot respond with good grace to spiritual values if we do not first meet their basic *physical* or *emotional* needs they are experiencing.

Assuming Proper Perspective

Often pastors and leaders believe addressing the basic needs of people, such as the physical, mental, or emotional, do not fall within the primacy of the local church's mission. This incorrect perspective has caused them to avoid spending time, energy, and resources on the matter of the human needs of their members. This evasion has created a severe imbalance in the church with many hurting people thus drifting away from the church. When people make contact with our churches, whether they are new believers or new members, they find themselves on some need-level. That is natural.

We have to be careful though that we do not misunderstand what we mean when we refer to the *needs* people have in this regard. We will certainly miss the mark if we are under the impression that all people are forever looking for a handout. Oftentimes it could be the opposite; it's not so much about receiving as it is about giving. One meaningful way people's needs could be met in this regard is by the church providing them the opportunity to be involved in practical acts of ministry. They have received specific spiritual gifts from the Holy Spirit and desperately desire to share what God had graciously given them.

The truth is that many people indeed have needs that have to be met and these oftentimes start with requirements of a physical nature (hunger, thirst, etc.) Our approach should be to view the providing of these needs as the entry point for people to connect to the church, so we have the opportunity to help them to advance to the next level of advancement in their lives. To a great extent, it explains why we should be knowledgeable of what people are facing in life.

After having said that, I want to make abundantly clear that I do not intend promoting the idea of focusing on the needs of people over the importance of Christ's mission for His Church. As I unfold the position, you will find that my premise in doing so is instead to utilize people's life-circumstances as an instrument of connecting with them and helping them discover the true meaning of life, which is available only in Jesus Christ. Meeting their needs is step one; helping them find security should be the next.

Let's Sharpen the Focus

It may be helpful for us to take a brief glimpse at the social sciences to understand our viewpoint more clearly. Psychologists and sociologists accept that there are absolute necessities of life all humans possess. While having studied this subject several years ago, I remember that Psychologist Abraham Maslow conducted an in-depth study of the basic human needs that exist among all humankind. Consequent to his research, Maslow cited five particular requirements of all people. He developed what has broadly become known as *Maslow's Hierarchy of Human Needs* which has been designed more vividly in a pyramid, showing five levels of progression. The science of human behavior widely accepted his model while both secular as well as Christian leaders broadly quote him in their writings. Although Maslow later in his life added three more levels, his five-level-hierarchy remained the foundation of his theory over several decades.

Maslow identified the following five basic needs all people have:
1. Biological and Physiological Needs
2. Safety Needs
3. Belonging and Love Needs
4. Esteem Needs
5. Self-Actualization

Maslow's Hierarchy of Needs

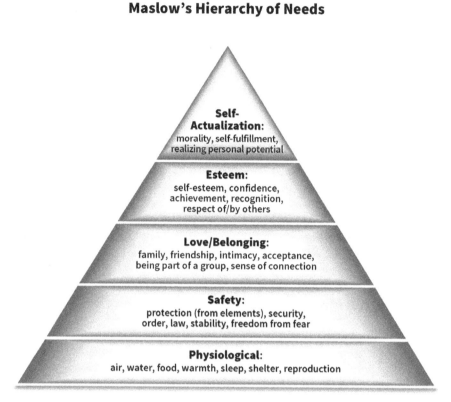

Self-Actualization:
morality, self-fulfillment,
realizing personal potential

Esteem:
self-esteem, confidence,
achievement, recognition,
respect of/by others

Love/Belonging:
family, friendship, intimacy, acceptance,
being part of a group, sense of connection

Safety:
protection (from elements), security,
order, law, stability, freedom from fear

Physiological:
air, water, food, warmth, sleep, shelter, reproduction

Image adapted from A. H. Maslow, *A Theory of Human Motivation* (1943)
by G. John A. Bosman II

A Realistic Perspective

Referencing psychologists in this discussion is unquestionably not an attempt to use a secular approach for effective ministry-outcome. It is instead an endeavor to deliberate this scientific viewpoint with an open mind in our quest of providing realistic and authentic care to each member of the congregation. We have previously stated that we cannot separate the totality of humankind in our ministry efforts and will, therefore, serve ourselves well by taking on a balanced perspective on the matter.

Our purpose for considering basic human needs is primarily an effort to evaluate our effectiveness of ministering to the wholeness of humankind and also to underscore the importance of a healthy balance between the spiritual and the physical when it comes to ministry execution.

As religious leaders, we will significantly benefit by looking through the lens of maturity and decide to remain objective as we together observe these psychological perspectives and not discard some of these aspects merely because they are scientific. Taking an academic approach is indeed not meant to abandon our Christian principles (or our commission of preaching the Gospel) and instead to fully embrace the field of psychology. That is not our intention. Let's instead ask the question: "What can we do as a local church to develop a culture of healthy balance in an attempt at reaching people who are hurting and desperate?"

Establishing Purpose

Referencing Maslow *et al.* in this context serves two primary purposes: *First*, the research substantiates that these basic human needs do exist and are not merely the wild fabrications of some ideologist's imagination. *Second*, I am referencing these findings because I want to launch from this accepted academic platform to present basic human needs from a *Christian perspective*. My focus remains on: (i) connecting with people in their life-circumstances, (ii) understanding why people act the way they do, (iii) finding ways to develop believers to function at their optimum level, and (iv) changing from being dysfunctional to being functional as a body of believers.

Although there may be some apparent overlap between established needs and Christian needs, my emphasis may be somewhat different and not necessarily scientific (however experientially undergirded). The basic *needs* may not be fundamentally different, but the Christian *response* to these may likely vary from the secular-sociological perspective, as one would expect. That does not mean that I am attempting to juxtapose a physiological position over real spiritual values, which again, I am not.

We hold that the Bible states that no individual attains greatness without having their sinful-will broke. That is where real life begins. We base this reality on the Holy Spirit creating a nature-change in each of us, not just a habit-change. Reaching people means reaching them at the point in life where they find themselves. Our responsibility begins by engaging with people at their level from where we then apply evangelism-principles which continues through developing people to become all God wants them to be.

Maslow's Theory

Maslow's theory proposes a developing hierarchy. It suggests that a person's needs should be met on the most basic level before the individual will strongly desire (or focus motivation upon) the next or higher-level needs. With that in mind, we can somewhat understand why people often stagnate in their spiritual development and seldom advance in their church involvement. If they have basic needs they are struggling with, and the church does not respond accordingly, we stifle their growth and progress, which usually results in feelings of uncertainty, insecurity, apathy, and sometimes rejection. In many cases, such persons then feel inadequate and experience a sense of worthlessness and assume that the church does not care or has no resolve.

Eric Fromm speaks of the dilemma of modern man when he says, "Our approach to life today becomes increasingly mechanical. Our main aim is to produce things, and in the process of this idolatry of things, we transform ourselves into commodities. People are treated as numbers . . . The question is whether people are things or living beings . . . At giant centers of production, giant cities, and great countries, men are administered as if they were things . . . But man is not meant to be a thing; he is destroyed if he becomes a thing, and before this is accomplished, he becomes desperate and wants to kill all life . . .. People living in such a system become indifferent to life and even attracted to death."[23]

Eric Fromm's viewpoint still holds good today. With the over-emphasis of programs, driven by enthusiastic visions, we should be careful in our churches that we do not once again unintentionally see people like objects, or things, and not as human beings. We can be so focused on reaching our goals that we inadvertently misuse our people by utilizing them for *our* purposes and objectives instead of helping them develop values in their own individual lives. If we spend our energy on reaching goals and not changing lives, we are missing the mark.

When someone has become no more than a name on a membership roll, or just another church-visitor or attendee, he/she becomes a thing, rather than a person. If it's all about numbers, we are driven by the wrong incentive. It should never be about how many people are in attendance, but rather about how many people we are touching for Christ. It should never just be about the number of people

---

23   As quoted by Oscar Feucht in his book *Everyone a Minister* (St. Louis: Concordia Publishing House), 141, taken out of Eric Fromm, *The Heart of Man* (New York: Harper and Row, 1968).

who respond to a call for salvation, but more about how many people are we discipling. It should always be about people as individuals and not about abstract statistics. The Bible says the Lord knows us by our names, not by our numbers.

A Christian Perspective of Human Needs

Even from a Christian perspective, we realize that all people have the same five basic human needs we mentioned before, that fundamentally do not change geographically, genetically, or even culturally. How they are satisfied and how we approach them may differ, but if we are normal, living human beings, the needs themselves remain.

Christianity is not driven by psychological principles but entirely by spiritual values. The Apostle Paul made sure that the Corinthians understood that their conversion to Christ was not the result of some physical, emotional, or intellectual persuasion, but rather by the inner working of the Holy Spirit.

> And my speech and my preaching were not with persuasive words of human wisdom, but in demonstration of the Spirit and of power, that your faith should not be in the wisdom of men but the power of God (1 Corinthians 2:4-5).

A changed life is brought about by the work of the Holy Spirit, and Him alone. Man, cannot add anything to it—and indeed, should not. It is the responsibility of the Church to provide spiritual growth to its members through discipleship and other means, but then likewise realize the importance of also ministering to people's needs in the natural, by providing authentic care. We must be careful that we do not become so heavenly minded that we are of no earthly good. At the same time, we want to clarify that we are not promoting a form of *social gospel* either. It is instead a matter of living out by example who we are in Christ. Paul seems to have a good understanding of this when he says that those who are followers of Christ should ". . . Be careful to devote themselves to doing what is good" (Titus 3:8 NIV).

Care Ministry

One of the most significant challenges we face in our churches is finding ways to stay connected with our members. This action is vital because that is the only way whereby we can know what our people are facing and understand the valleys through which they are walking. It also helps us to discover how we can best serve the body of Christ and involve people in a ministry that fits their spiritual gifts.

In our *Care Ministry Network* concept, we have designed a workable system, whereby church members are trained to stay in touch with a designated number of people within the congregation. We firmly believe when it comes to caring for people that *caring* goes way beyond shaking someone's hand on a Sunday morning or talking to the people we like or fellowshipping with the people who are like us. It's what happens after we say the last amen that matters. Honestly, genuine *Christian caring* only finds proper meaning once we reach people within their environments and touch them within their community.

Achieving this objective calls for developing a genuine and sincere friendship that becomes the catalyst for people to grow, develop, and reach their full potential. When left alone, on the other hand, people become disenchanted and begin to drift away from the church, seeking to fill the vacuum in their lives through alternative ways.

One of the essential reasons churches today have become ineffective in many areas is because they have become afraid to move outside their protected environment. For the most part, people are deeply involved in their private little church "bubble." They enjoy being there. But the truth of the matter is that the more they isolate themselves from their community, the less they can function in the real world. Through providing genuine care, we become engaged with people around us and primarily show that the Church is not an exclusive club for perfect people.

Life Outside the Sanctuary

Our model of providing care and meeting people's needs is confidently not an action that should only take place within the confinement of the four walls of a church. The activities that take place within the church building in our care ministry model is the least of the process we propose. It's not so much what happens on Sunday that matters, but even more so, what happens between Sundays that's important. We can see the power and effectiveness of the concept by how it functions outside of the church facility. If we desire to be faithful to our core mission of being Christians, we should show compassion to all people, regardless of where they live or what may be the level of their social stance.

> Dietrich Bonhoeffer says "Nothing that we despise in the other man is entirely absent from ourselves. We must learn to regard people less in the light of what they do or don't do, and more in the light of what they suffer."[24]

---

24   Phillip Yancey, "Middle East Morass," *Christianity Today* (2006): 128.

The way we see people, and especially the way we treat them, will determine the level of the relationship we develop. Once people sense a congregation's acceptance, they begin to show trust and readily respond to interaction, which often results in their lives being profoundly transformed by Christ. When will we learn to accept people for who they are, not for what we wished they were? Sometimes it appears we want to scale the fish before we catch them. We want to change people on the outside before the Holy Spirit has renewed them on the inside.

It is by *loving people*, regardless of where they find themselves, that we can lead them to *love God*. Most individuals in any given church today accepted Christ based on an existing relationship they developed with someone who shared their faith with them before they even came to our church. This truth underscores the importance of meaningful relationships and sincere friendship. If we are serious about developing significant associations, it may be necessary for us to learn some principles which beyond what are presently is the norm in most of our churches.

Engaging with Behavior

I previously made mention of Abraham Maslow and his *Hierarchy of Human Needs*. So, contemplating these identified necessities for life on an accepted basis, let's view these *Basic Human Needs* from a *Christian Perspective* and apply them to ministry in the local church. It will be most helpful to understand why people act the way they do. I intend to take most of the stated levels and describe them in simple ways in an attempt to make them useful and applicable to daily ministry.

Understanding the Mission

As we approach a subject such as this in the ongoing functioning of the Church, we fully understand that meeting the needs of people should never eclipse the Great Commission. There must be a healthy balance, with the goal ultimately being spiritual.

Addressing the needs of individuals should be part of our identity in Christ and should not merely be a form of *bait* to attract people. That means that when people, for example, are hungry or thirsty, our driving force should primarily be actually to provide them with the required necessities. We should follow up with these actions driven merely by Christ-like compassion even if the opportunity does not prevail in introducing them to Christ. The seeds we sow in love will ultimately produce a harvest.

After we have met people's necessities, we should make every attempt to lead them to the ultimate, which is Life in Christ. If on the other hand, we only do our Christian duty by meeting people's needs but never make any attempt to introduce them to Christ, we have changed our mission to that of just another social agency.

Churches cannot meet all the needs of all the people all the time. That is just not possible, and neither is it practical. But what is critically important is for the local church to be acutely *aware* of these needs so we can better understand why people respond the way they do, and even more so, to discover how we can effectively minister to them and help them develop personally.

If we look at the ministry of Jesus, we will notice that it was not necessarily His preaching that attracted the people. In fact, they did not always understand what He was saying. It was through meeting their needs that Jesus drew them: providing food, accepting them, loving them, touching them, and healing them. The compassion Jesus bestowed upon people was remarkable and became the stimulus of His ministry. I believe He was exemplifying how we should likewise approach people in everyday life.

Evaluating Human Needs

1. Biological and Physiological (Physical) Needs

Social scientists describe physical needs as the most basic and obvious necessities all people have and do not need much explanation. These are the bare requirements for human survival and the development of the individual as an organism and personality and can be summarized using the acronym T.H.R.E.A.T.S. (thirst, hunger, rest, excretion, air, temperature, and sex). All normal people have these needs and if not provided, causes anxiety, trepidation, and apprehension.

Although Maslow's Pyramid shows physiological needs at the bottom level, it exceeds all other requirements and remains the most basic of all necessities. If a person, as an example, is on a deserted island with no food or water, security or esteem does not matter. Such persons do not care what others think of them; their priority need is survival. It's only after they receive the basic needs met, that things like safety and security, or whatever, comes into play.

While it may not necessarily be the local church's ministry-priority, we cannot deny the distinct emphasis the Bible places upon our responsibility of providing in the physiological necessities people have. "For I was hungry, and you gave Me food; I was thirsty, and you gave Me drink; I was a stranger, and you took Me in; I was naked, and you clothed Me; I was sick, and you visited Me; I was in prison, and you came to Me" (Matthew 25:32-38).

1.1 Hunger

Out of the above list, hunger is apparently the most dominant factor, and until we meet this requirement, an individual has little drive to pursue any of the other needs. That is one of the reasons in our international ministry, we feed people at our mass crusades in Africa.

During our last Gospel Festival, we passed out 10,000 loaves of freshly baked bread. The responses of desperately hungry individuals who ran as fast as they could—some on human-made crutches cut from tree limbs—falling, bleeding, and weeping—was indescribable and will never be quickly forgotten.

> People don't care
> how much you know
> until they know
> how much you care.
> *John C. Maxwell*

Not all congregations will see meeting the need of hunger as their primary mission, but it indeed should be the responsibility of the leadership to ensure that everyone has food available to take care of themselves and their own families. In the days that lie before us, the church is going to have to prepare to play a significant role in meeting more of the physical needs of their people. Political pressure is driving society toward unfamiliar territory, and the need for people to firmly connect with each other in meaningful relationships is going to become increasingly more critical. These demands, including natural disasters, will require each congregation to have a *system of care* that ensures that they connect every member to someone who will be available to identify and, either personally provide these needs, or find appropriate support.

Meeting Needs Builds Ministry

To some inner-city churches, *feeding and clothing* have become their primary driving force to connect with people outside the church.

It has become the catalyst for attracting people and then introducing them to Jesus Christ. The late Dr. E. V. Hill was a guest at our church some years ago. I was so impressed by the outreach ministry he ran in Los Angeles with his *soup kitchens*. There are more people on their way to heaven today because of this outreach that we will ever know. And it all started with hungry people in search of satisfying their need.

Dr. Hill was wise enough first to identify and then meet their particular need. In doing so, he created an opportunity to introduce people to the real *Answer*—Jesus Christ! These days we cannot neglect to equally mention the powerful ministry of Pastors Tommy and Matthew Barnett with their compelling vision of a Dream Center—also, coincidently, in Los Angeles. They have been successful in even touching the lives of scores of people enslaved to all kinds of addiction and abuse. In both cases, they connected with people on the level of their physiological needs and then used the opportunity to develop them to the next level.

Even Jesus was Concerned About the Basic Needs of Humankind

Before He sent away the crowds who came to hear Him preach and teach, Jesus would often instruct the disciples first to feed the people. In one of Jesus's most famous miracles, He feeds a massive crowd of 5,000 people with just a few loaves of bread and some fish (Mark 6:34-44). He said to His disciples, "You give them something to eat" (Mark 6:37). On another similar occasion, Jesus said, "I have compassion on the multitude because they have now continued with Me three days and have nothing to eat" (Mark 8:2).

Jesus exemplifies a caring attitude towards people for us to understand that all people have needs that we have to meet if we desire to minister to them. We make a terrible mistake when we ignore the needs people have. Jesus's goal was regeneration, and His teachings revolved around a Kingdom to come. But in His humanness, He also realized that people were natural beings and still needed the necessities of life. Jesus did not, and we shouldn't either, only concentrate on the spiritual aspects of people's lives. How dare we say we should not spend resources, time, or energy on people's needs?

But then, of course, we realize that meeting physical needs is not the ultimate. It is only the doorway to the eternal purposes God has for us on this earth. Humankind's *greatest need* is not physical food, but rather the spiritual. Jesus said that "Man shall not live by bread alone, but by every word that proceeds from the mouth of God" (Matthew 4:4). Finding the *Bread of Life* through salvation is the first level, or entry point, for every person to start their development in Christ. If we do not meet this need, there will be no further advancement in a person's spiritual growth. The fact is that people often come looking for their physical needs to be met but also encounter the reality of the Holy Spirit, who changes their lives forever. We just need to maintain the correct perspective.

Let's Look at the Rest

Evidently, hunger is not the only physical need people have, so let's briefly consider some other aspects to be aware of:

1.2 Sanitation

Now actually excretion does not sound spiritual to me! But the fact is, it's a real human need, and you can't get away from it. We cannot even think of having a gathering of people of some sorts without providing proper sanitation. It also becomes more critical when it comes to our church services. The worship can be out of this world, and you can preach like no one else, but when people *have to go, they have to go!* And if you don't have adequate, clean, good-smelling restrooms that meet people's expectations, they may not come back. They may forget your sermon, but the smell lingers on and on and on!

A good example is when people attend a church for the first time, the women, especially, first look for the restroom. It's their comfort zone. If you've won them here, they're willing to venture further. Lose them here, and you may as well give it up. That's why I have always advocated that the ladies' restroom should match the most beautiful hotel in the city.

1.3 Sex

Now come on, what responsibility does the church have with this one? Well, again, it's the *awareness* of needs that are important. Since we know it's a basic human need, it is most certainly the Church's responsibility to give clear direction on how to handle the aspect of sex. We too often ignore the importance of addressing an issue such as this, and as a result, leave people in an unjustified vacuum.

It's unfair to our people not to provide sound teaching on an important subject such as this. We also owe it to our young people to teach them about the Scriptural expectations concerning abstinence from sex, and furthermore sincerely caution them about the physical and emotional dangers of having sex before marriage.

We should teach our single adults that fornication is wrong, dangerous, and sinful. We should warn our married couples that infidelity is breaking a covenant, which God hates. We also need to give practical teaching of how couples should experience intimacy in marriage scripturally. The Bible is clear on these subjects.

Now, getting down to the questions you asked in your letter to me. First, is it a good thing to have sexual relations? Certainly—but only within a certain context. It's good for a man to have a wife, and for a woman to have a husband. Sexual drives are strong, but marriage is strong enough to contain them and provide for a balanced and fulfilling sexual life in a world of sexual disorder. The marriage bed must be a place of mutuality—the husband seeking to satisfy his wife, the wife seeking to satisfy her husband. Marriage is not a place to "stand up for your rights." Marriage is a decision to serve the other, whether in bed or out. Abstaining from sex is permissible for a period of time if you both agree to it, and if it's for the purposes of prayer and fasting—but only for such times. Then come back together again. Satan has an ingenious way of tempting us when we least expect it. I'm not, understand, commanding these periods of abstinence— only providing my best counsel if you should choose them (1 Corinthians 7:4-6 MSG).

Psychologist Darwin was emphatic that sex is the most potent driving force of all and that it will overrule every other impulse. We contend that a Spirit-born person has the power to overcome whatever evil may come against him or her. But if we don't teach these things, people will continue to be hampered in their spiritual advancement and never learn how to be overcomers.

The pressure of everything that secular viewpoints present, can potentially create the impression with the Christian that sex outside of the marriage bonds is acceptable. This faulty perspective causes restraint in the spiritual dynamics of the church and keeps it from being healthy and fulfilling its mission. If the church does not give guidance in this matter, it may become a severe obstruction to someone who desires to advance to higher levels of leadership in the future.

Healthy teaching by the church, in this regard, is imperative. When we ignore this vital topic of human needs, we will continue to suffer the consequences of broken marriages and destroyed families in our churches, which always effects unity and well-being in our congregations.

1.4 Education

The good thing about education is that the church is familiar with it. We need to, however, realize that what's important is not only to educate people intellectually but even more so to develop them spiritually. This process should not only be presented to adults, but to all ages. From a Christian perspective, we prefer to refer to it as discipleship. But even at that, we should ensure that we are not only providing information but even more so, transformation. If the knowledge is all we are offering, spiritual obesity will be the result.

Every church must have a life-transforming discipleship track that will take people from where they are, to where God wants them to be. Develop people utilizing a process, having a definite goal in mind. And please realize that discipleship should never be an event; it should be a way of life. Any occasion has a beginning, and it has an end; discipleship has a start but should never have a conclusion.

Many of the other physiological needs, such as water to drink, air to breathe, etc., are mostly self-explanatory and could be interwoven in what I stated earlier. What is important is to remember that man is spirit, soul, and body. We must minister to the wholeness of humankind and as leaders help them develop to their fullest potential in Christ.

2. Safety and Security Needs.

Once we have sufficiently met people's basic needs, and have successfully introduced them to Christ, the natural progression for them is to find a place of safety and security in their newfound environment. Once again there are the spiritual as well as the personal aspects to consider, and both are important in a church environment.

Before moving on in their development, people need to feel secure in what they will be committing to for the future advancement of their lives. They need spiritual *security* in their lives and *stability* in their relationships. They do not only want to feel safe and secure in their environment but even more so regarding their spiritual growth and potential destiny.

Once they have been Born Again, the kind of safety and security people are after in a church is anchored in knowing that their church underwrites sound doctrine and that they can trust their pastors and leaders to teach and equip them according to biblical values and simultaneously protect them from false or wrong teaching. At this stage, it will be wise for a church to have some presentation of three or four one-hour seminars, teaching the basics of the faith, explaining who they are and what they believe, clarify what they require of members, and also how people may become involved in the activities of the congregation.

When people feel safe and secure spiritually, they are more inclined to buy into the vision of the church especially when they feel confident in the foundation of the church's beliefs or the spiritual convictions of their pastor. They want to make sure they can carry on their lives without any ambiguity and fear of the leadership leading them astray. This expectation naturally places a heavy responsibility on a pastor's shoulders. People do not trust anything that smacks of "flakiness." Their spiritual lives are way too meaningful for them to risk irrationality. Ask the Millennial Generation of our day. Integrity, honesty, and reality are high commodities in their viewpoint. And rightfully so!

It Goes Beyond the Spiritual

As they advance in their growth and their participation increase, people do not only want to feel secure about spiritual safety; they also want to know, for instance, that those who are responsible for the church's finances handle it correctly. Not everybody always wants to know the details, but they do want to be confident that the leaders utilize the money for the purpose they contributed. When people feel secure about the safety of the church's money-matters, their financial contributions will be both, more stable and more substantial.

Additionally, church members want to feel secure that their children not only are personally safe in the hands of church workers on all occasions but are also being taught correctly. Most parents have a higher expectation of the safety and security of their children than they have for themselves. All churches should place a high premium on their children's ministries and facilities. This aspect is all-important, especially to young families. For this reason, and many others, a local church just cannot afford to have people involved in ministry who have not passed a required background check, mainly when children are involved. Avoiding these principles, shake the foundation of safety and security and causes instability which in returns results in disunity.

Church members categorically also want to have confidence in their Lead Pastor's morality, marriage, and family relationships. This expectation is more important than many realize and is often seen in the overwhelming responses of people when a pastor falls from grace in the sins of immorality, embezzlement, or some other impropriety. It is only in an atmosphere of trust and security that members feel comfortable, are at ease, and willing to fully participate and help fulfill the vision.

Knowing the Mission and Vision

Another point of creating an atmosphere of safety and security for church members lies within a clear understanding of the church's mission and vision. This knowledge causes them to not only feel secure in the present but allows them also to feel safe for their spiritual journey ahead. It is just when the mission and vision are clear that people feel secure in participating in the execution of the dream. "Write the vision . . . make it plain . . ." (Habakkuk 2:2). People unite behind a vision and will join you on a journey if they understand the destiny. But once they're on the bus and don't know where it's going, they will get off at the first stop. "Where there is no vision, the people perish . . ." (Proverbs 29:18 KJV). The NKJV gives another interesting perspective: "Where there is no revelation, people cast off restraint . . ." (Proverbs 29:18 NKJV). This translation could in effect mean that when people lose the vision, they abandon (cast off) their commitment to ministry and forsake their loyalty.

Personal Safety and Security

It's almost impossible to address safety and security without considering the actual aspects of these matters for all who attend our churches. Since 9-11 our entire approach concerning personal safety and security has changed. Today you can hardly enter a large public building without having to pass through some form of security scanner or search mechanism. This requirement has even made its way to our universities, hospitals, and places of worship. Larger churches have armed security personnel at all their gatherings and have installed advanced security devices throughout their facilities.

In the face of recent attacks at our churches, it may now become necessary to instill some form of security in all our places of worship, even at smaller churches. This precaution may require church leadership to arrange for the training of some of their members in handling firearms and personal tactics in times of crisis. It has now become important enough for us to realize that spending money on security is not an expense, but an investment in the lives of our members. Not taking these measures are probably going to hurt church attendance shortly and will sincerely influence the outcome of our efforts.

3. Love and Belonging Needs

After people have become followers of Christ, and are satisfied with their safety and security expectations, the next step for them is to experience acceptance as well as a sense of belonging from the company of believers. They experience loving and belonging best through the love they receive in the congregation within the context of a group. People need an environment where they feel cared for and know they could also care for others. All people have an innate desire to *love* and also to *be loved*. People cannot efficiently survive without meaningful expression of affection. God created humankind for community. The need for love is so strong that it, for instance, becomes the upper mold of character in a child's life and becomes the key ingredient that shapes a human being in an emotional sense.

Dear friends, let us continue to love one another, for **love comes from God**. Anyone who loves is a child of God and knows God (1 John 4:7 NLT) (Emphasis added).

It is a fact that God created humankind for friendship and relationship. That is why He said, "It is not good that man should be alone . . ." (Genesis 2:18). He then created Eve as a close companion for Adam. Following this scenario, we notice that God, the great Creator, personally understood the need for fellowship and, for this reason, showed up at the end of every day to meet with Adam and Eve (Genesis 3:8). There is a certain good feeling we get when people show they care for us and, likewise, when we can care for others in return. In church circles, we readily refer to this as *fellowship*—a term that is more fitting in a Christian environment than anywhere else because it brings with it a relationship that goes beyond mere acquaintance.

Connecting and belonging are crucial components of growing a church. We understand that if people do not make at least six close, personal friends within six months after they have joined a church, they will disassociate themselves from the congregation and move on. The fundamental reason this plays out as it does is that people cannot live without significant interaction with other people. Bonding through friendship is essential to people, and we have to concentrate on ways to accommodate this human necessity. No man is an island to himself.

God created humankind for fellowship! To Adam and Eve, not even live animals could fill the ticket in the Garden of Eden. Talking to the monkeys or chasing after the rabbits were just not enough. It didn't fill the vacuum. It had to be a person. It was beautiful Eve, and not Bambi, that made Adam say, *Wow!* when he took the first amazing look at her! Our needs are met only through connecting with real *people*.

God created man for fellowship! If we miss providing a meaningful community in our church relationships, people are going to look for it elsewhere.

3.1 Belonging

Let me share a few more thoughts on the importance of belonging. We should make every effort to make people sense that they belong. That is why joining a local church is so important. People want to connect with others who are of like-minded persuasion and have the same outcome in mind. Belonging meets the need for acceptance by one's peers and becomes the catalyst that produces unity and peace in the congregation. People who feel accepted feel part of the team and will, as a rule, give and do their best under all circumstances. Acceptance and belonging go hand in hand and can hardly be separated.

People who desire to connect, typically don't want to only attend church on Sundays just for the sake of being there. They want to feel integrally part of what is going on and, more importantly, know that their contribution and participation will make a difference to the overall effectiveness of the church. Those are the people that will move the proverbial mountain. Ignore them, and you're sure to lose them. When people are appreciated, they feel valued, and value breeds commitment.

Until people honestly and rightfully feel they belong and are part of what's going on, they will never fully support the church with their finances, talents, time, energy, and other resources. They will, at best, remain an audience, but did we not say we are not raising up an audience, but raising up an army?

3.2 Church Membership

Church membership is important—again! It's part of the process, and it's part of *belonging and acceptance.* It's a colossal mistake for pastors and churches to think that membership is no longer relevant or that it is no longer the "in-thing." There may have been a time when it seemingly didn't matter much, but not so anymore. The pendulum has swung back the other way. Leaders are acknowledging the importance of committed members again. And the focus is *not* on numbers as much as it is for inclusion. There is no more practical way for people to experience a sense of belonging than to be accepted as members of a local church.

Church membership should mean much more than mere names on a roll or some qualification to vote in a business meeting (where applicable) or to function in some ministry position. Membership should be a defined *covenant relationship* that exists between the church and its members with a clear understanding of expectations. And I cannot stress enough how essential it is for these expectations to be clarified, understood, and implemented. People must grasp this and agree to it. You cannot expect people to become members if they do not know what the church requires of them or to what they are committing. When people become Christians, they commit themselves to Christ, and by becoming church members, they commit themselves to each other (2 Corinthians 8:5).

In our *New Members Conferences,* I always clearly defined what the church would provide for its members, taking time to share the vision and what they could expect from their church and what the benefits are of membership. Then we reversed the role and stated what the church requires of its members and clarify how they could help the congregation fulfill its mission. It's covenant—it's two-sided. The Bible asks the question, "Can two walk together unless they have agreed?" (Amos 3:3).

3.3 Set a Standard

It is of vital importance to have a standard for membership, and it's imperative not to set the bar too low. If expectations are set low, the commitment level of members will be minimal, their participation will lack, and so will their giving and involvement. Low expectations add no value to the relationship. As a requirement for membership, all people should have an explicit profession of faith in Christ as Savior, should have been baptized in water, should attend a *New Members Conference,* commit to supporting the church financially, and declare their willingness to be involved in some form of ministry. We are not looking to add more passengers to a cruise ship; we are looking for soldiers to join the battleship.

Receiving people into membership is the most transparent act of demonstrating *acceptance.* It creates stability in people who will remain faithful despite whatever may transpire in the church. Individuals with no commitment, or even little commitment, are usually the first to abandon ship. The more you can make people feel they are needed and that the mission depends on them, the more buy-in you will have from them and the more cooperation you will experience. The most efficient way you can add value to people and make them feel needed is to involve them in meaningful ministry. This action is what makes people loyal, committed, and involved. That's what gives people the buy-in that develops unbreakable cohesion. Said in another way: people have a need to be needed.

3.4 Acceptance

Acceptance is a crucial component when it comes to the aspect of love and belonging. You will find that some of the people in your church have a higher need for acceptance than others. Where they have come from, and how their lives have developed, will mostly determine where they find themselves on the ladder of recognition.

Let us never lose sight of the fact that scores of people come to church with broken lives and torn reputations. Many have gone through the mill of life, are bruised, and feel profoundly rejected by the world, society, their peers, and even their family. They come looking for hope and acceptance, desiring to be restored and loved. The pain of their past has made them gun-shy and frequently cause them to struggle with low self-esteem and low self-worth.

People who walk through our doors on Sunday may look fine on the outside but often are broken on the inside. They are dealing with stuff they don't know how to handle. The church always seems to be the logical place to go. Therefore, we should guard against legalism and accept people for who they are not for whom we wished they were.

Many times, even after people have received Christ and have received forgiveness of their sin, they struggle to get rid of the shackles of shame. They know God has forgiven them but find it hard to forgive themselves. They struggle with self-acceptance and are desperate for acceptance by others. This reality is where people in the church can play such an influential role because preaching alone cannot adequately fill that need. They must experience acceptance through genuine personal relationships and received into the community of their church family.

On the bright side, it appears people with a high need for acceptance are usually easy-going and pleasant to have in a group.

They are cooperative and self-sacrificing and will often go beyond the call of duty. They make the best servant-leaders. But be aware at the same time they are, unfortunately, vulnerable and easily hurt if they sense rejection. They will silently walk away and finally disappear. In most cases, it's hard to get them then back again.

4. Esteem Needs

Most people need healthy self-respect and high self-esteem to advance in life. This level is more challenging to reach and will not happen until a person is first accepted and experiences the sense of belonging and love. This group indicates the need for position and acknowledgment and belongs mostly to those who have the gift of leadership.

People who desire to stretch to the esteem level have a high expectation of acceptance. Their need is to be needed. *Acceptance* is, at first, confidence in yourself and then, secondly, to be recognized by others. People in this category thrive not only on accomplishments but rather on the successes of their achievements. It's the acceptance of their peers on the level they function in that builds their esteem.

People of this nature are highly motivated and usually have strong personalities. Pastors and leaders should identify such individuals, recognize them, and train them to be involved in leadership positions for the future. It is essential to have this category understand the church's vision and share the pastor's heart. Ignoring these people and suppressing their giftedness robs the church of dynamic advancement and simultaneously cause anxiety and frustration to the individuals. It is much easier to be a leader of strong leaders than to be a leader of weak leaders.

Many people, on the other hand, are satisfied to merely remain on the level of being part of the congregation (belonging) and don't care if there is no further development. They function best when they are among their peers and give their best when they are part of the team. If a title, for instance, would endanger their relationships with their peers, many individuals will shirk away from accepting such opportunities. In fact, in many cases, people in search of acceptance are troubled that titles and positions may potentially isolate them from their peer group and hurt rather than help them in the inclusion of the team.

Church Elections

The need for acceptance and striving to build esteem are the main reasons I detest elections in churches. I have presided over too many meetings where I have seen the results of elections. It's probably not intended to be that way, but it almost seems as though these meetings are purposely set up for someone to fail. Someone is going to lose and feel rejected. I have yet to see any election, on any level, that did not cause deep-seated hurt, pain, or rejection. And experience has shown that those who the group does not choose, for the more significant part, lost their enthusiasm and personal drive and, in many cases, dropped out from involvement altogether.

The active development of meaningful relationships is what builds self-confidence and self-respect and positions individuals to excel in their endeavors. Equipping people for ministry is one of the most excellent tools the church could ever foster to develop the abilities and potential of its members. This application is the biblical way of helping believers advance their self-esteem and build self-respect.

5. Self-Actualization

Self-Actualization, the final need-aspect in our discussion, is the most significant of all. Maslow, in his original pyramid of five, has *Self-*

Actualization as the fifth stage of human needs. By that, he suggests that a person has an inherent need to want to reach the highest level possible and become all he can be. His viewpoint is that *Self-Actualization* is the development of one's potential by striving to achieve it at any cost. This category refers to the need for personal achievement. All the other lower need-levels depend upon the viewpoint of others, but this high-level group relates to the development of the individual personally. These people are exceptionally goal-oriented and tend to drive the mission of the organization devotedly.

From a Christian perspective, we believe that humankind's highest ambition should be to cultivate a close relationship with God—there is no question about that. Humankind was created to glorify Him. For a person to become all you can be, one needs to be reconciled with God through repentance of sins, acceptance of Jesus Christ as Lord and Savior, and be born again through the work of the Holy Spirit.

The Bible states that when this happens, you become part of God's family with all the benefits attached. You become a new creature with a unique destiny and unlimited potential in Christ (2 Corinthians 5:17,18). You are freed from the burden of the world and elevated in a spiritual sense to a level you would never be able to reach by yourself. There is no higher or more fulfilling level a person can ever achieve in life.

Through the Holy Spirit, we can live in the fullness of Christ for it's "... in Him we live, and move, and have our being ..." (Acts 17:28). You have not lived until you have found life in Christ. By Him, and Him alone, you can become all you can be. "Jesus expressed a Christian perspective of self-actualization when He said, 'I am come that they might have life, and they might have it more abundantly.' (John 10:10.

KJV) This concept of abundant living presents a new dimension of life that Maslow could not share from the context of secular writing.[25]

We believe that once a person has found Christ and had committed his or her life to Him, He provides all the other things (needs). "But seek first the kingdom of God and His righteousness, and all these things shall be added to you" (Matthew 6:33).

God First

Many of the need-levels mentioned earlier, other than the physiological, can best be reached by first having an encounter with God. For instance, when we talk about our need to love and be loved, we realize that we cannot truly love others until we first love ourselves—"Love your neighbor as you love yourself." And we cannot fully comprehend loving ourselves until we have first experienced the love of God. It is only when we have a relationship with Him that we can become whole, and it is only through that wholeness that we can become who we are supposed to become. The more familiar we become with God's love, the more capable we are of developing affection for others. The Bible says, "He who does not love has not become acquainted with God . . . for God is love" (1 John 4:8 AMP). Simply put, it says you cannot truly love others until you understand the love of God.

The True Source of Life

We believe that only God can give people the deep awareness of how infinitely valuable and precious they are, and what a glorious

---

25   Gary M. Gray, *Christian Growth and Leadership* (Austin: Church Management, Inc.).

destiny He has for them. Only God can see and meet the unfulfilled needs a person may have, even when they may not personally recognize it. Only God can ultimately fix a broken heart. Only God can mend the battered mind. Only God can fully restore a broken life.

Increasingly, life-giving churches today are those who genuinely care about, understand, encourage, and enable their members to become all they can be in Christ. And furthermore, for them to fully accomplish their spiritual goals—way beyond the traditional mold, the religious patterns, and the learned behavior. Paul admonishes us to *earnestly desire the best gifts* (1 Corinthians 12:31a). Substantial church growth is the result of members developing their own personal and unique spiritual gifts and building the Church.

Cutting edge pastors are teaching their members to *discover* their gifts, then leading them to *develop* those gifts, until they can *deploy* those gifts. And their churches are *exploding*—because this is the full expression of Ephesians 4. There is no other more profound way to add value to people's lives, which, at the same time, affects eternal values.

Every believer has three stages of growth they should go through spiritually: *First*, they are fed by someone else. *Secondly*, they nourish themselves. And *thirdly*, they feed someone else. This process is the complete fulfillment, which is spiritually found only in knowing Christ and what Maslow would describe as *Self-Actualization* in a secular sense.

Finding the Ultimate

Since we thoroughly realize that we will never attain to perfection here on earth, we should continually strive to reach for what Paul calls *the more excellent way* (1 Corinthians 12:31b) The Holy Spirit nurtures an innate desire within the heart of every believer to advance by developing others also to grow spiritually and arrive at maturity (the third stage of their spiritual journey mentioned above).

Maslow called this further level *Transcendence*. But to us, it falls into the category of discovering and developing our spiritual gifts and functioning within the body of Christ. Being "born again" does not mean the believer has proverbially arrived. We should realize that we are not saved just to escape hell; neither were we saved just to go to heaven. God adopted us into His family with a purpose, and that goal is to glorify Him, build His Church, and expand His Glorious Kingdom.

Summary

1. The levels of needs people experience in their lives provides the church with the most excellent opportunity to connect with people. We can accomplish this without applying religious jargon or the confinements of a church building.

2. Our ultimate goal should be to connect with people to help them advance to a higher level. From the fundamental level of physical needs, we endeavor to lead people to a place of safety and security. The ultimate safety a church can provide is salvation through which we attain new life and shape a divine destiny.

3. Our Christian message and instilled spiritual culture compel us to accept people into our fellowship and have them experience Christ-like love which in return creates a sense of belonging within them and infuses value into their lives.

4. As people develop in their walk with God and discover their spiritual gifts, the church should provide every opportunity for them to be involved and also advance in ministry. The achievements the reach, along with the activities, and commitment they display, builds their confidence (esteem) and gives them boldness to do more for Christ.

5. Through developing their leadership skills and showing full devotion to the cause of Christ, people reach a level of personal accomplishment and then not only devote their time to themselves but as a result of their spiritual growth and dedication to the Lord, equip others to likewise become fruitful in the Kingdom of God. Not many people reach this level in the local church, but this should be the goal of every believer.

Conclusion

Realizing that we should minister to the *whole* person, we have identified the importance of understanding that all human beings have basic human needs. God created us that way. We have further established that man's need for God is the most significant need and is where our ultimate focus should remain.

In a real world of church life, there will always be someone who finds themselves in at least one of these needs-categories. One comforting thought is that not all people have all these needs all the time. If that were the case, we could never have made headway. It is comforting that people's needs are often not in the realm of wanting to *receive* something, but rather to give and to provide. The real question we should answer is: How willing are we to consider these aspects as we provide devoted ministry in the local church?

While psychologists advocate that a person's inner passions are what drives him, we believe that it's the Holy Spirit that drives the desires of a truly born-again child of God. We have been accepted into the family of God and live by a different set of rules and hold to different values. Our desires and satisfaction do not lie within physical pleasure but rather in spiritual gain. We find our most significant benefits in His presence, and in Him, we fully understand what love is all about. Building close bonds with Him is enjoying the highest level of relationships we can ever desire. The Bible says it best when it says that Abraham was a friend of God.

Caring for people goes a long way, and sincerely loving them covers a multitude of our faults and failures. The heart of the matter that remains is that the responsibility of congregational care is so vast that it should be done by all God's people alike. As Mel Steinbron always said, "It takes all of the people of God to do all of the work of God" (sic).

10

THE ROLE
OF THE PASTOR

In this chapter, I am going to challenge some of the perspectives many people have concerning congregational care. As the chapter heading states, we will emphasize the role of the pastor regarding pastoral care and reflect mainly on his or her vision and influence in this regard. The positive stimulus of the pastor is imperative since the role he or she plays in the launching of this ministry is most significant. If the vision for this care model is not alive in the lead pastor's heart, it will function for a while, and then fade away. Most every time the care ministry concept has failed was directly related to the neglect of the pastor's influence.

Care Directors will lose their effectiveness because the members will not be enthusiastic about a vision the pastor does not embrace. They need to see and feel their pastor's passion before they will become excited about the concept. But do not, however, erroneously assume from this statement that we have designed our care concept to increase the burden of the pastor because that is assuredly not the case. On the contrary, it is purposely developed to lighten his or her load.

While we understand that this ministry should be the earnest desire of the pastor and certainly be the extension of his/her vision, the church members are the ones who eventually run it and affect the actual implementation. We have, however, designed the system in a way whereby there are strong accountability and feedback, so the pastor never loses touch.

A vital key to the success of this ministry is not only in the formidable concept but even more so through practical, in-depth training and development of the church members. Without thoroughly equipping them, this ministry will not be as applicable as it could be. And it's the aspect of training that requires the devotion of the pastor. It is launched by him or her but continued through the leaders who are in place according to the designed structure.

What needs to be underscored, to all involved, is the fact that through the *Care Revolution* process, there is a definite paradigm shift taking place. In this movement, church members are trained and taught that the ministry of congregational care will gradually move from the pastor to them. The pastor's role is to develop, empower, and encourage their members to be actively involved in caring for one another. An excellent partnership then forms between the pastor and the members with outstanding results that follow.

As mentioned in a previous chapter, we are dealing with the church's culture, which we cannot frame without the direct and active leadership of the pastor. This ministry should not only have the *approval* of the pastor but also, and more importantly, enjoy his/her input, as a mentor and coach. Once church members know that their pastor, as the leader, will do his/her part in the fulfillment of the vision, they will embrace the idea and wholeheartedly become involved.

In church after church, it amazes us to see the large numbers of people who enthusiastically participate in this ministry in a relatively short span of time. The reasons for this phenomenon may be multiple, but I believe at the heart of why so many people are getting involved in this movement is because this ministry's time has come. It's addressing a long-felt need and providing a surprising response to Jesus's command to *love your neighbor as yourself.* The *Care Revolution* has proven to release incredible enthusiasm once leaders cast the vision to the entire body.

Across the nation, it has become evident, now more than ever, that pastors are keen and willing to train their people based on Ephesians 4 and other Scriptures. Instead of using different measuring instruments, people today evaluate pastors by the church members they equip and raise up for ministry. In this process, we have found that the one challenge most pastors face in this regard has always been the lack of appropriate material with which to equip and train their people to care for one another especially. The result is that, for the most part, it was never enthusiastically implemented, and many times been left undone; with overworked pastors, frustrated members, and dying churches remaining.

It's for these above reasons we are now making resources of different kinds available to pastors and leaders as tools for expanding their ability to care for God's people. We are entering an exciting season and will soon see the Church arise again as never before.

Few things are as helpful to a leader as having adequate knowledge on a particular topic when it becomes time to cast a vision. Sharing an idea begins by having a sound strategy, which should include a game plan that a leader can articulate clearly and succinctly. If church members do not see distinctly where the dream is taking them, they will not readily accept the responsibility of making the trip with their pastor. They need to grasp the big picture to which they can connect emotionally and logically, so they can work together with their leader to reach the goal.

The Pastor's Philosophy of Ministry Development

In the paradigm shift we are talking about, and for this change to take place, pastors should be committed and enthusiastic about developing their people for ministry. This persuasion will first require them to trust their people and secondly to accept *equipping the believers* as a biblical principle. The most efficient way of encouraging people to be trained is for the pastor to be involved in the process of development personally. It's entirely understandable that others will be part of the equipping progression also, but it's the initial contribution of the pastor—his or her investment into their member's lives—that releases the eagerness among the members to participate. As it is often said, "People buy into the leader before they buy into the vision."

Just as members have bought into the tradition of ministry being done primarily by the clergy, so have many pastors. As a result, it stands to reason that we should eradicate this erroneous belief from our persuasion. Changing this mindset calls for discipline, but the fruit of doing so is so vast that we cannot afford to ignore it. The personal involvement of the pastor by training and developing people to be involved in congregational care sends a loud message of the pastor's commitment to this ministry-shift.

The following points may prove helpful as we together build the foundation of people-involvement:

1.   **Ministry is a shared responsibility.** The foremost point we should settle in our minds as pastors first, is that ministry does not exclusively belong to the credentialed ministers—also known as the clergy or professionals. Ephesians 4:11-14 remains a significant and Scriptural basis for our conviction to explain that every believer is a minister. The balanced way to observe this premise is by conveying the notion that members do not just help their pastor in the ministry but provide actual ministry. As pastors, we take on the crucial role of trainers and enablers who turn members into ministers.

     We must develop and then include our people in ministry with us. Instead of keeping our life lessons to ourselves, we should alternatively, as pastors and leaders, utilize the experiences and insights we have gained in ministry as illustrations and examples in the instructions we design to develop our people for their roles in ministry. Many things in ministry are more *caught* than *taught*. If we believe this to be true, then we have to also accept the fact that meaningful training can only take place up close and not from a distance. Pastors have to develop strong relationships with those they train.

2. **Training should become a priority.** For church members to be involved in fruitful ministry, they have to be trained. We have for too long placed people in roles of ministry without ever taking time to equip them. That is a sure recipe for failure and is most likely one of the major reason people no longer want to be involved in ministry. Preparing or training God' s people for the work of the ministry should become the priority of all credentialed ministers and should be done on purpose. If not, there will be no life in the church. The key to building a robust and healthy church is by raising up more and more people to be involved in ministry. That is God's way, and there should be no other way.

Training, developing, and utilizing our people will change our churches like few other things will. It releases excitement, life, and enthusiasm that becomes contagious and even raises the spiritual climate. We should never see equipping people as an appendix to everything else we are doing; it should be at the forefront. That's the life of the church!

3. **Share the principle of ministry partnership.** We should not only hold the belief but also clearly communicate the strategy of membership involvement to the entire congregation. Pastors should take the lead and distinctly and explicitly teach the biblical premise of ministry-partnership—everyone should be involved,

and everyone should know. The more we preach and teach this principle, the more we will create the awareness among congregants.

If shared-ministry is not understood, and the biblical principles not undergirded, many people may think the pastors are attempting to shun ministry responsibilities by shifting their obligations to church members. You have already heard me say it, and you will still hear about it often, but the truth rings clear: *Every believer is a minister,* and everybody should understand it.

4. **Keep the vision before the people.** The pastor should consistently and publicly share the benefits of *people caring for people* openly to the congregation, so members will become more and more eager to accept ministry from each other and not only from the credentialed ministers. Constantly sharing the vision and announcing the positive affects also becomes a stimulus for more people to become involved in this specific ministry.

Keeping the vision alive is best done by often including the benefits of members caring for another in sermons. It is also helpful to have members share testimonies of the worth of the ministry with the congregation and even by including pertinent information on the church website, in the bulletins, newsletters, etc. Celebrating victories in this way too encourages the Care Pastors to continue in their calling of caring for one another joyfully. If we do not share the vision consistently, the care ministry will begin to wane and could even potentially die. Remember, it's initially a new concept, and it takes time before it becomes part of the church's culture.

Help church members understand that the Lead Pastor is not implementing a care ministry because he or she doesn't care, but because they **do** care. One person can only be at one place at a time.

5. **A system of care requires people to function together as a team.** People should be trained to not operate in ministry as lone-rangers but rather with a team concept in mind. For the concept to be practical, people should never function on their own, but always as part of the whole. The *Care Revolution* concept includes a built-in system of continuous connection between care pastors, care shepherds, and the leadership as they function together as a solidified team.

It almost seems needless to say, but after we have trained church members, they should be released into ministry by delegating certain responsibilities to them. Although pastors should delegate the ministry of care, they can never totally let go of it either. Although there should be levels of leadership built into a care system, the lead pastor still watches over the outcome of its workings. It should remain a direct outflow of that which is close to their hearts—the care of people. That is the reason we emphatically teach that the Care Pastors do not *replace* the pastors; they *represent* them.

Powerful Dynamics

Once the pastor has effectively set the value of member involvement in their care ministry, the entire concept will thrive and with certainty become compelling. You won't have to explain the basics of the volunteer ministry repeatedly; it will take on a life of its own. Instead, you will be able to continue to build upon the firm foundation of a Scriptural truth that,

Two are better than one because they have a good reward for their labor. For if they fall, one will lift up his companion. But woe to him who is alone when he falls, for he has no one to help him up. Though one may be overpowered by another, two can withstand him. And a threefold cord is not quickly broken (Ecclesiastes 4: 9-12).

Letting Go of a Clergy-Dependency Mindset

As mentioned before, to some pastors the thought of equipping the saints for ministry comes easy, but for others, it takes a little more consideration. It even becomes more perplexing to some when the thought of training church members to be involved in actual congregational care, forms part of the process. It could be downright terrifying for some to think of relinquishing a role that we all have traditionally accepted to be exclusively that of the ordained clergy. It calls for enormous courage to come to the point of shifting ministry of this stature to unlicensed and non-ordained members "who have nothing but a love for Jesus, a heart for people, and a willingness to be taught."[26]

Preparing for Expected Growth

Practical experience has shown that if we provide the proper care for people, as we should, and in particular with the right motive in mind, we will assuredly reach and attract many more individuals. It's the gospel message that reaps people, but it's the *love your neighbor* message that keeps them.

When the implementation of our congregation's care ministry became known in our city, it not only attracted hurting and lonely people but became a catalyst for many who erroneously thought the Church was a closed circle reserved just for an exclusive group of individuals. It furthermore created trust in people's minds who may never previously have responded to the message of the church. The result was that scores of people who were hooked on drugs, alcohol, and other things, had confidence that we cared, and believed in us to help them. Couples whose marriages were on the rocks, parents with rebellious teenagers, people of all ages with broken lives and shattered dreams, showed up because we had become known as the caring place.

As incredible as it may sound, when you apply biblical care, it becomes a powerful incentive for evangelism. I cannot even begin to tell you how many people became devoted followers of Christ just because they knew we were genuine and that each person was valued. Never lose sight of the fact that six out of ten individuals who come

---

26   Carl F. George and Warren Bird, *How to Break Growth Barriers* (Grand Rapids: Baker Books, 2017), 117.

into our churches have already experienced conversion somewhere else. They are like ripe fruit just waiting for us to pick them; they merely need a congregation with people who show they care.

It was this influx of so many people that became one of the main reasons we had to find a way to connect individuals with each other and the church. We realized that if we did not have a workable system, people would fade away and we may never have known about it. And this is where many churches miss it; they never prepare for the expected growth. It's a huge mistake to leave the preparation of your members (to connect with people) until the influx has begun. You have to start training them well in advance in anticipation of the coming harvest. The primary reason for this is that experience has shown it takes more than one person to handle a crop.

It Goes Beyond

If we are serious about multiplying disciples, we have to realize that the role of the pastor should be much broader than that of merely being a lone-shepherd. Carl F. George and Warren Bird in their book, *How to Break Growth Barriers*[27] has an interesting observation. They suggest that if pastors desire to see their churches grow and for disciples to multiply, they should change their roles from being a *sheepherder* (sole-caregiver) to being a *rancher-shepherd* (a developer and coach).

Among other things, George says being a traditional pastor means that he or she is the primary caregiver of the entire church and attempts to meet all expectations by being by trying to be ever-present. He says they consistently think in terms of being more accessible to the church and finding ways to make themselves more available—even when they

---

27   Ibid

272 | THE CARE REVOLUTION

are exhausted. He says that by following this pattern, it provides them with some feeling of satisfaction and makes them feel indispensable. Pastors in this category are often driven by guilt rather than mission.

> The spotlight on their crisis intervention, hospital calls, and other pastoral acts prevents their seeing the support roles church members can provide that are essential to effective care. It is one thing to tell a church member that her husband has died. It is another for friends and relatives to live with that widow through the two years of grieving that she needs to surrender her spouse to death.[28]

Carl George goes on to say that sheepherders tend to see the local church as made up of individual members rather than visualizing ministry done from the perspective of a workforce. Thus, developing people to affect the whole is not part of their persuasion. Progress becomes bottlenecked because sheepherders fail to fulfill a manager's role; they are too busy keeping the work close to themselves. Where this belief exists, churches will just not grow.

By contrast, George says, "the pastor as minister-maker (rancher) gives more significant and more careful attention to organizational needs than to personal and professional needs. Rancher-pastors make sure the flock measurably receives pastoral care, primarily through systems of non-clergy-dependent, mutual self-care. The typical forum for this kind of one-another nurture is a small group . . ."[29]

---

28   Ibid, page 101

29   Ibid, page 106

For care ministry to be applied by members, it is imperative that all in the congregation understand the concept and is never left in the dark. Rancher-pastors "set the expectation that the members of the church will give and receive care among one another. A ministry coach will hold up this standard in such a way that everyone understands this is how they do it."[30]Although our intention is not to replace pastors through our congregational care system, their goal should be to work themselves out of a job by enabling their people to function well without them.

Reasons for Failure

There have been different models of congregational care presented in the past, but most of them failed. The main reasons for failure can be summarized as follows: (i) the workers were not trained and equipped, (ii) the workers were left to do ministry on their own, and (iii) because the concept did not make provision for the caregivers themselves to receive care.

The valuable component of providing nurturing and care for the workers should never be left out of the equation. Carl-Bird underscores this when they say, "... the ministry coach (rancher-pastor) sends people, not one by one—because they would require regular maintenance and nurture—but team by team, so that they can keep themselves nurtured, maintained, and high in morale."[31]

In our model, we provide levels of leadership to ensure that all people receive care, and none are left out.

Where does all that leave us? A pastor and a church have to realize that God may want them to handle many more people than

---

30   Ibid, page 107

31   Ibid, page 108

they are ministering to at present. Being satisfied to remain at the status quo level cannot and should not ever be entertained. The most encouraging truth is the fact that there are undoubtedly many people in the church God wants to use who have the necessary giftedness to provide care to others. All they need is to be trained, acknowledged, and released.

Therefore, it becomes crucial to recognize that we should not only consider those who need care but also bear in mind those in every church who have the giftedness and desire to serve in the body of Christ through providing care to their fellow church members. That means that if we disregard this ministry, we most assuredly also deprive some faithful people of fulfilling their call. Doing so, we stand the chance of losing them to another church where they would be accommodated to function in their calling. This truth makes it evident that every church needs to implement a caring system such as this, regardless of the size of the church. We need to consider both sides of the spectrum: those who *need* care on the one hand, and those who have the giftedness to *provide* care on the other. Both are important, and we should consider both.

A Sheepherder or a Rancher-Pastor

It is entirely conceivable that by shifting paradigms and including their members, pastors and churches can reach more people than they could ever think possible. And here is the bottom line: *Sheepherders* provide all the pastoral care by themselves. They attempt to be everything to everybody and seldom see the big picture. A *rancher-pastors,* on the other hand, remains in their role as shepherd of the flock under Christ but raises up other shepherds out of the membership to provide ongoing congregational care.

If the sheep multiply,
the shepherds should
multiply also!

The rancher does not live within the limitations of today but sees the possibilities beyond present-day confinement. Their fulfillment does not lie within what they can do themselves, but primarily on what they can get done through others. The rancher-pastor always seeks occasions to empower their people and celebrates the expansion of their caring for one another.

> Dr. Peter Wagner says, "The shepherd-mode can function well up to the 200-member barrier, but not above it. Pastors whose job satisfaction is highly dependent on a shepherding ministry are typically small church pastors. A rancher mode can take the church through the 200-member barrier. The essential difference between the sheepherder and the rancher-pastor is not whether they care for the sheep—they are in both cases if things are going as they should. The difference is in who takes care of the sheep. The sheepherder must do it personally (with restrictions); the rancher delegates the pastoral care to others."[32]

This perspective brings us to the realization again that the significant role of a pastor is to train, develop, and equip God's people for the work of ministry. This application will enable them to

---

32   Dr. Peter Wagner, *Church Planting for a Greater Harvest* (Ventura: Regal, 1990), 113.

accomplish more significant ministry through people who will effect ever-widening circles of influence.

> Being a *rancher-pastor* does not mean you are no longer a pastor (shepherd) to the congregation, but it does say that you have a wider-spectrum-vision for caring for the flock and are coaching members to accomplish the task. You remain a shepherd, but you function on a different level. It does not have to do with roles, offices, or calling; it refers to the active application of caring for the sheep entrusted to us most efficiently. It has to do with a mindset more than anything else.

> Of course, we have a choice. We can stick with the *status quo* and continue to provide pastoral care in the way we always have. Or we can lift our horizon, get outside of the box, and be willing to make the shift to a higher potential. There are most likely people in your church God wants to use more significantly who can help you build the church you have always dreamed about, but because the traditional way of doing things has trapped you, it has hindered you from turning those people free to function in God's blessing.

Where You See Yourself

Whether a pastor should change from being a sheep-herder to a rancher-pastor is a personal choice and will mainly depend on their calling and ultimate pastoral goals. It's not for others to determine. Taking either position should not be a prerequisite to implementing a workable system of care. That should be a given. The question is: do you want to stay where you are or do you want to reach for the stars? Answering that question will determine where you will be five years down the road. "God wants to give you a spiritually healthy church with a positive, faith-oriented, biblically sound approach to your community, under Christ, such that if someone joins you, he or she will be significantly better off for having done so."[33]

There is nothing that gets a church off of a plateau or away from stagnation as efficiently and as steadily as getting people involved in ministry. Typically, recession sets in when church members get bored, don't feel needed and have the impression the church seems to be going nowhere. In the business world, they usually change leadership when a company or industry reaches a plateau, and sometimes in the church, it may also be necessary—but it does not have to be that way.

> Stagnation sets in
> when people
> get bored.

We have the great opportunity of relying on the Holy Spirit to reignite new vision and passion on our inside and, through prayerful consideration, begin to steer the church into a fresh, enthusiastic, and dynamic ministry dimension. And I know you, as a leader, will have to become bold! Perhaps you will need to change your entire thinking about looking at the Church and the roles of believers. But this I know: Once people have put their toes into the water of ministry, joy is going to explode in the congregation as they fulfill their calling. To

---

33   Carl F. George and Warren Bird, *How to Break Growth Barriers* (Grand Rapids: Baker Books, 2017), 114.

278 | THE CARE REVOLUTION

positively advance the Kingdom of God it sounds advisable to change our paradigm and shift the focus from the pastor being the sole care provider to instead becoming an equipper, developer, and coach of many care pastors.

Teamwork Makes the Dream Work

Inherited tradition and established church culture have caused many pastors to bow down before the pressure of unreasonable and unscriptural demands and are bending backward to fulfill every expectation. When pastors have to do everything in the church, they become incapable of doing anything else. Studies have shown that the primary root of burnout in many pastor's lives is because of them not being able to say *no* to the demands on their time. This pressure, unfortunately, creates a co-dependency which people abuse and some pastors embrace. The sooner we can change this pattern, the sooner our churches will become healthy and grow.

Jay E. Adams in his excellent book *Shepherding God's Flock* says it like this:

"When a pastor on his own tries to do the work of an entire congregation,

a. He fails because he does not have the blessing of Christ upon this program; he has substituted (well-meaningly perhaps, but none the less highhandedly substituted) a human plan for the divine one.

b. He fails because he does not have the many opportunities and contacts that only the members of his congregation have.

c. He fails because he spreads himself too thin, trying to do too much as one person. It is nothing less than pride for any one individual to think that he is capable of doing what God has said is the work of an entire congregation.

d.   He also fails as pastor-teacher. In spreading himself so thinly over the works of evangelism as well as that of shepherding and teaching, he does none of these things well. His sermons suffer, his members are not cared for, and even the fruit of evangelism usually is minimal.

e.   He fails—and this is the most significant failure of all—because, wittingly or unwittingly, he has disobeyed and thereby dishonored the Chief Shepherd by whom he had been "given" to the Church in order to shepherd and teach so that the sheep might discover, develop, and deploy their own gifts. Thus, he fails to equip each member for his own "work of ministry."[34]

There is too high a demand on churches in this modern-day to be the New Testament churches they were designed to be for us not to break the mold and begin developing our members to being included in actual works of the ministry.

Empowering People

Once the wave of people involvement rises, the flow of blessing is released, and you can't stop people from coming to church unless you do something foolish. As a pastor, you will experience freedom and joy from shared ministry and be motivated beyond description as you see God's people blessed and strengthened by each other. Once they have

---

34   Jay Adams, "Shepherding God's Flock," Zondervan, 1974, 1975. Used by permission of Zondervan. www.zondervan.com.

caught the vision, they will be the ones that will bring the people. As we have heard it often said before, "Shepherds don't produce sheep. It is the sheep that begat sheep."

As more and more of our people were equipped and released, I can remember well how often I stood on the platform of our church seeing how the people were filing into the sanctuary. It sometimes seemed as though a bus had just pulled up and dropped them off. With tears in my eyes and with great gratitude, I would often turn to my wife and say, "from where are all these people coming? It's not because of anything I am doing!"

Church members can reach people whose names the pastor may never even have known. But the truth is that they will never rise beyond the level of the leader's maturity and his or her conviction of releasing people into ministry. It's not always easy to change the paradigm, but once you have tasted the sweetness of the fruit, you will never want to go back.

Dr. John C. Maxwell says, "Everything rises and falls on leadership."

As Goes the Pastor (leader), So Goes the Church.

The truth is that many of your people have gifts, talents, and abilities you may not even know. They have wisdom, insights, and perspectives that we, as credentialed ministers, may not have. But once we blend their skills and perceptions with ours, a potentially explosive situation arises. I cannot see any reason pastors would even think of doing ministry without having their people partner with them.

A visionary pastor is the one who will prioritize his/her time and vision around a system of member-development so they can accomplish more excellent ministry. These pastors always search for opportunities to empower their people, so they can together reach the common goal. The active principle of shared ministry is undoubtedly going to become the catalyst for churches to break through the barriers that have kept them back. Effective pastors these days are not evaluated by what they can do themselves. Their achievements depend on what they can get done through other people. Their fundamental goal is to see how many ministers they can equip and not merely how many members they can gain.

11

THERE IS A SHIFT
GOING ON

Whether we are part of an established congregation or whether we have planted a church, we are all still in some way or another guided by what has customarily been developed over the years before we got where we are today. These long-gone philosophies have wittingly or unwittingly influenced some of our ministry thinking and biased many of our decisions. Unfortunately, many pastors and churches have gotten stuck in that milieu and find it difficult to let go, even though most of these values are no longer relevant to our day.

Loren Mead once said that we need to *reinvent the* Church, and I think he is correct. The changes we need to make are so vast that it won't help us much to merely change the songs we are singing or modify the title of deacons to elders or to stop wearing coats and ties, and start wearing cut-offs and flip-flops, or whatever modest ideas we may configure. It's a paradigm shift that is necessary, and as Mead says, we are going to have to "reinvent" our congregations.

Looking Back

It would, in all fairness, be unreasonable for us to criticize those who have gone before us and find fault with the methods they used in their day. When the early frontiers, as an example, set out from the East Coast of the USA on their way out West, the only form of transportation they had were horses, buggies, ox wagons, etc. Other than walking, there was no other alternative. They traveled over mountain tops, crossed flooded rivers, faced steep and treacherous cliffs, and had to cover unbelievable distances through valleys and deserts. It took them a lifetime to get where they wanted to go, and many never made it. But that was their only known means of travel.

Today, in the twenty-first century, however, if you want to travel from New York to Los Angeles and choose to go on horseback or travel in the *sleep car* of an ox wagon, it won't make any sense. You will be entirely out of touch because there are jet planes these days to get you there in much less time than it takes just to load an ox wagon. Times have changed and so have methods.

Sometimes it appears that many in the church-world are still trying to reach their destiny by yesteryear's approaches and applications. They are stuck in past performance. But if we want our churches to become relevant, we should begin to do some things differently. As the saying goes, "If you want something you've never had; you have to do something you've never done." Sure, we can still go cross-country by horse and buggy, and we may eventually get there. But is that what we want to do? Just because it worked then, certainly does not mean we should still do it the same way today. Life has moved on, and so should we!

From the Pan into the Fire

Let's be careful though; in their quest for bringing change, leaders often decide to jump outside of the proverbial box and deliberately attempt to do everything they can to steer far away from the traditional conducts they have inherited. And I am all for that. But if we're not watchful, it won't take long before we develop a culture of its own and find ourselves in the same position we were in before—stuck in a rut. It may look different and sound different. We may change names, titles, and slogans, avoid religious terminology, and create a non-churchy atmosphere. We can build cute coffee bars in the foyer, and wear skinny jeans, but if we forgot the path we have come, and we avoid looking ahead, we would inevitably be in a groove again—just in a different culture. We should always remind ourselves that we, as the Church, have not yet arrived. We should remain open and innovative but continue to follow the leadership of the Holy Spirit. Let's never change just for the sake of change, but instead, seek to remain relative and valid and contemplate the future.

There's a Shift Going On

I am convinced that this is the Church's finest hour and if we approach it correctly, we are going to see more growth and advancement in the Kingdom of God than ever before. There is a shift that is taking place in the Church, and it's an exciting and healthy shift. Life-giving churches are going to explode in growth, and it's not all going to be transfer-growth either.

World systems are
failing miserably

and people are
losing confidence

The systems of the world are failing miserably, and people are losing trust in the pillars they had once trusted. Their financial system has failed them, the political policies have failed them, their power systems have failed them, and the list goes on. We are facing a financial crisis, a hunger crisis, a housing crisis, a criminal crisis, a moral crisis, a marriage crisis, an education crisis, a political crisis, a constitutional crisis, and who can tell where it will all end?

We do not have the answers to all these questions, but what we do know is that all these factors have caused an unbelievable uncertainty and insecurity in our societies. The mainstays the world has depended upon are coming down with a crash, and the astute are now looking for an established alternative to meet their need, and in their search, they are beginning to discover the only constant that has remained is the Church.

The Church, regardless of its human-induced faults, is still God's chosen channel of blessing and has been for more than 2,000 years. In their search for authenticity, the world is not looking for religion; they are looking for reality. They are in pursuit of power that is greater than their own. They are in search of significance and stability, and if we get our act together, they are going to find it in our churches. But only those churches that are preparing for the coming harvest will benefit from what is about to transpire. Pastors and church leaders must make every effort to build spiritual silos and barns to retain the ingathering when it comes. The Lord of the harvest certainly will not send grain to those churches that have not prepared to take care of the souls.

Sharpening the Saw

Although many people believe the Church has become irrelevant, and some even venture to say that in twenty or so years the Church may most likely not exist, I am unquestionably not there. Although many churches are struggling, I do not believe that we have lost everything. There is hope, and there is a solution, and the Church is becoming more relevant than ever. Pastors and church leaders are awakening to the quickening of the Holy Spirit and are, as Stephen Covey suggests, "sharpening the saw." They are not satisfied to stay with the status quo and are anxiously adjusting to the challenges of the day.

The churches that are making significant headway are those where the leaders are enthusiastically enlisting and equipping their people to be involved in ministry. They are giving the ministry to the people and are investing more and more of their time, energy, and resources in developing and equipping their members, while at the same time, meeting their needs. Management consultant Peter Drucker also believes churches are facing difficult challenges and concludes that those that will survive and thrive in the twenty-first century are those who are "pastoral." He defines *pastoral* as giving attention to the needs of people.[35]

There is entirely no doubt in my mind that there is a definite and positive stirring going on in the Church and the focus is on taking care of the household of faith. This aspect is the only sensible way to create a healthy body, which will be able to reach a hurting and dying world and care for the new babes in Christ. It is entirely possible that we have worked so hard and depleted so much energy in what

---

35   Peter, F. Drucker, *The New Realities* (New York: Harper & Row, 1989), 200.

we have done that we have in the process neglected to take care of the flock. It is quite possible that we have focused our attention so heavy on multiplying our programs and chasing numbers that we have forsaken our Christian duty of paying attention to our brothers and sisters around us. We may have become so attentive to our own necessities that we never see the hurts and pain of those around us in church. To get the Church ready for the most significant harvest of all times, to restore the church to health, and cultivate a loving community, we should discern the Lord's Body and make sure that nobody is losing their strength, nobody is getting afflicted, and none are perishing. Gathering for communion creates the ideal situation for us to pause and pay specific attention to our fellow church members (1 Corinthians 11: 29-30).

Updating the Paradigm

Member-involvement is the dynamic future of the church. One of the primary ways whereby we can get large numbers of people involved in a short span of time is by including them in congregational care. It not only meets a need in the congregation but also brings boundless fulfillment to people who have a desire to minister to people personally. Once we grasp the value, power, and energy of people caring for people, our churches will grow and become what they should. The paradigm needs to shift seriously and quickly from church members supposing that they have *hired* a pastor to do ministry on their behalf. They have forced their pastors to develop an unbiblical standard by doing what the members were supposed to do and unwittingly quenched the life of the church.

Another misconception that has settled in the minds of many of our church members is that they are not capable of doing ministry.

In their minds, the *professionals* are the heroes who should perform *the real ministry*, while the members are merely spectators, watching the experts operate. They think that the pastor's purpose is to *do* ministry while their role is to *receive* ministry. Neither of these viewpoints is correct and describes a church that is out of biblical order. It is creating an "us and them" position instead of a united front of the collaborative ministry. This viewpoint also explains why so many vocational ministers are frustrated, angry, and burnt out. But traditionally it is what we have inherited.

> There is a poor return
> of investment in all
> we are spending

This faulty, unscriptural, and traditional thinking is the reason the amount of energy and resources spent in our churches are not producing matching results. It is frightening to calculate the sums of money we utilize and the working hours we spend in the activities of "running" the church without any noticeable results. It reveals a shocking statistic when you compare the total expenditure of the church to the souls we add to the Kingdom of God at the end of any given year. The results just do not validate the expense! No secular business will survive with such an outcome.

God's plan has always been a comprehensive plan for all believers to be involved in ministry, both vocational and volunteers. As simple as it may sound, the church must rise to power and once again become a living organism and not an institution or a dead organization. The dead bones should live again!

The Church Is Alive, and History Proves It

When I was in school, I disliked history with a passion. To me, it was as useful as a broken coffee pot. I thought it was only an unnecessary burden to try to remember birth dates of people I didn't know and learn about places I didn't like. Who cared about who fought which battle, and why? How wrong I was! Today, I love history and regret that I did not spend more time on the subject. Church history, and especially the Reformation and beyond, gets my attention quickly. I have read many books on the subject.

If we go back to the early years of the church, we will discover that it was not a dead organization. Instead, it was a vibrant, dynamic, living organism. People worked together, prayed together, and worshiped along with great enthusiasm. They helped each other, depended on each other, and cared for one another. Together they experienced the power and presence of God and saw Him perform mighty deeds. The result was that they added significant numbers of people to the church, even daily. What was especially noticeable was the fact that *all* the believers were involved in ministry. There were no such things as *professionals* or some priestly order. They were all ministers, and the church moved ahead with a high power, making tremendous progress in one country after the other.

The Good News swept over Europe like a tsunami of blessing. The Church was operating per God's ordained order, the Holy Spirit was truly at work, and the saints functioned happily with the Gifts they had received from God. The Church powerfully blazed ahead in the way Christ had intended it to when He said, I will build My Church, and the gates of hell shall not prevail against it! (Matthew 16:18)

But over time, some years later, the Evil One devised a plan through the church hierarchal leaders of that time with the intent of stopping the conquering power of the church. The Emperor (Constantine) who had *converted* to Christianity made a decree, called the Edict of Milan. Through this proclamation, he returned the sequestered property that was seized from the Christians back to them and legalized Christianity by advocating that people could become Christians by merely being baptized or joining the church without any act of dedication or commitment.

> An illegitimate
> church that has
> no power and
> no eternal results

At one point, Constantine marched his entire army through a river as a means of baptism and then declared them all to be Christians. This action resulted in an *illegitimate* church that had no power and no eternal results. The requirement of forgiveness of sin and life transformation through the death of Christ was made null and void. Repentance was no longer obligatory to be part of the Church, and by order of Constantine, they removed the ridicule and persecution from the followers of Christ. All people were required to do was *join the church.* Of course, the church exploded in growth—membership was the favorite thing around—but in the process, the church lost its effectiveness.

History tells us that Constantine then came up with what he thought was a brilliant idea of appointing leaders to oversee these substantial religious gatherings and to lead the services. This position seemed to have been the answer. However, slowly but steadily it resulted in the ministry being taken away from the believers (saints) and placed into the hands of these *expert leaders*. It led to the eventual loss of the power of member-involvement. It was no longer a vibrant body and a shining light, but rather a lifeless religious organization that had no more purpose than a watch on a dead man's arm. This juncture became the moment when the pendulum swung far away from the involvement of the Saints, to where the ministers were *doing* ministry, and the members were *receiving* ministry. The Church gradually took on more of the form of an organization than a living organism. Church members were declared unqualified to read or understand the Bible, and ultimately only the priests were regarded capable of handling God's Word.

Ever since that time the Holy Spirit has been prompting the church to get back to the full understanding of ministry, as Christ had intended; not only by a select group of people but by the entire body of Believers working together. There can never be two classes of Christians—the priests and the members.

The First Reformation

The First Reformation was God partly dealing with the church to return to the essence of ministry, which meant that all who are Christ's should be involved in ministry. God was not through with the Church then, and He is not through with it now in this twenty-first century either. Looking back, we can see today that, in general terms, *the Restoration* was the reinstatement of the priesthood of the believer with everything it entails.

God gave Martin Luther spiritual insight into the truth (or error) of his day. He realized that the Church was no longer living up to its Godly expectation of ministry by all believers and was also much disturbed by the fact that people were made to understand that they could find forgiveness of their sin through their works by applying some form of penance.

Even more disturbing was the belief they promulgated that ordinary believers had no free access to God and was required to go through an earthly priest to do so. This viewpoint virtually meant that the people did not come to God on the merit of faith in God, but by way of the priests. Luther believed the Church had perverted the doctrine of redemption and grace.

> After an extended period of religious doubts and guilt at what he saw as his failure to obey God's Law, Luther found relief around 1518 through a sudden conviction that Justification came through Faith (and not by works). He believed that salvation is a divine gift of grace; that Christ represents God's forgiving mercy, and that the soul, free from the burden of guilt, may serve God with a joyful obedience. Luther drew up the Ninety-Five Theses and fastened them on the door of the Castle Church in Wittenberg, on October 31, 1517.[36]

This action of Luther gave birth to the restoration of the Church which led to the Protestant Movement. With all and everything that was in him, Luther roared against the posturing and domination of those who functioned as priests in an unscriptural way, and even more so, to the detriment of the believers. Luther believed that the Bible was the only valid authoritative. He understood that all believers are also priests and therefore have the freedom to approach God through Jesus

---

36   Merriam-Webster's Encyclopedia of World Religions (Merriam-Webster Incorporated, 1999), 672 (Parenthesis added).

Christ, the High Priest, and did not need an earthly priest as mediator. In the same vein, he came to understand that all of God's people should be involved in ministry. *The Priesthood of all Believers was a cardinal principle of the reformation of the 16th century.*[37]

The biblical truth that all believers are priests denied the validity of a select elite priestly class within the church. The Reformation liberated the believers from the oppression and timidity of the current church order.

> "All Christians," says Luther, "are truly of the spiritual estate, and there is no difference among them, save of office alone. As St. Paul says, we are all one body, though each member does its own work, to serve the others. This is because we have one baptism, one gospel, one faith, and are all Christians alike…"[38]

John Calvin stated that Christ ". . . Once for all offered a sacrifice of eternal expiation and reconciliation; now, having also entered the sanctuary of heaven, He intercedes for us. In Him, we are all priests (Rev. 1:6; cf. 1 Peter 2:9), but to offer praises and thanksgiving, in short, to offer ourselves and ours to God. It was His office alone to appease God and atone for sins by his offering."[39]

I also found the following statement John Calvin made so fascinating that it is noteworthy: "Based on Calvin's formation,

---

37   Ibid. p.885

38   Philipp Schaff, "History of The Christian Church," Retrieved from http://www.ccel.org/s/schaff/history/7ch01.html.

39   "The Priesthood of All Believers," Grace Valley Christian Center (n.d.), http://www.gracevalley.org/sermon_trans/1996/Priesthood.html.

the priesthood of all believers emphasizes the participation of the entire Christian community in Christ's ministry. To confess Christ's name to others is the believers' **prophetic** task. To pray for their salvation is the **priestly** function. To disciple people is the noble **mission** of the believers. Apparently, Calvin's concept of the universal priesthood of believers provides a theological foundation for the ministry. Furthermore, his formulation of the concept encourages ministry involvement of every member of the body of Christ."[40]

It is interesting to note that during the First Reformation the church gave the *Bible* back to the people and restored both the doctrine of justification by faith and the priesthood of all believers. Looking back, we will regretfully discover that the position of the Priesthood of the Believer, *as* it pertains to *ministry involvement*, never came to its full right. It was only many years later that some aspects thereof came to fruition. For the past 1700 years, the Holy Spirit has been nudging the church to bring full restitution to this paramount function within the Body of Christ.

The Church in the Twenty-First Century

The good news is that there is presently a renewed unction of the Holy Spirit at work, awakening the Church with greater force to get the ministry back into the hands of all the people of God.

Findley Edge said, "The church is facing problems because its work is being done by the wrong people."

---

40   HTTP://www.awf.nu/en/Priesthood-of-all-Believers (Emphasis added).

There is a noticeable shift of ministry-responsibility taking place. Pastors and leaders of life-giving churches, along with their congregants alike, are realizing that the Church can only flourish when we do ministry through the proper working of each part (or member) of the body of Christ. Utilizing the giftedness and availability of all the saints is God's way of building the Church. Today, churches are breaking free from their encumbrances and releasing people to become actual priests within the body of Christ.

Every believer has a vital role to play in God's plan for the Church. No one has been called to be a spectator in the grandstands or a casual passenger on the bus. When a person is part of the covenant of grace, he or she functions with a purpose, and that goal is always to glorify God and do His work on this earth. And the magnificence of this is that God has given each believer a significant gift that fits into the overall working of the congregation. What is also essential is to note that not every person necessarily receives the same gift(s) and will therefore not necessarily fulfill the same function or be involved in the same ministry. That is why it is so essential for us to provide the opportunities for people to get involved in many diverse ways. 1 Corinthians 12:7 states, "A spiritual gift is given to each of us so we can help each other" (NLT).

1 Corinthians 12 verses 4-30 gives us an expanded description of how each member functions in his or her assigned ministry role and underscores the importance of each task as it works together in the Body. What is striking in this teaching that Paul gives, is that there is no such thing as more important or less important gifts or functions within the body of Christ. They are all important. You do not have to have an official title or job

description to operate in any form of ministry in the church as a believer.

Pastors and
ministers are not
necessarily synonymous

We often say *Every Believer is a Minister,* and that is, of course, correct, but we need to understand that it does not mean that every believer is a Pastor. As the Holy Spirit is refreshing the involvement of believers in ministry, we should be careful not to see *pastor* and *minister* as synonymous in this sense. *Pastors* as mentioned in Ephesians 4:11 are those specifically called into vocational ministry, have been trained and taught, and have been ordained by the laying on of hands. They have an important task of shepherding the flock and equipping people for ministry. *Minister*, on the other hand, includes all who are God's people that are involved in serving in some capacity of ministry.

In that same vein, we realize that while all believers are ministers, it does not mean that all believers are necessarily *leaders* either. Leadership is a gift, through which such person guides others to function in their roles of ministry to reach the common goal. What is quintessential here is that God has set each believer to operate in the body of Christ as it pleases Him.

Each body, whether it be a physical body, or an organizational body has a head, which indicates leadership. And each such entity can only have one head because a body with more than one head is a monster. I am saying that to clarify that although we are all ministers, there are most definitely different roles and offices. There is such a thing as a leader among the leaders. It has nothing to do with importance; it all entails function (Read again 1 Corinthians 12). One member cannot operate without the other, whether it's the head, the heart, or the hand. They are all needed to complete the body.

The Day of the Saints

There is every indication that the twenty-first century has become the season of the next *Reformation,* and in this whole process, God is restoring the Church to its fullness. We have arrived at what some scholars are calling *The Day of the Saints!* I stated earlier that during the First Reformation the Church gave the *Bible* back to the people, but now in this present-day Reformation, the Church is giving the *ministry* back to the people. This action is evoking anticipation as few other movements in the Church. Today, in many parts of the world, pastors are once again equipping their people and are enthusiastically giving the ministry back to them—and the results are remarkable!

And when I say they are giving the *ministry* back to the people I don't mean just singing in the choir, shaking hands at the door, receiving the offering, or taking care of the babies in the nursery. Not that these things are not necessary. They are essential and valuable, and people should keep doing it—and we thank God for them! But by "ministry," however, I mean a whole lot more than mere volunteering.

For most people in most of our churches, showing up, singing, praying, giving in the offering, and doing some act of kindness from time-to-time was their extent of ministry. And truthfully, in most of our churches, that was all the church expected from their congregants (and many did not even do that!) So, they did what they understood to be their duty and were consequently satisfied. People did not know how to function differently. What they were doing was the way the church operated. And amazingly enough, the church did grow, despite this awkward style of functioning. But it's no longer working. Times have changed, and people are chomping at the bit to become involved in the ministry of their churches.

Actual Acts of Ministry

By "giving the ministry back to the people," I categorically mean that church members are the ones who are going to be doing actual acts of ministry. They should be winning the lost, discipling new converts, going outside the walls of the church, praying for the sick, teaching the Word, going on mission trips, caring for the flock, doing great exploits for God, planting churches, and the list goes on. I believe that it's through membership involvement that the next great move of God is going to be released. And I am not implying that it's only going to be a time of refreshing or even a revival; it's instead going to be a powerful ministry movement that will shake the world.

Market Place Ministry is going to be a dynamism of the Holy Spirit that's going to inspire people to enter the business community and touch people in every stratum of life. It is already powerfully taking place in many areas and is poised to accelerate exponentially. We have to be aware of this and be fully prepared. The identifying characteristic of this ministry is to function outside the walls of the church, seeking the lost through innovative methods and unique places.

Martin Luther, way back when, seemed to have had a good grasp of laity involvement when he said, "The idea that service to God should have to do only with a church, altar, singing, reading, sacrifice, and the like is without a doubt but the worst trick of the devil. How could the devil have led us more efficiently astray than by the narrow conception that

service to God takes place only in church and by works done
therein . . ." [41]

Equipping and Discipleship

We all realize the importance of discipleship—the process of
making believers become fully committed followers of Christ. Pastors
and leaders are becoming more and more aware of this all-important
calling of the Church and are delving into reading, researching, and
studying so they can implement this part of the *Great Commission.* In our
quest for doing what is right in our process of discipleship, we should
make sure that we are not just providing *information* but even more
so, *transformation.* By this I mean that we should not only provide our
people with spiritual, or biblical content week after week, that is void
of developing them to reach their spiritual goal of becoming ministers.

Sometimes pastors come up with the most excellent biblically
sound teachings, well prepared with notes and PowerPoint, but there
is no progression. They continually move from one subject to the
other. In other words, they are faithfully feeding their people, but they
are not taking them from point A to point B to finally get to Z. In
this way, the people become overfed and spiritually obese. They are
enjoying good food but are getting no spiritual exercise.

Instead of only providing information, if Pastors would instead
develop a defined process of transformational discipleship to where
they take their people from a starting point and gradually move them
through the Word with an objective of ministry involvement in mind,
it will make all the difference. This process then opens the door for

---

41   Martin Luther, quoted in *Theological Foundations of Bible Study, Train Two
       Leaders Manual,* Board of Parish Education, The Lutheran Church, Missouri
       Synod, 25.

people to be equipped for the work of the ministry and progressing to spiritual maturity. This development is the way a church grows and becomes relevant.

We must understand that equipping the saints for ministry is absolutely an integral part of the discipleship process. I am convinced that unless a person has been trained, empowered, and released into ministry, the discipleship cycle is not complete. It starts with cultivating (nourishing) new believers, taking them through spiritual growth, and teaching them the precepts and concepts of the Word, which should culminate in each believer being part of the collaborated efforts of the church (ministry involvement).

Functions of a Healthy Church

Developing believers to become ministers in the church has become essential. The New Testament teaches us in several places that all believers have received gifts and talents given by the Holy Spirit. We do not accept these as accolades, but instead with the purpose of utilizing them in building up the body of Christ as we work together in reciprocal interdependence.

In the book of Ephesians Paul describes how the Church should function and puts everything into perspective for us. It will help us to pause for a moment and digest the full implication of this statement:

And He Himself gave some to be apostles, some prophets, some evangelists, and some pastors and teachers, for the equipping of the saints for the work of ministry, for the edifying of the body of Christ, till we all come to the unity of the faith and the knowledge of the Son of God, to a perfect man, to the measure of the stature of the fullness of Christ;

that we should no longer be children, tossed to and fro and carried about with every wind of doctrine, by the trickery of men, in the cunning craftiness of deceitful plotting, but, speaking the truth in love, may grow up in all things into Him who is the head—Christ— from whom the whole body, joined and knit together by what every joint supplies, according to the effective working by which every part does its share, causes growth of the body for the edifying of itself in love (Ephesians 4:11-16).

1. Paul mentions five particular gifts in these verses. Sometimes they are referred to as the Five-Fold Ministry Gifts, and sometimes as the Equipping Gifts (verse 11).

2. It is the task of the Five-Fold Gifted ministers to equip the saints for their work of the ministry (verse 12).

3. They should, however, also personally remain involved in the work of their God-given ministry (verse 12).

4. Their duties also further include the edification of the body of Christ, establishing the unity of faith, undergirding sound doctrine, developing (perfecting) the Church in the fullness of Christ, encourage maturity, and promoting cooperation between the members of the church.

Verse 11 says that Christ *gave* these people to the Church, which means they are *gifts* to the body of Christ. It is noteworthy that Christ gave specific *people* with specific callings as gifts to the Church to lead and equip the rest of the body of Christ. They were not given to do all the work of the ministry or to get all the attention of the worshipping saints. This statement also lets us understand clearly that these people (gifts) are not hirelings of a congregation, but emphatically God's gift to the church who we should receive as such. This perspective flies in the face of so many people who say, "We have hired a pastor to do the work of the ministry." There are few greater deceptions than this to stifle the health and growth of any church.

It is the responsibility of those in the Five-Fold ministry (apostles, prophets, evangelists, pastors, and teachers) to not only fulfill their particular calling but also furthermore to have an obligation of equipping the saints (church members) to also function in these respective ministries. It is the proper working of each part of the Body of Christ that makes the Church grow.

1. Apostle – develops a church to be Apostolic
2. Prophet – prepares a church to be prophetic
3. Evangelist – trains a church to be evangelistic
4. Pastor – equips a church to be pastoral
5. Teacher—teaches a church to be educational

Practical Application

When we consider the Evangelist as an example, we realize that this person's gift is to *evangelize,* which means to win souls and lead people to Christ. But his or her added responsibility is to teach the *believers* then how they too might be involved in the work of evangelism. It does not mean these people become *vocational evangelists*; it states they have become soul winners. We deprive the body of Christ when we do not equip and develop our people according to the giftedness God has graciously bestowed upon us in the Five-Fold Ministry.

The same principle applies to Pastors. They should shepherd, lead, and guide the flock, but then, in addition, go beyond, and teach the saints (church members) how to care for one another. I am convinced that by our not completing the cycle of ministry-development we have hurt the mission of the Church, ourselves, and assuredly our members. Restraining believers from the ministry has been the most ingenious ploys of the devil.

There is a reason God gave unique equipping gifts to some people and designated specific ministries to all members of the local church. There should always be a healthy balance between the different gifts and ministries as given by the Holy Spirit. What should be understood is that there is no such thing as a two-tier caste classification. There are different ministries with different roles and functions, but all form one body with one singular goal. This view is the only way the Church will be efficient, and the Body will become mature.

Katartismos

Remember, in chapter four I made mention of the word *katartismos*? So, before I close this section, allow me to go back there and reflect on it with you. *Katartismos* is indeed a fascinating word which describes a fitting analogy when applied to the process of development we are considering regarding the equipping of the saints.

Let's go back for a moment to the Scripture we referenced previously: "When He had gone a little farther from there, He saw James, the son of Zebedee, and John his brother, who also were in the boat mending their nets" (Mark 1:19). In the Greek, the action-word for "mending" is the word "*Katartismos*" which means: to *restore,* to *prepare,* or to *equip* (make ready). What is striking here is that it is the same word Paul uses in Ephesians 4:12 when he describes the process of equipping or *preparing* the saints for the work of the ministry. Since the Bible describes the Church as *the Body* of Christ, it is interesting to realize that the same word, *Katartismos,* is also used to describe the action of a doctor setting a broken bone.

When we look at this interesting word, *katartismos*, it becomes thought-provoking:

1. "Mending their nets" describes the enduring process of the disciples repairing their nets and mending the holes which were usually caused by sharp rocks in the ocean. They obviously did this, so fish would not get away, and they consequently do not lose the catch. This task was essential in as much as it makes no sense to cast nets into the water knowing there are holes and tears in them.

This tedious process of mending nets serves as an excellent metaphor when we compare it to our responsibility of preparing people for ministry, especially congregational care. Through our ministry of caring for others, we are mending the nets so none of our members fall through the cracks and we likewise not lose one single soul through our evangelism efforts. The church will not grow if we do not mend the nets and close the holes. In spite of the challenge to develop a system of care, we cannot leave the task undone.

2. "Setting a broken bone" describes the procedure of a physician adjusting a bone and setting it back into its proper position with the intent of it functioning as it

should. A broken bone will not correctly heal if the physician does not place it back into its rightful position and will subsequently cause the whole body to hurt.

The description of setting a bone is a fitting analogy of restoring church members back into their correct positions in the body of Christ to function as they should. It refers to a process of restoration, healing, and recovery.

3. "Equipping" as used in the mentioned verses relates to preparing the nets so that they will function effectively during the next operation. The fisherman just cannot afford to cast their nets into the sea if they have not first prepared them for the task. Not only should the holes be sewn up, but the entire functioning of the net should be evaluated to ensure a successful outcome.

This application is another apt description that defines our obligation to equip (prepare) our people for ministry thoroughly. It is by developing them that people can function in the gifts God has given them. Prepared church members are the catalysts for preventing people from falling through the cracks or slipping through the ever-daunting back door.

Let's just take a moment and take a closer look at what "mending"
or **"equipping" teaches us?**

The purpose of the fishermen mending their nets is to increase the effectiveness of their efforts. It is not a waste of time. In fact, the more time they spend preparing their nets, the more efficient they will be in preserving the catch when they are out fishing. Preparing people for ministry is undoubtedly tedious, but it is time well spent. It serves no purpose to spend all our time, resources, and energy on trying to build the Kingdom of God, but never prepare the people to be effective in retaining the harvest.

1. **Preparation is a Continual Process.** Fishers never quit mending their nets. It is never a completed task. When they pull in the nets, their first responsibility, after taking care of the catch, is to fix the tears caused by the rocks and other instruments which occurred during their mission. This repeated task makes us understand that nets are always under construction. They continually need mending.

   Juxtaposing that reality over our notion of preparing people for ministry, we understand that equipping people is likewise an ongoing task. A significant portion of a pastor's responsibility is to develop the people, which is a job that never ends. The product is never final. There's never a time when a person is wholly equipped or entirely discipled. For the sincere believer, the school is never out.

2. **Preparation denotes action.** Fishers don't mend their nets just to make them look attractive or put them on display. Instead, as soon as they have fixed the nets, they go out fishing again. The whole intention of "mending" is to prepare the nets for more work.

Being equipped for ministry likewise is not merely to
gain more knowledge, or even to receive a certificate—
but rather to become more functional in the church.
The purpose of equipping people for ministry is for
them to be active within the body of Christ. It has
little value if we train people and then not use them in
ministry.

Likewise, the reason for setting a bone is so it can be "fitly joined"
and function as it was created to operate. It's not meant to be a cosmetic
fix merely. It is evident that broken bones cause pain and discomfort
and stifle the growth of the body. When the physician sets the bone,
he knows the whole body is eventually going to benefit. The analogy
is striking when we realize that people within the body of Christ who
are out of place, have not only become dysfunctional but even more
so, causes the entire body to hurt. The Bible says, "And if one member
suffers, all the members suffer with it;" (1 Corinthians 12:26).

3. **Preparation Defines Extension.** When the fishermen
    mend their nets, they are doing so with the intent of
    going out to catch more fish. They do not sit back and
    keep counting how many fish they had caught. They
    desire to continue with their passion. They know that
    the more time they spend in preparation, the more
    significant their results would be in the future.

So, why do we as pastors equip the saints, and why do
we prepare them? We do it, so our people can become
extensions of our ministry and fulfill Christ's Mission.

Our people can go where we can't go, they can reach people we may never be able to reach, and they can alleviate the pain of hurting people whom we have never met. As pastors, we can only be at one place at a time, but by taking time in preparing our people, we duplicate our efforts and live out the expectation of the Church being a living organism.

12

LET THE BIBLE SPEAK

It would be senseless for us to promote such a compelling concept and not have a biblical foundation upon which to build. Describing a scriptural basis will be our focus in this chapter. I feel convinced that most pastors, and even church members, will appreciate us focusing on this crucial phase of the journey. As we establish the biblical principles of the *Care Revolution,* we need to clarify that this concept, and its local church application, the *Care Ministry Network,* does not advocate any denomination's doctrines or systems of belief. There are no hidden dogmatic tenets that could be offensive to anyone. Christian churches of all persuasions can therefore safely implement the principles of this concept. We hold that "loving your neighbor as yourself," cannot, and should not be legislated, but preferably applied as the actual expression of who we are as the Church.

We are going to touch on some diverse aspects of this concept that may potentially raise an eyebrow or evoke some questions. One such issue may arise, not so much from the idea itself, but rather from questioning whether it is biblically correct to have non-credentialed people serving in the role of pastoral care towards other members. Others again may wonder whether the church should even actually be concerned about spending time and resources on caring for established church members who have been part of the church for a long time. Pastors often assume they should instead exclusively devote their time and energy on first knocking on every door in the community before they would even think of attending to those who are already in the church—other than for crisis moments. Now that is irrational. No church will ever arrive at the place of having knocked on every door in their community. That goal will never be reached, for many reasons.

While we concur and underscore that winning the lost and making disciples are the mission of the Church we cannot, and should not, neglect the whole counsel of God, which includes ministering to the entire being of humankind. It is, in fact, impossible to separate the ministry of care from the process of spiritual development. We do not, however, advocate a Christian elitism where only Christians matter to God and that we should direct all our efforts exclusively to them either. Evangelism, discipleship, and caring go hand in hand.

When Jesus initially called Peter, He said, "Follow Me, and I will make you (a Fisher) of men" (Matthew 4:19). Jesus called him to catching people (evangelism) before He called him into caring for the sheep (pastoral care). This method strikes a compelling balance between the two ministries: "Win them and nurture them!" We should never have to decide whether we are going to *reap* people or whether we are going to *keep* them. It's not a matter of either-or, it's a matter of both.

Scripture does indeed place a heavy emphasis on taking care of the flock and therefore needs to be underscored as being a vital ministry in the local church. When people come to Christ and become part of the

Church, they can readily accept that they would be loved, accepted, prayed for, and encouraged. After all, that is the charge Peter gave to the church leaders in 1 Peter 5:1-4.

The Early Church

Acts 6: 1-7 is a vivid picture of a local church finding themselves in a critical situation. This account describes the challenge set before the leadership in the early church and how they handled the situation. The church was multiplying, and with growth came difficulties the leaders may not initially have fathomed. Some of the members became disgruntled about the fact that all the people were not receiving adequate care. We see in this account that when they confronted the Apostles with the issue, these did not send the people away by saying, "You have been part of the church long enough, take care of yourselves! We have to look out only for those yet to be saved." Instead, they recognized the need and put a plan of action into motion. And what they put into place became a model for us to follow to this day. Naturally, they did not reject the importance of spiritual values either. We should always have a healthy balance of ministry.

> Not much
> has changed
> since then

It is incredible, but it still holds true today in the modern church. As soon as a church begins to grow, challenges always loom up. As I have heard it said, "Every level has its devil." Make no mistake, my friend, the price of growing a church is hard work. It doesn't come easy, and it doesn't happen without a price tag attached to it either. But the result and the abundant fruit are worth it all. Once everyone and everything is in place, there can be no greater joy in the whole wide world.

The people in the early church, described in Acts 6, did the right thing and referred the identified problem to those who could effectively deal with the problem—the leadership. It still amazes me to see how God has placed particular ministry-gifts in place within the Body of Christ. They are all necessary and of equal importance. Members have their functions, and leaders have their roles

The Apostles recognized the problem, defined their personal responsibilities as spiritual leaders, and then appointed deacons (ministers) from among the believers to provide the necessary care. This action proved to be successful. Everyone was satisfied, there was peace among the people, and the outcome was enormous growth in the church. The people could not do it on their own, and neither could the leaders. Both elements were required.

Let's follow the steps in Acts Chapter Six:
1. The church begins to grow
2. Murmuring arises
3. They identify the problem
4. They prioritize the ministry
5. Church members (laity) are appointed to do the ministry
6. The clergy commissioned them
7. They implemented their ministry, and
8. A revival was the result.

When the entire church functions in the biblical way it was intended to, and there is divine order, peace will prevail, and a healthy church will be the outcome. It is when churches function outside of the order of the New Testament that they experience strife, tension builds up, and power struggles develop.

Acts 2:42 gives us great insight into what the primary emphasis of the Early Church was. It says, "They spent their time learning from the apostles, and they were like family to each other. They also broke bread and prayed together" (CEV). We can safely say today that the believers in the Early Church lived *in community.*

The people's focus was:
1. Teaching
2. Caring
3. Fellowship (Community)
4. Breaking bread (Communion), and
5. Praying.

Today we have complicated everything so much that people do not understand the actual value of ministry. People are busier than ever before, and our packed church programs are hindering the effectiveness of our ministry. The more significant problem lies in the fact that our busyness is robbing us of the opportunity to consider our fellow church family.

The New Testament Outlook
The Scriptures make it clear that the Lord, Jesus Christ has high expectations of believers to take care of "the household of faith." We will do well to discover these truths. After all, people are the ones for

whom He gave His life. I cannot for one moment believe that Christ was concerned only about their salvation, and then for them to not have a warm, loving family to take care of them. That is the reason Jesus established the mandate for Peter, the Elders, and finally the Church-at-large, to care for the flock before He ascended to Heaven.

In evaluating the scriptural validity of taking care of God's people is emphatically stated in the New Testament and was declared as a high priority by Jesus as well as some of the chief Apostles.

Let's briefly look at some of the statements:

1.   The mandate Jesus gave us: "A new commandment I give to you, that you love one another; as I have loved you, that you also love one another" (John 13:34).

2.   The Lord's Prayer: "I do not pray for the world but for those whom You have given Me" (John 17:9).

3.   The charge Jesus gave us: "Take care of My sheep" (John 21:6).

4.   Peter's exhortation: "Be shepherds of God's flock that is under your care…not because you must, but because you are willing, as God wants you to be…eager to serve…being examples to the flock" (1 Peter 5:2 NIV).

5.   Paul's admonition: "Keep watch over yourselves and all the flock of which the Holy Spirit has made you overseers. Be shepherds of the church of God, which he bought with his own blood" (Acts 20:28 NIV).

These scriptures, as examples, lay a solid foundation for taking care of the people that God has entrusted to us. Looking carefully at each of these verses will enlighten us to the depth of this vital ministry and helps us to evaluate the priority it should enjoy in the local church.

It is striking, for instance, in point #2 above, that Jesus, who came to die for the world as a ransom for sinners, in this crucial moment was not praying for the world, but instead found it necessary to concentrate on those the Father had already given Him. It certainly does not mean that Jesus did not care about the world, but in His Priestly Prayer, Jesus spends time upholding them that have committed to Him. There is a time to concentrate on the lost, but then there is a time to focus on those He has already given us.

Let's further consider some pertinent verses to establish the authenticity of congregational care:

It is true that the Bible interprets itself. We never base truth on one single scripture alone. There always should be more references in different places given by various authors of the Bible to constitute the essence of a passage. Let's, therefore, look at a few selected verses on this subject, including those we have mentioned before so we can have them all together. As a useful tool, we will take one verse at a time and then use *different translations* for clarity and comparison's sake to consider the particular truth contained in them. Take time to consider each translation; it will truly enrich your understanding of the necessity of providing care to the congregation.[42]

---

42   I do not intend this specific portion of the chapter to be casual reading. I propose this information to be primarily geared towards pastors and leaders (including small group leaders) plus those who desire to make a more in-depth study of the Scriptural validation. See it more as a reference tool.

Galatians 6:10:

KJV. "As we have therefore opportunity, let us do good unto all men, especially unto them who are of the household of faith."

NIV. "Let us do good to all people, especially to those who belong to the family of believers."

WENT. "So then, when we can, we should do good to all people. But most of all, we should do it to those who are in God's family."

MSG. "So, let's not allow ourselves to get fatigued doing good. At the right time, we will harvest a good crop if we don't give up or quit. Right now, therefore, every time we get the chance, let us work for the benefit of all, starting with the people closest to us in the community of faith."

CEV. "We should help people whenever we can, especially if they are followers of the Lord."

NCV. "When we have the opportunity to help anyone, we should do it. But we should give special attention to those who are in the family of believers."

NIRV. "So, when we can do good to everyone, let us do it. Let us make a special point of doing good to those who belong to the family of believers."

1 Peter 5:2.

NIV. "Be shepherds of God's flock that is under your care, serving as overseers—not because you must, but because you are willing, as God wants you to be; not greedy for money, but eager to serve."

NKJV. "Shepherd the flock of God, which is among you, serving as overseers, not by compulsion but willingly, not for dishonest gain but eagerly."

MSG. "I have a special concern for you church leaders. I know what it's like to be a leader, in on Christ's sufferings as well as the coming glory. Here's my concern: that you care for God's flock with all the diligence of a shepherd. Not because you must, but because you want to please God. Not calculating what you can get out of it but acting spontaneously. Not bossily telling others what to do, but tenderly showing them the way."

AMP. "Tend (nurture, guard, guide, and fold) the flock of God that is [your responsibility], not by coercion or constraint, but willingly; not dishonorably motivated by the advantages and profits [belonging to the office], but eagerly and cheerfully."

CEV. "Just as shepherds watch over their sheep, you must watch over everyone God has placed in your care. Do it willingly in order to please God, and not simply because you think you must. Let it be something you want to do, instead of something you do merely to make money."

NIRV. "Be shepherds of God's flock, the believers who are under your care. Serve as their leaders. Don't serve them because you have to. Instead, do it because you want to. That's what God wants you to do. Don't do it because you want to get more and more money. Do it because you really want to serve."

WENT. "Take good care of God's people. They have been given to you to care for. Do this, not because you must do it, but because you want to please God."

John 21:16

WENT. "He asked him the second time, `Simon, son of John, do you love me?' Peter said, `Yes, Lord. You know that I like you. I am your friend.' Jesus said to him, `Take care of my sheep.'"

MSG. "He then asked a second time, 'Simon, son of John, do you love me?' 'Yes, Master, you know I love you.' Jesus said, 'Shepherd my sheep.'"

NKJV. "He said to him again a second time, 'Simon, son of Jonah, do you love Me?' He said to Him, 'Yes, Lord; You know that I love You.' He said to him, 'Tend My sheep.'"

Acts 20:28

NKJV. "Therefore, take heed to yourselves and to all the flock, among which the Holy Spirit has made you overseers, to shepherd the church of God which He purchased with His own blood."

MSG. "Now it's up to you. Be on your toes—both for yourselves and your congregation of sheep. The Holy Spirit has put you in charge of these people—God's people they are—to guard and protect them. God himself thought they were worth dying for."

WENT: "The Holy Spirit has made you leaders over his people. Watch yourselves. Like one who takes care of his sheep, so you must take care of the church people. They are the Lord's people. He gave his blood for them."

John 13:34

NKJV. "A new commandment I give to you, that you love one another; as I have loved you, that you also love one another."

MSG. "Let me give you a new command: Love one another. In the same way, I loved you; you love one another. This is how everyone will recognize that you are my disciples—when they see the love you have for each other."

A new commandment I give you (My disciples): Love one another (Parentheses added).

John 17:9

NIV: "I pray for them (My disciples). I am not praying for the world, but for those you have given me" (Parentheses added).

NLT: "My prayer is not for the world, but for those you have given me, because they belong to you."

AMP. "I am praying for them. I am not praying (requesting) for the world, but for those, You have given Me."

We will be most successful in developing healthy churches when we discern the hurts and needs of people more closely. "God has made the body, so more care is given to the parts that need it most. This is so the body will not be divided into parts. All the parts care for each other. If one part of the body suffers, all the other parts suffer with it. If one part is given special care, the other parts are happy" (1 Corinthians 12: 24-26).

Even Ephesians 4:11-16 emphasizes the vital role of believers who are in the household of faith. In these verses, the Five-Fold Ministers are called to prepare God's people for the work of the ministry. And surprising enough, the purpose is not solely for evangelism, outreach, discipleship, or even missions. The goal of this equipping is to build up the body of Christ, to promote unity among the believers, and bring them to spiritual maturity.

And he gave the apostles, the prophets, the evangelists, the shepherds and teachers, to equip the saints for the work of ministry, for building up the body of Christ, until we all attain to the unity of the faith and of the knowledge of the Son of God, to mature manhood, to the measure of the stature of the fullness of Christ, so that we may no longer be children, tossed to and fro by the waves and carried about by every wind of doctrine, by human cunning, by craftiness in deceitful schemes. Rather, speaking the truth in love, we are to grow up in every way into him who is the head, into Christ, from whom the whole body, joined and held together by every joint with which it is equipped, when each part is working properly, makes the body grow so that it builds itself up in love (Ephesians 4:11-16 ESV).

Paul helps us to understand the importance of putting a process of ministry into place for people to grow spiritually and to develop their spiritual gifts for ministry.

- These verses in Ephesians 4 show us:
- The Lord has given particular equipping gifts to the church (apostles, prophets, evangelists, pastors, and teachers) to
- Equip, develop, and prepare God's people (the saints) for works of service (ministry), to
- Build up the body of Christ,
- Establish unity of the faith,
- Increase the knowledge of the Son of God,
- Reach maturity, and to
- Reach (attain) to the whole measure of the fullness of Christ—which means that the body should function in proper order.

Every church must have a solid strategy to equip their people for ministry, which in our genre is to take care of one another. If it's not applied intentionally, it won't happen. When the Apostle Paul describes this process and refers to the body of Christ being "built up," he has something like a construction team in mind that is building a house and regularly maintaining it.

A simple, free translation of Ephesians 4: 11-15 may read as follows:

Jesus Christ Himself selected some people in the Church to function as apostles, prophets, evangelists, pastors, and teachers to coach the team how to build and maintain a spiritual house; encouraging them to work together and educating them to understand more about the principles of Jesus Christ—to the point where they become skillful and function, as they should. The reason for this is so that every member will mature and grow up, know the truth, be able to stand firm against the aggression of divisive people and to take up their responsibilities with the rest of the team (By Author. Not a literal translation).

Taking Care of the People of God is Scriptural

The need for well-thought-out congregational care that includes the entire membership is demonstrated to us by Jesus in the parable of the lost sheep. He cautions us by stating, "Even so it is not the will of your Father who is in heaven that one of these little ones should perish" (Matthew 18:14). Every member of the congregation is valuable and deserves to receive care!

Considering all the scriptures as mentioned earlier and the clarity it conveys concerning the necessity of caring for God's people, makes us stagger at the thought that a significant number of churches today do not have an intentional system of care for their people. And they will never be able to have an efficient system if the pastor is the only one providing care. It is practically impossible.

The *Care Revolution,* through the leadership of the Holy Spirit, is bringing the focus back on these essentials of the Word of God regarding this subject. The leaders of the Early Church were involved in the active care of the people. We are coming to the full understanding that the mission of the Church is not only to win the lost and disciple them but indeed also to nurture and care for them. As Mel Steinbron says, "Pastoring follows evangelism in the spiritual order just as nurturing follows birth in the biological order."

I am convinced, since I have seen it over and over, that it takes a healthy, nurtured, and cared for church to have the vigor and strength to continue making new disciples. A sick, neglected church just does not have the energy to win the lost. Look around you, and you will see it is a fact. Growing churches have cultivated a culture of care and developed people with a loving attitude. And by loving people, I don't mean cliquish people, but genuine caring people. It's not about them; it's about others. Loving people—is one of the most beautiful marks of Christianity.

Care is not primarily an emotion; it is an act of compassion. If you can love people, you can care for people. It doesn't take a professional to love—it only takes a person that has experienced the love of Christ. Our churches are full of people who have the giftedness to come alongside their pastor and provide the care that is essential. When we affirm people, equip, and release them to provide genuine care, they will honor the Great Commitment and bring the church back into balance.

As a Lead Pastor, I have always concentrated on the healthy balance between the Great Commission and the Great Commitment. It has become evident to me that the one supports the other. Some churches seem to major on the one at the neglect of the other, not realizing that both are equally important to build a healthy church. God expects pastors and leaders to have compassion for the physical as well as the spiritual needs of people.

An Old Testament Model

Exodus 18: 13–26 provides an excellent model for establishing a system of ministry, which we can equally apply to the *Care Ministry Network.* It is, in fact, a model for total mobilization of all believers in a congregation. Even though Moses was a great leader, and called of God, he was apparently not providing adequate care for His people. He was overworked and frustrated and was attempting to do everything himself. Verse 13 says Moses worked from morning till evening, and if you continue to read the next few verses, you will notice that the people came to him to resolve all their matters. He was trying to be everything to everybody. His modus operandi sounds much like that of a modern-day pastor.

Jethro, his father-in-law, noticed the tragedy of this failing leadership. Although Moses was giving all that he had to offer and became fatigued and discouraged, the people's needs were still not fully met. Despite all his efforts, many of the people were neither heard nor helped. I can just imagine Iky and Rebekah standing in line waiting for Moses to give them pre-marital counsel. By the time they reached him, they no longer needed pre-marital counseling, they needed advice on their 401(k).

Noticing his calamity, Jethro then gave Moses the classic model of delegation along with a plan for making the most of the abilities of all the people. Moses took Jethro's counsel and instigated a practical organizational structure, which simultaneously ensured that he would himself also survive.

Every local church has a *Moses*, called the Pastor. I do believe that God raises up a plurality of leaders to lead a congregation, because there is wisdom in a multitude of counselors. But I also hold that there is always a leader among leaders, the person that Christ has given to the church (Ephesians 4:11) to be the pastor. God never speaks to a committee; He talks to a person. Even in the Sanhedrin, there was a Chief Rabbi among the Rabbis. In the Book of Revelation, it often states, "And to the angel of the church . . ." which indicates that there is one leading voice (pastor/leader) in every church.

Any pastor and church can learn from the advice Jethro gave Moses to develop an efficient organizational structure for ministry. God has entrusted us with the responsibility of developing people spiritually and leading them to be actively involved in meaningful tasks within the congregation. This requires an understanding of how to systematize our churches and how to connect people with each other.

Steps of Delegation Jethro gave Moses (Exodus 18: 17-23):[43]

Let me give you the natural steps that Jethro instructed Moses to do and then add some of my own comments:

---

43   Unless otherwise indicated, these Scriptures have been taken out of the New King James Version (NKJV) of the Bible.

1. "What you are doing is not good . . . you will only wear yourself out . . . the work is too heavy for you; you cannot handle it alone . . ." (verses 17–18).

Moses was doing ministry the way modern-day pastors are traditionally functioning, with one person trying to meet the ministry needs of all the people. Not only is it impossible, unrealistic, and impractical; it is indeed unscriptural. Pastors attempting to do ministry alone wear themselves out and often lose the joy of their calling. A single pastor may still be sufficient until the membership reaches one-hundred, but after that, it becomes virtually impossible. We should learn how to involve all God's people in the work of ministry.

2. "You must be the people's representative before God and bring their disputes to Him" (verse 19).

The priority Jethro sets to Moses, is his responsibility, as the leader, to stay in touch with God on behalf of the people. Communicating with God and spending time in His presence remains the most successful strategy for any pastor or leader. Before we do anything else, we should first develop a personal relationship with God. The pastor is the Shepherd who supports the people through prayer and spiritual upliftment. His or her counsel should not be based on the wisdom of man but rather on revelation from God. Knowing how to take the burdens of the people to the Lord and leaving it there is the most effective way of displaying Godly leadership.

3. "You shalt teach them . . . the work they must do" (verse 20 KJV)

This directive Jethro gave Moses, is precisely what Paul is also saying in Ephesians 4:11-12. It is the Pastor's responsibility to equip (teach/train/develop) their people for their specific roles in ministry. Every believer should be involved in works of service in the church; that is the biblical model. Preaching and teaching on the subject of ministry-involvement should be followed by intentional training and development of church members so they can come alongside their pastors to do the work of the ministry. Pastors equip the believers who in return do the work of ministry.

4. "...And show them . . ." (verse 20)

The best way for pastors to develop and train their people is not only using note outlines and classroom teaching but more appropriately by demonstrating ministry to them in practical ways. This can be done by relating real-life experiences and even by modeling how we could and should execute ministry. I have said it in a previous chapter but allow me to say it again—"Ministry is often more caught than it is taught." You cannot show someone how to ride a bicycle by simply having them read a book or watch a DVD. You have to let them get on the bike and have them learn in a practical way how to succeed. People likewise learn ministry best through personal involvement. Another way of "showing them" is by connecting a learning member with a more mature member to experience on-the-job training.

5. "Select capable men (and women) from all the people
   . . . who fear God . . . trustworthy . . . who hate
   dishonest gain" (verse 21—parenthesis added).

Jethro underscores the necessity of required benchmarks for people to be involved in the work of ministry. It is never a good idea to merely include people in roles of ministry without first having agreed-upon standards of expectation and explaining requirements. The higher a person advances to a leadership level, the more we should clarify and agree upon the qualifications.

In the case of our care system, there are certain specific giftedness and characteristics required as prerequisites for church members to function in these roles and should be taken into consideration when selecting them. Not all people have the appropriate giftedness to function as care pastors.

6. "Appoint them . . ." (verse 21)

Doing things in proper order remains the requirement for a successful outcome in any organization. People should not just randomly pick up a role and function on their own volition. People need to be selected, authorized, and commissioned (appointed) publicly by the leadership (elders) to operate in their respective capacity. The principle here is: if people are not under authority, they have no authority. This act of the equipping process puts the seal on our efforts and allows the church body to recognize those that have been prepared for works of service. Authority is never assumed—it's given.

7. Place them "…over thousands, hundreds, fifties and tens" (verse 21).

In this statement, Jethro describes the functions of an organization, which is crucial for every church. Every church needs a structure, which requires (i) levels of leadership, (ii) lines of authority, and (iii) avenues of communication. People need to know to whom they are *accountable* and for whom they are *responsible*. They furthermore also need to know with whom they are *in relationship with*—their peer level. The most helpful tool in this regard is an *Organizational Chart*, which after we have designed it, should reflect all the previously mentioned aspects.

Developing these levels of leadership and structural associations, allow us to connect every person in the congregation to each other and sensibly place them into smaller groups who in turn relate to a designated leader. This is the only way we can provide hands-on ministry to every member of the congregation. We can only offer authentic care when we do it in a group setting—smaller gatherings of people under the careful eye of a Care Pastor.

8. "… have them bring every difficult case to you …" (verse 22)

This statement illustrates that the pastor remains God's delegated authority in the church who continues to play an important role. The pastor can delegate a task but never his or her leadership. To develop and release people into ministry does not mean the pastors are no longer involved in the work of the ministry. They do not forsake their leadership role or relinquish the vision. The fact is that every ministry should be the extension of the Lead Pastor's vision. The significant things still end up on the pastor's desk. Some decisions and tasks just cannot and should not be handled by members. The difficult cases remain the responsibility of the pastor.

9.   ". . . The simple cases they can decide themselves."

There are assigned functions and responsibilities church members could fulfill in their line of duty. They can handle ongoing congregational care efficiently and should have some rights to make specific decisions on their own. They are trained and equipped for this purpose.

This step Jethro gave to Moses, as well as the previous one, underscores our notion in the care ministry that the Care Pastors do the *congregational care* while the Pastors do the *crisis care*. The people do the attainable part while the pastors continue to do the challenging part of pastoral care.

Three things are evident: (1) a definite act of delegated authority, (2) a level of trust in those the leadership has appointed, and (iii) a willingness by the members to accept the responsibility of the delegated task(s).

Results of Ministry Delegation:

"If you do this . . . you will be able to stand the strain, and all these people will go home satisfied."

Moses listened to Jethro, did all he had said, and the results were spectacular. It is only when the enormous task of ministry is spread among all the believers that we can be effective. The evident key Moses applied was to appoint capable leaders to help him guide the people and then placed everyone in smaller groups, which made it easier for all to stay in touch. Moses no longer had to provide care to all the people, and neither did they have to wait for him to have their needs met. There was now a system in place, and the positive results were evident in satisfied people.

It remains the key to effective ministry today. Congregational care demands more than most people could ever imagine. Pastors alone can only reach so many people, but if all of the people do all of the work of God, all of them will be satisfied.

Gary M Gray illustrates the dilemma and the solution well in the following two diagrams:[44]

---

44   Gary M. Gray, *Christian Growth and Leadership* (Austin: Church Management Inc.), 74-76.

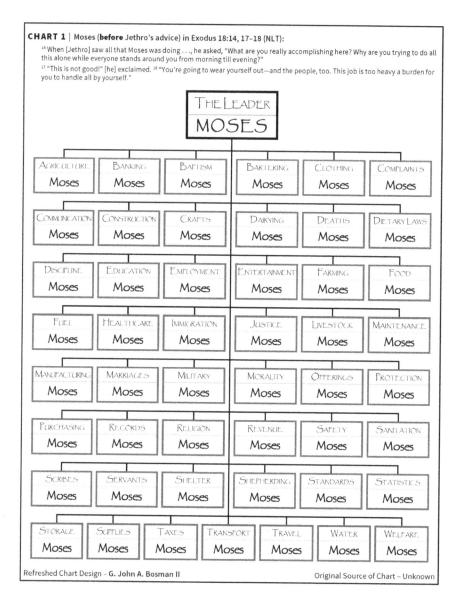

CHART 1 | Moses (**before** Jethro's advice) in Exodus 18:14, 17–18 (NLT):

[14] When [Jethro] saw all that Moses was doing . . ., he asked, "What are you really accomplishing here? Why are you trying to do all this alone while everyone stands around you from morning till evening?"

[17] "This is not good!" [he] exclaimed. [18] "You're going to wear yourself out—and the people, too. This job is too heavy a burden for you to handle all by yourself."

THE LEADER
MOSES

AGRICULTURE	BANKING	BAPTISM	BARTERING	CLOTHING	COMPLAINTS
Moses	Moses	Moses	Moses	Moses	Moses
COMMUNICATION	CONSTRUCTION	CRAFTS	DAIRYING	DEATHS	DIETARY LAWS
Moses	Moses	Moses	Moses	Moses	Moses
DISCIPLINE	EDUCATION	EMPLOYMENT	ENTERTAINMENT	FARMING	FOOD
Moses	Moses	Moses	Moses	Moses	Moses
FUEL	HEALTHCARE	IMMIGRATION	JUSTICE	LIVESTOCK	MAINTENANCE
Moses	Moses	Moses	Moses	Moses	Moses
MANUFACTURING	MARRIAGES	MILITARY	MORALITY	OFFERINGS	PROTECTION
Moses	Moses	Moses	Moses	Moses	Moses
PURCHASING	RECORDS	RELIGION	REVENUE	SAFETY	SANITATION
Moses	Moses	Moses	Moses	Moses	Moses
SCRIBES	SERVANTS	SHELTER	SHEPHERDING	STANDARDS	STATISTICS
Moses	Moses	Moses	Moses	Moses	Moses
STORAGE	SUPPLIES	TAXES	TRANSPORT	TRAVEL	WATER	WELFARE
Moses	Moses	Moses	Moses	Moses	Moses	Moses

Refreshed Chart Design – G. John A. Bosman II   Original Source of Chart – Unknown

MINISTRY DONE THE WRONG WAY

The above is the approach of a micro-manager style of leadership that frustrates both the leader as well as the followers. Take a closer look and see that Moses is involved in everything. Effective congregational care can only happen when there is a sensible structure in place, and people know to whom they relate.

No matter the size of a church, we must delegate ministry and develop levels of leadership. Without doing this, the ministry will never be efficient, and the church will never reach its full potential. The one most crucial thing church leaders can do is letting those they are leading grow to maturity. The key to an active, healthy church is to equip all believers for their work of the ministry.

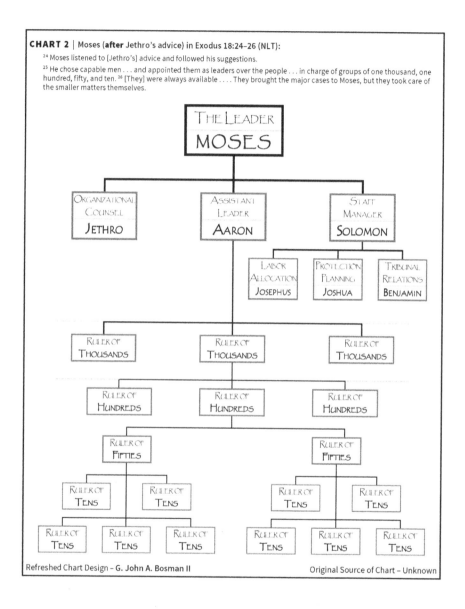

CHART 2 | Moses (after Jethro's advice) in Exodus 18:24–26 (NLT):

[24] Moses listened to [Jethro's] advice and followed his suggestions.

[25] He chose capable men . . . and appointed them as leaders over the people . . . in charge of groups of one thousand, one hundred, fifty, and ten. [26] [They] were always available . . . . They brought the major cases to Moses, but they took care of the smaller matters themselves.

THE LEADER
MOSES

ORGANIZATIONAL COUNSEL
JETHRO

ASSISTANT LEADER
AARON

STAFF MANAGER
SOLOMON

LABOR ALLOCATION
JOSEPHUS

PROTECTION PLANNING
JOSHUA

TRIBUNAL RELATIONS
BENJAMIN

RULER OF THOUSANDS

RULER OF THOUSANDS

RULER OF THOUSANDS

RULER OF HUNDREDS

RULER OF HUNDREDS

RULER OF HUNDREDS

RULER OF FIFTIES

RULER OF FIFTIES

RULER OF TENS

RULER OF TENS

RULER OF TENS

RULER OF TENS

RULER OF TENS

RULER OF TENS

RULER OF TENS

RULER OF TENS

RULER OF TENS

RULER OF TENS

Refreshed Chart Design - G. John A. Bosman II   Original Source of Chart – Unknown

MINISTRY DONE THE CORRECT WAY

The above sketch illustrates how Moses placed people on levels of leadership, and how he divided the tasks among the members. It's a great example of involving everyone in the work of the ministry. God never intended for the vocational ministers to do all the work on their own. That is why the Church is referred to as a body—with arms, hands, legs, feet, etc.—each one doing its part.

Design Member Involvement Around Productive Ministry

I want to make sure that we understand that a petition for ministry-involvement is not a plea for more programs. In the past, we have assumed that the more the church grows, the more activities and programs we should provide. But if we're not careful, we will hurt rather than help our churches. Again, it's not about *more* programs, but instead *productive* and purposeful ministry. Churches today will most certainly be more successful if they simplify their programs rather than complicate them with packed calendars. *Simplified churches* are the life-giving churches that focus their momentum on a few things they can distinctively do best and will emerge as the most effective churches in the future.

13

THE RESTORATION OF THE MINISTRY OF THE PASTOR

Paul says in Ephesians 4:11, "and He gave some to be pastors . . ." and thereby includes the ministry of the Pastor as one of the Five-Fold Ministries Jesus gave to the Church. We said previously that some scholars refer to this present season in the Church as *The Day of the Saints*, and I agree. But I emphatically also believe this is *The Day of the Pastors*—a season wherein the role of pastoral ministry is being restored to its rightful position as Christ intended it to function.

The saints cannot adequately function without the pastors as little as the pastors can operate without them. This statement rings especially true when we refer to the implementation of this exciting, fresh movement, called the *Care Revolution*. That does not mean that the other offices in the five-fold ministry do not play a role because they do. But it is the pastor that has the primary task of fulfilling the shepherding-role in the congregation and therefore the one to equip the believers to do the same.

The Five-Fold Ministry Restoration

I have often read about the different seasons of the restoration of the five-fold ministry, but I cannot distinctly remember a definite period of the restoration of the *pastor*. Perhaps it's because the emphasis on the ministry of the pastor never really diminished over time to the same extent, the others may have. For as long as there have been churches, there evidently had to have been pastors. There has, however, been a definite shift in the role of the pastor that will have to be revisited and brought back to the biblical position.

Some church history scholars believe the restoration of the pastor took place during the Latter Rain Movement in the 1960's. Chronologically it makes sense, but in all reality, it seems as though it was more of an emphasis on the restitution of the leadership-role of the pastor. During this time, there was a strong conviction by many to emphasize the autonomy of the local church. This persuasion necessitated that someone take the lead, which, understandably, identified the pastor as the obvious person. I am inclined to settle for this belief. Others again point to the Charismatic Movement as being the moment of the restoration of the pastor. I have honestly tried to find that to be correct. I am not suggesting these scholars are wrong, but from my perspective, the Charismatic Movement was instead the restoration of the *teacher*.

And since I am talking about both ministries here, let me say that I see a clear difference between the office of the teacher and that of the pastor. While I readily accept that all pastors should be teachers, I do not agree that all teachers are necessarily pastors. There are, for instance, many men and women who are gifted and *called*, as teachers, who are doing an outstanding job in our colleges and universities. Most of them will tell you outright that they are not called to be pastors.

I once heard such a teacher say, "Don't make me a pastor—I'll kill the people!" I'm sure he wasn't serious about killing the people, but I do know for sure that he knew he felt convinced he could not be a pastor. It was not his calling. Then I also know of many teachers who, for instance, have effective itinerant ministries and go from church to church, but they again will tell you they are not evangelists. They are teachers.

It is accurate to say that pace-setting pastors formed many large churches during the time of the Charismatic Movement, but it was more of a pragmatic movement combined with the gift of *teaching* that brought about the consequence. I do not find any evidence of any significant emphasis on the restoration of the shepherding aspect of the congregation. You would have been hard-pressed to see a general restitution of "Feed My sheep . . ." (John 21:16), or "heed to . . . all the flock, among which the Holy Spirit has made you overseers, to shepherd the church of God, which He purchased with His blood" (Acts 20:28) or even "Shepherd the flock of God which is among you . . ." (1 Peter 5:2). The Charismatic Movement was a most exciting time, and while they obviously did not disregard the role of the pastor or the functions of shepherding, it was not their emphasis.

Genuine Shepherding

To make it clear, it is the restoration of the pastor, as *shepherd,* that needs our attention. In this regard, allow me to unambiguously state that the concept of congregational care as we promote it in the *Care Revolution,* should not be confused with the *Shepherding Movement* of the seventies and eighties. That is not the mode of shepherding I have in mind, and neither was that a model of the restoration of the ministry of the pastor. I do not regard the function and premise of what the

Shepherding Movement upheld as being the Scriptural description of the role of a pastor, and positively not an excellent example of pastoral care either. That movement panned out to instead be an abuse of authority and functioned by manipulation, which in most cases was a disgrace and became hurtful to the body of Christ. No wonder it died. Even though we advocate levels of leadership and lines of authority in the Care Ministry Network, we do not embrace the notion of manipulation or an individual having domination over people.

Recognition

When it comes to focusing on pastoral care, I gratefully recognize the great work of individuals such as Dr. Mel Steinbron, who towards the end of the eighties, rendered a great service to the body of Christ in bringing the matter of pastoral care, provided by church members, to the attention of the church in America. His books and his ministry have been influential, and I am aware of many churches that have followed his model and have been successful in their efforts. His teachings brought forth a renewed passion for genuine, biblical congregational care. His passing in July 2017 left a void in the church-world.

One of the ways I have learned to evaluate the restoration of a ministry is to look at the fruit it produces. When the ministry of the prophet, as an example, was renewed, it ignited the prophetic in other people, and it affected the entire body of Christ. The same happened earlier during the restitution of the ministry of the evangelist; everybody wanted to be an evangelist. Then there was a time when everyone wanted to be a teacher and did not want to be known as a pastor. Lately, many want to be an apostle, whether they have the required gift or not. The benchmark is: what is the fruit they produce?

I also want to be careful that it does not sound as though I am suggesting that all pastors have forsaken their role of being good shepherds either, or that this essential ministry-gift had died. There have always been great men and women of God who have been tremendous and faithful shepherds of the flock—and there are undeniably still many thousands. My father was a pastor before I was even born. I know what it takes to be a faithful servant of God, twenty-four hours out of every day. What I am underscoring is the necessity of an overall resurgence of the active ministry of pastoral care, and I don't suggest pacifying the saints, but caring about each of them sufficiently and intentionally.

This Was Not Good

Since I have been around the block a few times, I have seen the season of pastoral abuse that was going on. Instead of displaying the heart of a true shepherd we have all observed and heard of some pastors during the eighties and even into the twenty-first century, who have taken advantage of the Church in ways that did not always bring glory to God. I know my heart is pure and my spirit is not judgmental, and I ask that you hear me out. I love pastors; I do; I've been one for most of my adult life. And not *all pastors* have been guilty of what I am about to share either. They are not to blame, and I am thankful for the sacrifices they make.

Part of the reason we have not seen real pastoral ministry demonstrated in movements of the past is that we have come through an era in the Church I call the "Stardom Syndrome!" During this time, people elevated the *image* of the pastor, but not the actual *function* or ministry of the office. And sadly, their followers encouraged and applauded their actions—at least initially. Pastors became competitive in their attitude, trying to see who could attract the most people to their ministries.

They dared not include too many others around them because it would have taken away from their prominence too much. In so many ways they became untouchable, unavailable, and unreachable. Their congregants could no longer get close to them and consequently felt like strangers. The personality on the platform did not match the same person on the floor. The people liked the one on the platform!

It was a race to see who could build the most significant and most talked about church in the nation in the shortest span of time—attempting to break everyone's records, including their own. It was all about numbers. But the fact is that Jesus never called us to build a crowd; He invited us to build a Church. Now please understand, I am keenly aware of the fact that you must attract a crowd before you can build a church, but the bottom-line question is: what is our motive? What is our calling? What is our purpose?

> The church exists primarily not to increase its membership but to bring men and women to Christ.[45]

> Changed from flocks
> to frenzied
> entertainment
> seekers

During this unfortunate season, many church members were changed from flocks to frenzied entertainment seekers waiting for the next show. Instead of caring and nurturing God's people, the pastors

---

45   Oscar E. Feucht, *Everyone a Minister* (St. Louis: Pillar Books for Concordia Publishing House, 1974), 81.

were in search of the next flavor of the month. Scores of people were coming, but just as many were leaving, because nobody cared. The back door was as wide open as the front door. And sad to say, many of these so-called pastors are no longer even in the ministry today. But should we be surprised?

It brought with it unimaginable pain and heartache, and the result was that many churches in America today are stagnated or are in severe decline. There have been too many things going on that caused distrust, hurt, and a loss of confidence. People have been abused spiritually, mentally, and financially and got burnt in their experience with the *church*.

I am thankfully not begrudging pastors of large churches. As a pastor, I led a large church for a long time myself. That's not the argument. The real point should be our attitude towards the people God sends us. The ones for whom He died. And to maintain a right balance we know there are, thank God, still huge mega-churches today with great pastors who certainly do not fit the mold I have described. I believe that the unfortunate period I referred to above is (hopefully) behind us.

While there was a time in the past that everything revolved around the church, it is no longer the case. If all the people who once attended church will all return, we won't have enough church buildings to accommodate the multitude. This being the case, we will do well to consider taking the ministry to the people, instead of them having to come to a facility to receive such. When we go to them, they will be willing to come to us.

One final point on this subject: Personally, I am *almost persuaded* that this faulty pastoral-role could probably also be to blame for the *Many sons, but no Fathers Syndrome*. We suddenly found that there were many sons, but no spiritual fathers in the Church. Could it be that the "stars" were so busy building their kingdoms that they did not notice the cry of those who were coming behind them? There was minimal, if any, coaching or mentoring taking place. And sad to say, they passed over an entire generation and now anointed men and women of God are going all out trying to catch up and reach the next generation—frantically attempting to coach them back. And thank God, in so many ways it is occurring powerfully.

Let's Bring Back the Focus

With all the changes of ministry emphasis in the church, including the restoration of specific ministries, it almost seems as though the *glamor* (used carefully) of being a pastor has been somewhat misplaced. One of the significant shifts we are facing in the church world today is the apparent changing role of that of the Lead Pastor. Amazingly some pastors do not want to be known as *pastors* any longer and prefer to be called, or identified, by some other designation.

Research provides evidence that most credentialed ministers love to preach and teach, but fewer prefer to *pastor*. In a recent survey, taken among 232 senior (lead) pastors, it shows that they, on the whole, see themselves as *teachers* rather than *pastors*.

Megachurch pastors are **not** likely to see themselves as that: pastors. They're more inclined to view their role as preacher or teacher, according to a new survey.

In newly released findings from the Leadership Network's Senior Pastor Survey, 81 percent of senior pastors in churches view their role as "preacher/teacher" while only

16 percent see themselves as a "pastor, shepherd or spiritual guide."

Fifty-one percent chose the term 'directional leader,' and 33 percent described themselves as a "visionary."[46]

In that same vein, I am also now hearing of pastors who say they are pastoring the vision and not the people. Statements like these, and surveys as quoted above, make us want to ask, "Where have all the pastors gone?" And then immediately wonder—"Who is taking care of the sheep?" Positions like these emphasize why I am saying that we need to bring back the focus to the real, biblical function and role of the pastor-shepherd.

These comments are not meant to criticize modern-day pastors but are instead an honest and sincere attempt to call attention to the enormous challenge we are facing in the Church. We're not doing pastoral care with the same passion as years ago. Now, of course, that is not all bad, but it becomes alarming when we notice the neglect of church members who should receive the care the Bible expects us to provide. But hear me clearly: Pastors are essential, and their roles crucial!

There is presently a definite shift that's taking place—and that is what I am targeting in my overall approach.

The enormous pressure pastors face in the modern age may indeed have brought about some of the changing roles we see today. It is a known fact that being a pastor requires much effort, calls for hard work, and necessitates long nights. They must continuously try to be everything to everybody and can never assume to be human.

---

46   *The Christian Post,* Christianpost.com

That underscores the fact why more people in the church, other than the credentialed staff, should be trained and equipped to help in this mammoth task of congregational care. If we are going to be successful in this effort, we are about to see a movement rise that will blast the Church to a newfound level of relevance.

Traditional thinking could initially be the most active opposition we must overcome. Some pastors may feel threatened by the thought of equipping people for ministry, while the church members, on the other hand, may feel they are not capable neither worthy of being involved in ministry. The worst-case scenario and the most unbiblical is that some church members reckon they have *hired* a pastor to do the ministry on their behalf. I am still amazed to find this kind of thinking among American churches in the twenty-first century.

In many cases, there is going to have to be more of a shift in traditional thinking for some than there will be necessary for others. From what I have seen, there are some that may even see the transition to membership-involvement as something that is way out there. If done right, however, once we launch the *Care Ministry Network* and the effects become visible, these objections fade away quickly and cannot hold against the loving care given faithfully by gifted, equipped, and commissioned Care Pastors.

What is likely needed more critically now than ever before is that pastors again take on the role of *the pastor* and primarily function as shepherds in a defined way. But the added exciting facet of all that the Holy Spirit is quickening through *The Care Revolution* is that pastors no longer should do all the caring alone. They should instead equip their people to do the bulk of taking care of the flock and can do so without any guilt or fear. And just before someone says, "Poor guy, he thinks all a pastor has to do is providing care and loving people" let me quickly add that I, of course, realize that the tasks of a pastor are many, but shepherding the flock deserves high priority.

The New Testament Role of a Pastor

There are varied opinions of what the actual role of a pastor should be, especially in the twenty-first century. It seems as though the definition of a pastor's duties changes with every wave of restoration, and while every change contains a certain truth, it will serve us well to stay with the New Testament expectation as modeled by Jesus.

Although not complete, these following six essentials describe the *job description* **of a pastor well:**

1. Be a Worshipper – Develop a close relationship with God (Mark 1:35)

2. Be a Preacher – Preach the Good News of the gospel, as Jesus taught us (2 Timothy 4:2)

3. Be a Disciple-maker – Disciple believers under the leadership of the Holy Spirit Matthew 28:20

4. Be a Coach – Equip and Develop people for the work of the ministry (Ephesians 4:12)

5. Be a Shepherd – Meet the needs of the people (Matthew 9:36)

6. Be a Servant – Give your life as a sacrifice for the sake of the Kingdom (Mark 10:45)

We're Coming Back to the Heart of Caring

We have entered a most exciting time! I believe it's the season for the function of the *pastor* to be restored to its fullness with a particular emphasis on shepherding. The good news is that the Holy Spirit is quickening the Church to *take care of the flock* and a specific truth, which has always been in the Bible, is now being refreshed. And that requires **pastors** (real pastors) to come to the forefront and take up the charge.

That is why I am so excited about this *Care Revolution* that is set to help create a platform to influence the restoration of the ministry of pastoral care significantly. We are determined to be part of the solution instead of magnifying the problem. Our sincere prayer is that *pastors* will be proud to be called *pastors* again—and I don't mean the title, but the function.

A Divine Partnership

We have previously made the point over and over that providing adequate pastoral care is far too vast a task for one person to do alone. Not in the world we are living in today. It could have worked in years gone by but is downright no longer possible—and neither is it scriptural. It is likewise not possible for the paid staff to accomplish either. They usually concentrate on the specific ministries they have been brought onto the team to fulfill.

In his book, Everyone A Minister, Oscar Feucht aptly says it like this:

> An adequate ministry is not a one-man ministry. It is not even a corps of associated pastors. It is the whole church, congregation-by-congregation, mobilized and trained for mission. Only this strategy is adequate.[47]

---

47   Oscar E. Feucht, *Everyone a Minister* (St. Louis: Pillar Books for Concordia Publishing House, 1974), 80.

When we get our focus for ministry back where it belongs—on people—and realize the score of available talent sitting in our pews, a new day will dawn for the church and incredible potential will be released. A considerable disadvantage of exclusively utilizing paid staff to do pastoral care is the increased numbers of people it neutralizes and causes them to become mere spectators, robbing them of the opportunity to do ministry.

The traditional mindset that has prevailed over passed centuries is the notion that churches hire a pastor and then base their philosophy on an unbiblical and unhealthy understanding of the local church ministry. The expectation then rests upon the pastor to do all the ministry instead of the pastor equipping the members to do the work of the ministry. Rather than the pastor doing all the ministry, how about churches inviting a pastor to become their coach and trainer to train them how to do ministry? According to Ephesians 4:12-16, that is the biblical model. Ministry is not the responsibility of pastors alone, neither the members only; ministry is the task of all who are Christ's. As pastors, our responsibility is to recruit, equip, empower, and release our people and then lead them by example.

When we ignore church members' giftedness, there are several degenerative effects:

- The laity is not prepared or equipped for works of service in building up the body, as intended
- We deprive the members of becoming the Lord's instruments of meaningful service
- We stymie their potential usefulness for God
- We hinder them from serving and nurturing those who are hurting

- Those in the body needing love, encouragement, and exhortation fail to grow
- The "ever-present" pastor usually faces burn-out and discouragement, and furthermore
- We remove the process of spiritual development in people's lives with many ministry tasks left undone.

Developing people, on the other hand, results in such a beautiful time of restoration that we cannot even consider ignoring their involvement. Pastors and church members are forming a partnership in pastoral ministry that is becoming more and more of a revolution. It brings not only great release to pastors but also a marvelous sense of liberation to the members who are joyfully taking up their responsibilities. Remember: people need to be needed. Pastors who are still trying to do ministry on their own are killing themselves, missing God's plan, and robbing the people of great opportunities. Their churches will suffer and struggle, and they will never see the fruit they would wish to have.

Designing a New Way

One of the most effective and yet most challenging ways to re-ignite a church is by shifting the ministry to the people. It indeed calls for a new way of thinking and a new way of doing things, which entails change—and change is not always easy. But at the same time, we are made to understand that it often requires *change* to bring new life to a stagnant organization—as long as we don't keep on changing, because too many changes, too often, can prove to be detrimental. But basically, change is a good thing—everything that is alive, changes!

When you change
your mind,
you change
your life!

There is nothing that gets a church off a plateau or out of stagnation as efficiently and as quickly as getting people involved in exhilarating ministry. It is undoubtedly the most efficient way of releasing a spark of new life in a congregation, regardless of how long it has been in existence, or how long the pastor has been there. Stagnation typically sets in when members are bored, and the church seems to be going nowhere. In the business world they usually change leadership when a company or industry has hit a plateau, and sometimes in the church, it may also be necessary—but it does not have to be that way.

We have the great opportunity of relying on the Holy Spirit to re-ignite new vision and passion on our inside and through prayerful consideration begin to steer the church into a fresh, enthusiastic, dynamic, and unique ministry dimension. And I know you are going to have to become bold! You may initially run into resistance, and some of your peers may question your wisdom. Don't let that discourage you. Take on a winning attitude.

Perhaps we need to change our entire thinking of looking at the Church and the roles of believers. But this I know, once people have put their toes into the water of ministry, joy is going to explode in the congregation as they fulfill their calling.

I recently spoke with two businessmen friends about why it's hard to find a healthy church. Both are successful financially and are passionate believers. On the surface, they're what every pastor needs. After being active in a local church, they both became disillusioned with what they saw and how the church treated them. As they recounted stories of how pastors felt threatened by their dominant personalities and positions, I felt sorry for my friends (for never experiencing the community they sought) and for the insecure leaders they served.

Leadership has so wounded many mature Christians that they stay home on Sunday and "go to church" by watching . . . (some television preacher or live streaming). But this isn't Christian community. Aren't we supposed to assemble with other believers?

There are "sheep" that need to be nurtured, fed, and discipled in the things of God. It's the only way a believer can survive in this increasingly challenging cultural environment!

Until this happens, people—like my businessmen friends—will feel as if they're drifting. They'll never actually find their place in the body of Christ. And sooner or later, they will "vote with their feet" by going somewhere else—or worse still, nowhere.[48]

We just cannot stay with the status quo and lose these gifted people. They want to be involved in ministry more and more because

---

48   Short excerpts taken from Steve Strang's blog: Charisma News.com/
      Opinion/38101. February 5, 2013.

the Holy Spirit is quickening them to do so. They too have received ministries from God and are anxious to implement their gifts in the church and beyond. They are waiting to be included, trained, and sent.

Once you release people, you will stand amazed to see the body of Christ come alive and functioning in more significant power than ever before. And here is a little secret: when people "buy" into the vision, they willingly "give" to the idea. They will give time, energy, and yes, I do also mean money!

Once the wave of people involvement rises, the flow of blessing is released, and you can't stop people from coming to church unless you do something foolish.

As a pastor, you will experience freedom and joy from shared ministry and be motivated beyond description as you see God's people blessed and strengthened by each other. Once they have caught the vision, they will be the ones that will bring the people. As it is often said: "The shepherds don't produce sheep. It is the sheep that begat sheep."

It works!
I know it does

As more and more of our people were equipped and released, I can well remember how often I stood on the platform on a Sunday seeing how the people were pouring into our worship center. It sometimes looked as though buses had dropped them off. With tears in my eyes, and with great gratitude I would often humbly turn to my wife and say, "From where are all these people coming? It's not because of anything I am doing!"

You must realize that church members can reach people whose names the pastor may never even know. But the truth is that church members will never rise above the level of the leader's maturity and his or her conviction of releasing people into ministry. It's not always easy to change the paradigm, but once you have tasted the sweetness of the fruit, you will never want to go back.

The truth is that many of your people have gifts, talents, and abilities of which you may not even be aware. They have wisdom, insights, and perspectives that we as credentialed ministers may not have. But once we blend their abilities and ideas with ours, a potentially explosive situation arises. I cannot see any reason pastors would even think of doing ministry without including their people.

But let me also share a word of caution: Once you start with training and developing people for the work of ministry you cannot stop halfway, even when challenges emerge. I can assure you that it will release exploding excitement when you start equipping your people, and should you then stop, the discouragement that sets in is indescribable. But why would you want to withdraw?

The final results of preparing people for ministry is always astonishing and worth every effort. But yes, it takes hard work and tenacity to get the ball rolling initially. The temptation will still be there to instead slip back into the traditional way of doing ministry on your own, or at most have it done within the circle of your paid staff. Don't do it! This attitude has proven to be a huge mistake and is undoubtedly not what Christ had in mind.

And what's more is that it will toss the church right back into stagnation—and then changing leadership may be the only other viable option. Or, the church may well accept the status quo, stagnate, and gradually decline. Is that not where seventy-five percent of our churches in America find themselves?

God has given us the precious resources of gifted people. Let's involve them, develop them, and utilize them to the glory of God and the expansion of His Kingdom.

Time for Transition

Through many pages and chapters, I have taken you on a journey to discover the powerful concept of the *Care Revolution* and attempted to explain all of its relevance. I realize that I have cut the straps broad and have gone into much depth in some areas. The reason for this is that I wanted to present you with much more information than only a ministry application, however important that may be.

We have now arrived at the transition moment where we are going to move on from the philosophical and theological aspects of the overall *Care Revolution* to the practical application in the local church context. As mentioned in a previous chapter, we refer to this presentation as the *Care Ministry Network*.

As you begin to pray, plan, and prepare to launch congregational care in your church, reference this book often, because it will help you understand why we implement some of the things we do and furthermore undergird your vision when you begin to cast it to your leaders and congregation at-large. It should not only be a reference resource for pastors, but for all who will be involved in the ministry of care within the church.

I have found that when church members understand the background, as I have explained it, their commitment, participation, and steadfastness increase by several degrees. This conviction, added to their giftedness, makes it almost impossible for them to give up. People who don't know the root of the historical or the biblical journey, or even the philosophical, tend to view the care ministry as just another program, and their lack of enthusiasm shows quickly.

As a pastor, you may find material in this book that will provide helpful thoughts to you, as you prepare the congregation and equip your Care Pastors. There may even be some information you may find useful as preaching content and helpful tools to guide your people in finding their spiritual gifts.

As a church member, you will find this book educational and enlightening as you prepare to be involved in this cutting-edge, and Scriptural ministry called the *Care Ministry.* I will suggest you refer to it often and highlight the thoughts and principles that stand out to you. In so doing it will begin to become part of your life and shape a ministry within you that will become life-changing to you and most pleasing to God.

14

THE CHURCH IN ACTION

The triumphant Church Jesus mentioned in Matthew 16:18, is still the victorious Church and will remain as such until Christ returns. The Church is assuredly not going under, it's going over. We have no fear that the Church will diminish or fade into oblivion. As a matter of fact, the Church is only going to become stronger and more conquering in this season. More people are going to come to Christ over the next few years than we have seen over many decades. God has used great men and women of God, like Evangelist Reinhard Bonnke and *Christ For All Nations* (CFAN), to gather a great harvest of souls. To date, their ministry has won more than 77 million people to Christ, and the numbers are still growing.

Although *CFAN's* results have mainly been in Africa, there is every indication that evangelism is going to exponentially increase around the globe at this time. Bringing people to Christ does not complete the cycle; there also has to be discipleship and Christ-like fellowship included in the process. That is why a healthy local church is indispensable and will become more significant in the days ahead of us.

The challenge we are facing, and will have to address, is the fact that to a great extent, the modern-day church has evolved into an institute it was never really meant to be. The message is still pure and should never change, but we will do well to re-evaluate its methods. In many ways, we have seen the modern-day church develop into a conventional organization rather than a living organism. We have juxtaposed a worldly business model over the structure of the church and are frequently leaning towards a corporate model rather than the real Church Jesus had referenced. In some cases, some congregations, for instance, no longer even refer to elders and deacons, but instead to directors, as the official board. I don't think it will make much difference what you call them, but why move away from the biblical pattern? What are we trying to say? The danger is that we can easily develop a secular mindset that deviates from the original mission and embrace innovation over spiritual values.

To remove any misunderstanding, I want to clarify that I whole-heartedly believe that the business side of the church has to be run on sound business principles and should be in unconditional order. There should just be no excuse for sloppy administration or incompetent accounting in the body of Christ. I have always been a stickler for this. I unequivocally believe a church should have a credible organizational chart depicting levels of leadership, lines of authority and avenues of communication. It should furthermore run its affairs on an approved budget and operate according to sound accounting principles. So, I am not opposed to organization and administration.

We had a sizeable church with an administrative staff of approximately thirty-five people, twelve plus credentialed pastors, hundreds of other full-time employed staff which included our teachers in the pre-school and day school, which had a combined enrollment of well over eight-hundred students. I know what it's like to run a relatively large organization. However, I am extremely uncomfortable when it appears as though the church is led by a CEO-figure at the top with executive directors in the command calling the shots, embracing a secular mindset, and see little to no biblical principles applied.

My caution rests on the premise that we can mistakenly view the functions of the church as being no more than another business model. When that mindset takes root, you get a good idea why the church today is failing in especially the developed world. The mission of the Church is driven by the Holy Spirit who often operates in ways other than our fixated models. We have to, at all times, make allowance for Him to direct us in ways beyond our human comprehension. That is where *life* in our churches come from, and that is what sets us apart from any other organization. Take Him out of the equation, and all we have left is the ritualistic repetition of our stayed procedures.

We will do well to return to the mission and ministry-mindedness of the Church. The Church is still about ministry, and ministry has to do with people, and when we see our church members as contributors rather than ministers, we lose the driving force that makes a church great. It may be necessary to repeat: "The Church is not an organization, but a living organism."

Understanding the Power of Local Church Ministry

Christ commissioned the Church, and we are people under His marching orders. He is the King of the Kingdom and the Builder of the Church. And the glorious reality is that Christ did not choose angels to help Him build His Church; He selected frail, failing, faltering, imperfect people like you and me to assist Him in this great mission. What a privilege!

The Church is the body of Christ, and therefore the Church today shares the same mission and ministry-mindedness that characterized Christ while He walked upon the face of the earth.

While Jesus was on earth, there was nothing the Father accomplish, that He did not do through Jesus. In like manner today, there is nothing God does on this planet that He does not do through us—the Church. We are His hands, His feet, and His mouth. We are the ones to carry out the mission. We are Christ's representatives here on earth. If we fail to execute His mission, the message breaks down.

> Most assuredly, I say to you, he who believes in Me, the works that I do he will do also, and greater works than these he will do, because I go to My Father (John 14:12).

God's people, like Christ, are those who pour out their lives in service to others. Ministry is never about us; it's always about others. The responsibility for the Church's ministry is committed to the entire membership—all those who are Christ's disciples.

> But you are . . . His own special people that you may proclaim (declare) the praises (wonderful deeds) of Him who called you out of darkness into His marvelous light (1 Peter 2:9).

The obedience of the Church to her God-given mission determines the Church's health, strength, and growth. It is inconceivable to entertain the thought of ignoring what the Word instructs us to do concerning the building the Church. There is a reason there should be diverse ministries in the local church, and why there should be distinct leadership roles. The body of Christ, like the natural body, consists of many parts with different purposes. The clergy and laity share the same responsibility for the work of the ministry even though there are distinctions in their functions and offices, and their assignments may differ significantly.

Pastors, for instance, are called among many other things, to pray, study, preach, conduct meetings, develop leaders, equip church members, counsel the hurting, and cast vision to the congregation they serve. It stands to reason that one person alone cannot do the entirety of ministry that is required to keep a church healthy and vibrant. Believers should be equipped and trained to do the work of the ministry.

When Christ gave the Great Commission in Matthew 28, "Go ye into all the world . . ." He was addressing the entire known church and not only the leaders. It emphasizes the fact that the Great Commission (the mission of the Church) was not entrusted exclusively to the apostles, but to all who were members of the body of Christ.

With the refreshing and renewing breath of the Holy Spirit, there has never been a better time than this to remove the class distinction between the vocational ministers and the believers. What we should concentrate on is to restore the biblical truth of involving all of the people of God in executing actual works of ministry in the congregation. In many, if not most cases, it may call for us to again preach and teach about the *Priesthood of the Believer.* It is a fact that many people today do not have a clear understanding of what this statement means.

Clarifying the Terms

When we talk about ministry by all, we often use the word *laity* to describe the believers, or the members of a congregation (also called *saints* in the Bible). It always makes me uneasy to refer to believers as *laypeople,* because it can mean different things to different people. Most of the time it sounds like a degrading, which of course it is not.

The term *Laity* comes from the Greek word *Laos,* which is merely a word used to describe *people.* For the most part, in a biblical context, it refers to ALL the *people of God,* better known as Christians—the *called-out* ones. It is essential that we understand this. Paul, quoting Ezekiel 37:27, says, "I will be their God, and they shall be my people" *(Laos)* . . . (2 Corinthians 6:16) *Laity* is merely a term loosely used to describe those who are not in so-called vocational ministry. It indeed does not reference novices, and neither does it mean unqualified or unskilled people.

> The Apostle Peter says, "But you are a chosen people (Laos), a royal priesthood, a holy nation, a people (Laos) belonging to God. Once you were not a people (Laos), but now you are the people (Laos) of God" 1 Peter 2:9–10 (Words in parenthesis added) So, again, in its purest form then the word *laity* means *the people of God.*

Instead of using the word *laity* in this book, I have chosen to use the terms *believers, saints,* or *church members* interchangeably, and only in some rare occasions may have referred to the "laity." But at the same time, I do want you to understand that the term *laity* is not a wrong word. So, when I use it I want you to appreciate, I am not, in my mind, referring to a second-class of people. From a New Testament perspective, I am talking about *the people of God.*

The word *Clergy* comes from the word *Kleros* and is a term that we apply to individuals, called by God to serve in a particular ministry-role, vocationally trained, ordained by the laying on of hands, and employed in Christian ministry. It usually refers to those called into the five-fold ministry as mentioned in Ephesians 4:11, and could best be described as those who are principally set aside for service to God. Pastors are not called to serve in the role of a *priest* through whom the people should approach God, but rather to function as a shepherd and coach to protect, lead, and guide the flock.

Understanding the Functions

While all of the people of God, *Laos,* and *Kleros,* should be involved in ministry, we readily agree that there is a difference of function between them. Pastors are the ordained ministers who receive their vision from God to lead the congregation to fulfill the mission God had given them. Church members are called to support the vision of the house and make themselves available for training with the intent of serving others in ministry. Together, the pastors and members become the bulwark against the opposition of the enemy and the instruments who build the Church of the Living God. In the New Testament sense, all of God's people are called to be involved in the mission (the ministry) of the Church. You do not have to be employed (paid) by the church to participate in ministry. Being part of *the people of God,* you have the honor of being qualified to do the same works Jesus did while He was walking upon the face of the earth. There are also millions of people across the world that are involved in marketplace ministry, earning their income through secular employment, while simultaneously doing a great work for God in ministry even outside the confinements of a church building.

The recovery of the ministry of the laity can come only as the church revises its structure by training its people not to be institutional maintenance men and women but God's messengers in everyday life.[49]

To summarize all of the above, we could say:

- The pastor and staff are primarily called to *equip* the saints (the believers—the laity) for their work of the ministry.
- The believers are primarily the ones who are responsible for *carrying out* the ministry.

In many ways, our traditional methodology has hindered the growth of the Church by excluding the laity. But the good news is that the sleeping giant is awakening, and the Body of Christ is coming alive. The effectiveness of the church member's involvement, in a practical sense, goes far beyond the reach of an individual pastor or staff member. They should however always, follow the spiritual leadership of those God has placed over them. It is the umbrella of protection that authorizes them actually to implement what God has assigned them to do.

Understanding Ministry

Let's also take a closer look at the word *ministry* for a more precise understanding. In most instances where we translate the word ministry from the Greek, it uses the noun *Diakonia*. Those who serve in ministry are *Diakonos*. As you can readily observe, this is also the root word from which we get our modern-day term, *deacon*. The definition of ministry (Diakonia) merely is *service*, or *to serve*. Almost every use of the word

---

49   Oscar E. Feucht, *Everyone a Minister* (St. Louis: Pillar Books for Concordia Publishing House, 1974), 82.

ministry refers to a person or persons *doing ministry, completing a ministry,* or *having a ministry.* The emphasis of ministry is in the act of serving.

> For even the Son of Man did not come to be served, but to serve, and to give His life a ransom for many (Mark 10:45).

Local church ministry consists of those who God has called into the Five-Fold ministry (also known as the vocational ministers, or clergy) plus all the believers (also known as saints, or the laity). These are all called to be involved in ministry and represent the Body of Christ.

A New Reality

Many of our members who have been sitting idle in our churches for many years have done so because they never realized that all believers had received at least one or more spiritual gifts from God. But the truth is that they will never know this until they are being taught and helped to discover, develop, and then to deploy their gifts. If we do not teach these spiritual principles, it may explain why so many have become bored stiff in the church, and many have left. Pastors and churches that are open to genuinely enlist, equip, and involve their people in ministry are going to see an unbelievable explosion of growth, support, and excitement.

> So far as the Christian faith is concerned the solid handle in our time is laity religion. If in the average we would suddenly take seriously the notion that every lay member, man, or woman, is a minister of Christ, we would have something like a **revolution** in a short time; it would constitute both the big dose and the required novelty. Suddenly the number of

ministers in the average church would jump from one to five hundred. It is the way to employ valuable but mostly wasted human resources.[50]

A New Generation

The younger generation, called the Millennials, is looking for reality and is in search of significance. These young people want to be involved in what's happening in their world. If they do not find it in the church, they too will leave. It is the task of the pastors and leaders to raise the awareness of spiritual gifts and ministry involvement to their people so that everyone can be involved. Then there is the next generation, which we have indeed not yet identified. Perhaps they will be known as the *2-Kayers* since they were born after the year 2,000 (2K). Their primary focus is on their screens, whether it be a smartphone, iPad, iPod, or who knows what next, but the church has to begin to contemplate what will drive this generation.

There is a new zeal in the air as many cutting-edge pastors and leaders anticipate the leadership of the Holy Spirit, showing them how to empower their people. They are finding ways to steward their people so they can become the world-changers they are supposed to be and stop having the world change the Church to what it is not intended to be. God is quickening men and women all over the world who have been waiting for this glorious moment. They are ready to take on their assignments and enthusiastic to be released into the greater purposes and calling for their lives.

---

50   Elton Trueblood, *Your Other Vocation* (New York: Harper and Row, 1952), as quoted by Oscar E. Feucht, *Everyone a Minister* (St. Louis: Pillar Books for Concordia Publishing House, 1974), 58.

Discover Your Spiritual Gifts

It is essential that every believer knows what his or her gifts are so that they can function appropriately in the accurate position within the body of Christ. According to the New Testament, every believer has a spiritual gift; no one has been left out. The purpose of these gifts is so we can minister to others. Regrettably, many believers do not know what their spiritual gifts are and for the most part do not know how to discover their gifts. As a believer, you should make every attempt to discover the gift(s) that God has imparted to you. This is what will make you effective in the work of the ministry. It is quite possible that you have some dormant gifts inside of you that you are presently not using. Paul admonishes Timothy, "Do not neglect the gift that is in you" (1 Timothy 4:14). Some people may even be surprised to find they have more than one gift. But usually, most people have, what we call, a dominant gift, but no one has received all of the gifts. The Bible says there are diversities of gifts (1 Corinthians 12:6) with the intent of spreading these gifts among all of the believers so that we must work together to accomplish the full measure of what God desires to accomplish.

Paul makes some noted points in 1 Corinthians 12 concerning spiritual gifts. He affirms that:

1. We should identify our gifts (not be ignorant) (v. 1).

2. There are different kinds of spiritual gifts, but it's the same Spirit (v. 4).

3. There are different types of ministries, but we serve the same Lord (v. 5).

4. God works in a variety of ways, but it is the same God who does the work in all of us (v.6).

5. A spiritual gift is given to each of us, so we can help each other (v. 7).

6. The same Spirit gives great faith to each one (v. 9).

7. There are many parts (in the body), but the many parts make up one whole body (v. 12).

8. How strange a body would be if it had only one part (v. 19).

9. All members together are Christ's body, and each is a part of it (v. 27).

(Based mainly on the New Living Translation. Not all direct quotes)

A Spiritual Gift
is a special attribute
given by the Holy Spirit
to each believer
in the Body of Christ,
according to God's Grace,
for use within
the context of the Body.
(Peter Wagner)

Your responsibility as a believer is to discover your gifts, develop them, and then deploy them.

Ways to Discover Your Spiritual Gift(s)

Many believers are not involved in ministry just because they do not understand that they too are gifted to participate in ministry.

Others again may be aware that we have all received gifts but have never discovered what their particular gift may be and are therefore hesitant to engage in any form of ministry. When you were born you already had a gift; it was part of God's plan for your life and that's why you are on this earth (Psalm 139:13-16).

Here are some elementary, but practical actions that can be taken to lead people in discovering their spiritual gifts and broaden their thinking in becoming active ministers within their churches:

1. In a practical sense, you can discover your giftedness by recognizing your passion in life.

Whatever stirs your passion is a clear indication of the ministry-gift you have received. That which infuriates you the most is a clear sign of a calling to you to rectify it. Your assignment is any problem you were created to solve on earth. Similarly, that which excites or enthuses you most is an apparent evidence of what God wants you to do with your life. Not all people have the same passion, and that is the reason we sometimes cannot understand how it is that people do not have the same devotion to a particular cause as we are.

2. You will know what your real gift is when you become obsessed by it.

Once you have discovered your spiritual gift, excitement rises in your spirit and you constantly think about it. You think it, sleep it, pray it, until it becomes part of your lifestyle. One such gift is *Compassion,* most probably because there are so many people needed for this function.

"I beseech you, brethren, ye know the house of Stephanas . . . that they have addicted themselves to the ministry of the saints" (1 Corinthians 16:15 KJV).

This statement ". . . they have addicted themselves . . ." is indeed thought-provoking and is probably only mentioned as such in the King James Version of the Bible. It means:

- They cannot live without it.
- There is a driving force—a craving, a compulsion, a passion.

Webster defines the word *Addict*: To devote or give (oneself) habitually or compulsively to something.

A good analogy may be that just as a drug addict cannot live without drugs because of withdrawal symptoms; the believers should be so consecrated and devoted to ministry that they cannot live without it—doing it because they have an inner driving force and passion. You did not receive your spiritual gift as an afterthought of God, instead, it defines your purpose for being.

But you should . . . Fully carry out the ministry God has given you (2 Timothy 4:5 NLT).

Here Paul is emphasizing the importance and devotion one should have concerning ministry. Once a believer has discovered his or her gift(s), and have committed themselves to a ministry, they should do it with all their hearts and full devotion—*carry it full out!*

3. Another helpful way to discover your spiritual gifts is by getting involved in some ministries that seem attractive.

As you explore the different ministry areas, you will soon discover if it is a fit for you. If you are efficient, and it's fulfilling, it may be a clear indication of your gift. If it becomes monotonous or does not satisfy your longing, then it may not be where you need to serve.

You must have a passion for a particular ministry. But don't, however, try only one ministry and if it brings no gratification, give up on being involved completely. Find something else and continue until you find your fit. You will find something that fits your unique giftedness, I assure you, you will, and when you do, you will be so delighted!

4. Seek the counsel of mature believers.

Although this should not be your ultimate evaluation, it is always constructive to ask other people, who have been involved in ministry for a considerable time, to assess your effectiveness. Also, ask them to pray with you about your potential gift. Seeking counsel is okay.

5. Seek the confirmation of the Holy Spirit.

Remember, it is the Holy Spirit who gives the Gifts according to His will. You should have a confirmation on your inside that you are functioning in the right gift and should sense the inner-peace of the Holy Spirit (1 Corinthians 12:11).

Never do something just because other *people* think you should. Follow the inner witness of the Holy Spirit. You will know when you have found your spiritual niche.

6.   Make it a matter of prayer.

As you pray and ask the Lord to guide you, He will lead you to discover and identify your gift(s) and direct you in all your endeavors. God is faithful and wants you to be productive and fruitful (James 1:5).

7.   Take a Spiritual Gifts Inventory Test.

If you have not done so yet, we highly recommend that you take a Spiritual *Gifts Inventory Test*. Most people are excited to know that there are specific ways to discover their giftedness and are thrilled when they see the results that show they do have particular, identifiable gifts. Various options are available that are most effective. Your pastor is the most likely one that can help you decide what will work best for you.

You have to realize, however, that these inventories or tests are merely human instruments that are made available to help you discover your gift(s). There is nothing divine about them. They are, however, amazingly helpful and have helped and blessed scores of people.

Develop Your Gifts

"As each one has received a gift, minister it to one another, as good stewards of the manifold grace of God" (1 Peter 4:10).

Developing your gifts means to exercise them, and doing so consistently, you make them stronger. It's like a muscle; the more you use it, the stronger it gets. The way to exercise your gift(s) is by learning more about it and continually putting it into practice. Acquire some books, listen to CD's, watch DVD's or Podcasts, and every other way you can find to develop your gift(s). You may also find it useful to talk to other mature people who are functioning in the same gift.

The more you use your spiritual gift(s), the more potent and useful it will become, and the more comfortable you will be in applying this gift. Learn never to let go of your gift(s) for the simple reason that it is not functioning as you had thought it would. When this happens, ask the One who gave it to you, the Holy Spirit, and allow Him to guide you in the way you should be going.

Deploy Your Gifts

As a believer, it is essential that you *discover* your gift(s), but it is even more vital that you *use* the gift(s) God has given you. It's by using your gifts that they become efficient. To "deploy" your gift(s), in its simplest form just means to put them into a position of readiness; to be in a situation in which they can be utilized or put into service. "Having then gifts differing according to the grace that is given to us, let us use them" (Romans 12:6).

> If you do not
> use your gifts,
> you will lose
> your gifts

Don't Hang in the Air

If you are still uncertain about your spiritual gift, just get involved in some ministry that seems to match your passion and follow the leadership of the Holy Spirit. Do not allow Satan to hold you back in your uncertainty. Whatever you do, don't sit on the sidelines and wait; get up and get involved.

Pastors, on the other hand, must be perceptive to help their members *discover* their gifts, but then lead them into *developing* that gift, until they have finally *deployed* their gift(s) in useful ministry within the body of Christ. If we fail to involve our people in ministry, they become frustrated and discontented, and what's more is that it will ultimately lead to lack of spiritual maturity.

Being involved in ministry is part of the spiritual journey for those who have committed their lives to it. It is the means whereby believers develop their faith, and also learn to develop the characteristics of the Fruit of the Spirit such as love, patience, joy, and gentleness. This belief is most likely what Paul had in mind when he said, "from whom the whole body, joined and knit together **by what every joint supplies**, according to the effective working by which every part does its share, causes growth of the body for the edifying of itself in love" (Ephesians 4:16—Emphasis added).

Every member of the church should function in their respective gift(s), and responsibilities or else the church will be dysfunctional and never reach its optimum maximum. It is of vital importance for us to realize that ministry within the local church is crucial, but we must also fulfill our calling by living a life of mission. Ministry should never take place on Sundays only. It should become a way of life every day of the week wherever we go. Most of what happens within the Body should be preparatory for our mission outside the four walls of the church.

I cannot emphasize it loud enough: The Holy Spirit is elevating the message of all of God's people to be involved in ministry. Pastors and church members alike dare not ignore this call. People can no longer afford to sit in church every Sunday, singing their songs, listening to the preacher, praying their prayers, and going through the religious exercises, without ever experiencing the joy of being used by God.

Conclusion

One of the most significant responsibilities pastors have is to teach and train their people, enabling them, and then helping them to utilize their unique gifts to contribute to the Kingdom of God. Believers will experience true fulfillment as they give themselves to building the Church of Jesus Christ—against which the gates of hell cannot prevail. God said to Moses to tell Pharaoh, "Let My people go" (Exodus 5:1) This charge remains ringing in our ears in the present season of the modern-day church. It's a great time to be alive ". . . Who knows whether you have come to the kingdom for such a time as this?" (Esther 4:14). Don't miss your golden, God-given opportunity.

Final Word

Now that you have gained a good understanding of what the *New Proven Paradigm for Pastoral Care* is all about, it's time to set your sights on this great *Care Revolution*. There is no reason to want to be left behind. As a pastor and leader, the best way you can help your church and its members is by acquiring the appropriate training material and developing your people accordingly. The greatest church in your city is yet to be *built*, and there is no reason it cannot be the one you are pastoring.

Welcome to the *Care Revolution!!*

NEXT STEPS

1. A follow-up book called the *Care Revolution Handbook* is available.

The *Handbook for Pastors and Leaders* fully describes the step-by-step process of implementing the Care Ministry Network. The *Care Revolution Handbook* is written as an easy-to-understand guide for pastors and leaders.

The *Handbook* also provides a helpful addendum section containing proven support-material to assist pastors and leaders in effectively rolling out the care system:

- Appropriate Sermon Outlines – to assist pastors when casting the vision
- Preparatory Material – detailed guide for planning a successful Training Conference for members
- The Launch – the necessary steps to launch a practical care ministry network in your congregation after completing the Training Conference
- The Commissioning Service – how to publicly authorize and commission your church members to serve in care ministry
- Job Descriptions – the expectations of workers on each level of ministry
- Sample Letters – suggestions for step-by-step letters to be used by church administration throughout the training and development process

Our website has editable Word files available for the above documents, as well as the following downloads *(There is a nominal fee to download online material):*

- Application Form Template for Care Pastors
- Official Certificate Template to be issued to each commissioned worker
- Promotional Pamphlet designed for distribution among church members to introduce the Care Ministry Network

PLEASE NOTE: There is also a separate *Handbook for Participants* available for those attending a Training Conference. It's the same as the *Leaders Handbook* (above) but without the addendum material. It is essential that each participant has a copy.

2. Training Manuals

The third exciting mainstay in our care-ministry development is our collection of superb training manuals. A *Facilitators Guide* is designed specifically for the person(s) who will be doing the teaching during your Training Conference. The companion manual is called the *Participants Guide,* which is essential for each person in attendance.

www.cmni.org

*A free **introductory eBrochure** is also available on our website. It is a helpful tool for pastors and leaders to introduce the Care Ministry Network concept to their leaders and influencers.*

CPSIA information can be obtained
at www.ICGtesting.com
Printed in the USA
FSHW012327070320
67806FS

9 781946 453341